Government and Society in Nineteenth-century Britain

Commentaries on British Parliamentary Papers

EDUCATION

By the same authors:

P. FORD

The Economics of Collective Bargaining (Blackwell, Oxford, 1958)
Social Theory and Social Practice (Irish University Press, 1968)

P. & G. FORD

Hansard's Catalogue and Breviate of Parliamentary Papers, 1696-1834
   (IUP British Parliamentary Papers, General Indexes, Volume 1)
Select List of British Parliamentary Papers, 1833-99 (Irish University Press, 1969)
A Breviate of Parliamentary Papers, 1900-16 (Irish University Press, 1969)
A Breviate of Parliamentary Papers, 1917-39 (Irish University Press, 1969)
A Breviate of Parliamentary Papers, 1940-54 (Blackwell, Oxford, 1961)
Luke Graves Hansard's Diary, 1814-41 (Blackwell, Oxford, 1962)
A Guide to Parliamentary Papers (3rd revised edition, Irish University Press, 1972)

P. & G. FORD AND DIANA MARSHALLSEY

Select List of British Parliamentary Papers, 1955-64 (Irish University Press, 1970)

CELINA FOX

'Pictures from the Magazines', (with M. Wolff) in H.J. Dyos and M. Wolff (eds.), *The Victorian City II* (1972)

RICHARD JOHNSON

'Administrators in Education before 1870' in Gillian Sutherland (ed.), *Studies in the Growth of Nineteenth-Century Government* (Routledge & Kegan Paul, 1972)

ROY MACLEOD

Victorian Studies, advisory editor (Indiana University)
Science Studies, co-editor (Macmillan)
Archives of British Men of Science, co-editor (Mansell)
Social History of Science, editor (Frank Cass)

EDWARD MILLER

Prince of Librarians, The Life and Times of Antonio Panizzi of the British Museum (Andre Deutsch, 1967)
Short History of the British Museum (Pitkin Press, 1970)

GILLIAN SUTHERLAND

Studies in the Growth of Nineteenth-Century Government, editor and contributor (Routledge & Kegan Paul, 1972)
Matthew Arnold on Education (Penguin, 1973)
Policy Making in Elementary Education 1870-1895 (Oxford University Press, 1973)
Elementary Education in the Nineteenth Century (Historical Association, general series, 1971)

Government and Society in Nineteenth-Century Britain
Commentaries on British Parliamentary Papers

EDUCATION

Celina Fox   Richard Johnson   Roy MacLeod

Edward Miller   Gillian Sutherland (General
Editor)

Introduction by P. and G. Ford

IRISH UNIVERSITY PRESS

ISBN 0 7165 2211 X (case bound)
Library of Congress Catalog Card Number 73-92946

Printed in Great Britain by
Netherton & Worth Ltd., Truro

Contents

Prefatory Note

For permission to make use of copyright material we are indebted to The Controller of Her Majesty's Stationery Office, to the Trustees of the British Museum, and to the Bodleian Library.

The breviate notes on those volumes of Parliamentary Papers on the subject reprinted by the IUP, which follow each essay, are those prepared by the staff of the IUP to accompany the initial publication of the volumes.

Cambridge, November 1975   GS

Abbreviations

BM Add. Mss.	British Museum Additional Manuscripts		
C., Cd., Cmd.	Command Paper	mins. of ev.	minutes of evidence
Ch.	Chairman	PRO	Public Record Office
ev.	evidence	q. (qq.)	question(s)
HC	House of Commons	R. Com.	Royal Commission
HL	House of Lords	Rep.	Report
		Sel. Cttee.	Select Committee

Citations

The form used for House and Command papers is:

> session/paper no./volume no./volume page no.

Example:

> 1845(602)xii,331

If the title has not been given in the text, the form should be preceded by the title and description:

> title and description/session/paper no./volume no./volume page no.

Examples:

> Game Law. Sel. Cttee. Rep.; 1845(602)xii,331
> London Squares. R.Com. Rep.; 1928-29 Cmd. 3196,viii,111

References are to the *House of Commons* bound sets, *except* where the paper is in the House of Lords set only. From this it follows:

a. Where the paper is the report of a Lords select committee (communicated to the Commons) it must be marked HL to indicate this and to distinguish it from a Commons select committee:
Example:

> Sale of Beer. Sel.Cttee.HL.Rep.; 1850(398)xviii,438.

b. Where the paper is in the Lords papers only, HL should be added to the paper number. This can be done in the form HL(259) or (HL.259).

c. For a reference to a statement on a particular page of a paper, the title and description should be followed by the *printed* page number of the paper:

> title etc./printed page no./session/paper no./volume no./vol. page no.

Example:

> Finance and Industry. Cttee.Rep.p.134;1930-31 Cmd.3897,xiii,219

Where the reference is to the Irish University Press the citation is:

> IUP/subject/title/volume no.

Example:

> IUP Monetary Policy: General 4.

Introduction to Parliamentary Papers

P. and G. Ford

A fully comprehensive definition of parliamentary papers would include all those which form part of the necessary machinery of parliamentary government, even those concerned with the procedures of the day-to-day business. But from the point of view of the researcher three groups are of primary importance. The first group, the Journals, record the things done in parliament. The second group, the Debates, record the things said in parliament (the publication of the House of Commons Debates became known as Hansard throughout the world and was at first not an official but a private venture receiving public subsidy). The third group, Papers arising in or presented to parliament deal with the formulation, development and execution of its policy. It is to this third group, for many years known as 'Blue Books' because of the blue paper with which most of them were covered, that the name Parliamentary Papers became particularly attached.

After 1801 the papers were gathered together and bound in two separate sessional sets, one for the House of Commons and the other for the House of Lords. These volumes include reports of select committees, composed of a limited number of members of either House appointed to examine particular problems, and reports of royal commissions and committees of enquiry appointed in form by the Crown though on the advice of ministers or by ministers themselves. These latter have the double advantage of comprising persons from outside the House thought to be experts on the subjects in hand, persons prominent in public affairs or representative of some body of opinion, experience or interest, and of not being limited in their work to the length of a parliamentary session. All these bodies reported the results of their enquiries together with the evidence taken to the authority which appointed them. The reports of select committees and the papers which departments were required by Act to send to parliament, because they originated *in* the House were grouped into a numbered series as House Papers. Royal commissions reported formally to the Crown — even submitting massive volumes of evidence for it to read — and committees reported to the minister concerned. Because these were the work of bodies *outside* the House, the papers were brought to the House and incorporated in the Sessional Papers through the use of an historic formula which embodies much of the development of constitutional monarchy, 'Presented by Command'.

It was these committees and commissions which uncovered the evils of the work of children in factories and mines, the evils of bad housing and sanitation and of inadequate water supply in the new sprawling towns created by the Industrial Revolution, as well as the difficulties relating to monetary policy and the new phenomenon of recurrent trade depressions. The witnesses brought before the enquiring bodies included the victims of the new industrial conditions — little children who had worked in factories and mines, the exploited immigrants in the sweated trades, and the leaders of the early efforts to unionize workmen, such as John Gast in 1815, John Doherty in 1838 and the whole of the top leadership of the great trade unions in 1867-69. What is more remarkable is that the oral evidence was printed verbatim. Even Marx was impressed by the commissions' plenary powers for getting at the truth, the competence and freedom from partisanship and respect of persons displayed by the English Factory Inspectors, the Medical Officers reporting on public health and the Commissioners of Enquiry into the exploitation of women and children, into housing and food. There is no parallel in the world for such a series of searching and detailed enquiries covering so long a span of years and embracing every phase of the transition from a rural aristocratic society to an industrialized democracy. It is the most significant of these reports on a century of investigation, the 'policy papers', that are embodied in the Irish University Press series.

The method of personal examination of witnesses had occasionally to be modified when central hearings were not practicable. Before the Benthamite conception of a unified central and local government machine had been realized in practice, the central authorities often knew little of what was going on in the localities. The many thousands of parishes administered the poor laws in their own ways so that the *Royal Commission on the Poor Laws* (1834) had to send round assistant commissioners to carry out and report on a detailed standardized plan of enquiry. The *Royal Commission on Municipal Corporations* (1835) had to make district enquiries on how the boroughs and 'places claiming to be boroughs' conducted their affairs. The effect of adverse forces on agriculture could be country-wide: the *Royal Commission on the Depressed Condition of the Agricultural Interests* (1881-82), on *Agricultural Depression* (1894-97) and the *Labour Commission* (1892-94) looking into agricultural labour, each made use of assistant commissioners to find out what was common and what was different in the problems of the various districts. These papers are a mine of information.

There are also the various famous reports by great civil servants, such as Horner's on the enforcement of factory legislation, Tremenheere's on the state of the mining districts, bound in the sets under the heading of commissioners' reports, and Southwood Smith's on the *Physical Causes of Sickness and Mortality to which the Poor are Exposed,* tucked away in an appendix to an annual report.

Two aspects of these investigations — the membership of the committees and the importance of British constitutional procedure — are worthy of note. The fullness and considerable integrity of these penetrating investigations were remarkable in that in the first half of the century the members of the committees and commissions which made them were not, as they would be today, drawn from or representative of the great bodies of the working classes. On the contrary, they were from the wealthy and ruling groups, for the composition of the House of Commons reflected the fact that even after the Reform Act of 1832 the number of voters was still but a tiny fraction of the adult population. The Northcote-Trevelyan proposals for the reform of the civil service by replacing recruitment by patronage with open competition, were approved by a cabinet all of whom, said Gladstone, who was a member of it, were more aristocratic than himself. No doubt they had their blind sides. For most of the century they assumed the existing class structure without much question; and there were fields in which their approach to problems and the conclusions they drew were influenced not only by the prevalent social philosophies, but class ideals and interests, as in the investigations into trade unions, game laws, etc. No matter how experienced or impartial they may be, members of a committee come to the task of inquiry with patterns of ideas related to their time. The report is not just summarized evidence, but evidence as interpreted by the committee. In weighing a report, therefore, a distinction must be made between the evidence upon which it is based and what the members have contributed to it. But the facts elicited in the examination of witnesses were not covered up or hidden — because apart from pressure by reforming groups, the constitutional procedure was that reports and evidence should be submitted and printed verbatim (see P. G. Ford, *A Guide to Parliamentary Papers,* 3rd ed., IUP, 1972).

Further groups of papers are those which arose from the expansion of Britain overseas to control widely scattered colonial possessions and the development of areas of white settlement, Canada, Australia, and New Zealand. At the outset both kinds of territories were in some degree controlled from Whitehall. On the latter, beside formal committees of enquiry, there was a mass of despatches to and correspondence with colonial governors on the opening and sales of land for settlement, taxation, the administration of justice and the slow replacement of central control by primitive local representative bodies which eventually become the parliaments of self-governing dominions. In the case of the colonial possessions, after the Act abolishing slavery had been passed, the most striking feature was the immense body of papers which offer unique insight into the problem of enforcing this new political principle in widely scattered territories, differing in climate, crop conditions, land tenure, in the character and importance of slavery and in social structure. These are revealed in an immense volume of despatches, correspondence and instructions issued by the Colonial Office and the Foreign Office to colonial governors and their little Assemblies, which offered varying degrees of co-operation and resistance, and by the

Admiralty in orders to commanders of naval vessels engaged all over the world in efforts to suppress the slave trade.

The great body of material for the nineteenth century occupies some 7,000 official folio volumes. At the outset the problem of making it available had to be met by the Printer to the House of Commons, Luke Hansard, who kept it in stock and numbered the House papers. He was frequently asked by M.P.s and others for sets of existing papers on particular questions then under discussion in the House or by the public. This led him to take two steps. He made special collections of papers arranged in subject order, and prepared a series of indexes to the papers, some in subject and some in alphabetical order. But the passage of a century has enlarged the number of papers to be handled and the scale of the problems; and at the same time we now have to meet the demand not only of the politician concerned with the problems of his time, but those of professional historians and researchers ranging over the whole century.

To deal with the papers on Home Affairs the Fords' *Select List of British Parliamentary Papers 1833-99* includes 4,000 policy papers arranged in subject order, so that researchers can follow the development lines of policy easily through any collection of papers. But complete collections are few and far between and even ample ones not common. The Irish University Press Parliamentary Papers series supplies this deficiency first by reprinting all the major policy papers, conveniently brought together in subject sets, e.g. 32 volumes on Agriculture, 44 volumes on Industrial Relations, 15 volumes on Children's Employment, 55 volumes on Education, and so on. Secondly, it has retained what was the great virtue of the original enquiries by reprinting with the reports all the volumes of evidence. Thirdly, in those fields where despatches, correspondence and instructions are vital as in the case of the papers on slavery, Canada, Australia, New Zealand, as far as possible all the papers on these matters found in the British Parliamentary series have been reprinted, e.g. 95 volumes on Slavery, 36 on Canada, 34 on Australia.

The series includes the most commonly used official general alphabetical indexes from which researchers can trace papers referred to in the footnotes of scholarly works and in the references in parliamentary reports themselves. In addition to the official indexes, a special index[1] to the 1,000 volumes has been prepared which will also provide cross references, so that the official indexes can be used either with the official sessional sets or with the IUP reprints. Finally, indexes to subjects, persons and places (some of which are already published[2]) are being compiled for the papers in the IUP series.

1 *Checklist of British Parliamentary Papers in the Irish University Press 1000-Volume Series 1801-1899* (Shannon: 1972).

2 *Index to British Parliamentary Papers on Children's Employment* (IUP, 1973)
Index to British Parliamentary Papers on Canada and Canadian Boundary, 1800-1899 (IUP 1974).
Index to British Parliamentary Papers on Australia and New Zealand, 1800-1899, 2 vols. (IUP 1974).

ELEMENTARY EDUCATION: THE EDUCATION OF THE POORER CLASSES

Richard Johnson

Commentary

Introduction

But they are facts attested by Her Majesty's Government in the Blue Book presented to Parliament, and they cannot be disputed by anyone, I suppose? John G. Talbot (Cross Commissioner) to Thomas Smyth (witness).[1]

The rhetorical question of a royal commissioner prompts a return to first principles in search of a critical commentary.

What happened in history reaches the researcher through an intermediary. Sources that are called 'primary' derive directly from the activities of historical actors. The locations of these historical actor-mediators in their own society have shaped the versions of reality which they present. This has happened through the biographical clusters of experience which individuals have acquired and through group and class identities and more or less institutionalized rôles. These have carried some typical assumptions, interests and limitations of vision. No source is exempt from these tendencies since all have a human, therefore a societal and, commonly, an institutional derivation. In addition the form, medium, intention, and exact personal circumstance of communication have affected what it is possible to record. Genres of sources – statistical series, private letter, autobiography, novel and, not least, official document – each pose intrinsic difficulties of use. Testimony before a select committee of the House of Commons, for example, is a public, self-conscious and political event unyielding of nuances of motive compared with a private letter.

The concept of 'primary mediation' is less misleading than that of 'primary source'. Add the secondary mediation of researcher (another actor-mediator in a different society) and we have a measure of historiographical distance. The history of the books is twice-removed at least from past event or situation. And that itself was problematic enough.

Some of the distortions which will inevitably arise may be lessened by critical technique, care, honesty and explicitness in handling materials. There is, no doubt, a realm of fact that can be re-assembled by these means. Concern with meaning and explanation, however, forces historians to see that historical actors (like themselves) differ in their perceptions of reality, often irreconcilably. Each version may be situationally valid, impregnable to positive tests of 'accuracy' or 'authenticity'. If so, a better kind of history accepts and tries to explain differences of perception and attempts to reconstitute a whole, incorporating diversity, fixing on relationships. Completeness becomes a major test of objectivity.

An analysis like this needs testing against a particular source. It may certainly be applied to blue books; more fruitfully still to blue books dealing with education. It directs attention to situational and formal biases and to the whole question of the representation of relevant view-points. It poses the questions: whose blue books and for what? whose versions of educational problems do they portray? at what points are they misleading because incomplete? Perhaps they reveal only one side of a set of educational and social relations. If so, uncritical use may father really gross historical bias, grosser, perhaps, than that which technical inaccuracy fosters.

The Reports: an outline

The documents with which this essay deals form, in some ways, a heterogeneous collection. They span a whole era of educational, social and political change. The Brougham Select Committee of 1816-18, the first of the series, predated the philanthropic discovery of the northern, industrial city, the coming of parliamentary reform and the innovations in government of the 1830s. It worked against the backwash (not quite so turbulent since about 1803) of a counter-revolutionary disinclination to educate the poor at all. It was the first concentrated attempt, by parliamentary inquiry, to raise issues which were to vex the country for fifty years or more. The Cross Commission, by contrast, reported in the political context of adult male suffrage (very imperfectly realised) and of the growth of mass party, and to a society three-quarters of whose population lived in areas designated urban and whose children were required by law to attend state or state-approved schools. Similarly, if the post-Napoleonic-war years were the seed-bed of early and mid-Victorian attitudes to the poor, the Departmental Committee on London's pauper children of 1896 was part of the re-evaluation of these orthodoxies which marked the turn of the century.

The documents also take different forms: four select committees, three royal commissions and a series of inquiries within executive departments of government which did not necessarily, however, employ a departmental personnel. The 'Commission' into education in Wales belongs really to this latter category. It was carried out under the auspices of the Education Department, not under a crown or parliamentary commission.[2] There was, in fact, no royal commission on education until 1858.

Different types of inquiry tended to use different methods. Usually, the sole device of the select committee was the interrogation of witnesses before a committee composed of members of parliament. Three committees in the collection conform entirely to this model: Roebuck's of 1834-35, Slaney's of 1838 and the Select Committee on the Education of Destitute Children of 1861.[3] The committee of 1816-18 was a uniquely expansive affair, commission-like in scope, summoning witnesses but collecting massive returns from the parish clergy too. The three great commissions in the series – Newcastle (1858-62); Cross (1886-88); the Argyll Commissionn on Scottish Education (1865-68) – all secured returns from localities, voluntary organizations and individuals, Newcastle and Argyll also using on-the-spot investigation by assistant-commissioners, even sending them abroad.[4] The Welsh 'Commission' used local inquiry alone. Cross preferred its witnesses to do the travelling and called on over one hundred and fifty of them.[5] Membership of commissions was not restricted, of course, to members of parliament.

The inquiries were also very diverse in their terms of reference and scope. It is useful here to distinguish three periods. The early inquiries, up to and including the Welsh Commission, tackled huge provinces limited mainly by geography and by some omnibus social definition which embraced all sections of the working class, from artisan to 'casual poor'. The original brief of Brougham's polymathic enterprise was narrow enough: 'the education of the lower orders in the metropolis' with special reference to 'children of paupers who shall be found begging in the streets'.[6] To begin with, the committee conformed to a pattern of post-war inquiry – focussing on London, covering the linked issues of crime, 'mendicity', pauperism, prisons and police.[7] But by 1819, impelled by the chairman's ambitions, the committee had counted schools of all kinds in England, Wales and Scotland. It had even penetrated to Eton and Winchester linking them to the original brief as appropriators of endowments originally intended for the poor.[8] The select committees of the 1830s were a little less ambitious: that of 1834-35 examined 'the present state of the education of *the people* in England and Wales';[9] that of 1838, reflecting the industrial and provincial emphasis of the decade, looked at the education of children 'of *the poorer classes* in large towns'.[10] The Welsh Commission defined its clientele as '*the labouring classes*' (and also in terms of their ignorance of English).[11]

The early inquiries had the defects of pioneers. Resources were stretched by ambitions; findings, in terms of detail and coverage, were sometimes superficial, though no-one could make this charge against the Welsh Commission.[12] The reports anticipated or accompanied tentative first steps in state action – the beginnings of concern with pauper education within the framework of the new Poor Law Commission, the work of the first factory inspectors, the slow growth of the Education Department's grant system up to 1846. They owed relatively little to definitions of educational problems which law and administrative practice were to make more precise. They owed much more to the complicated politics of education and to anxiety born of social conflict. Together with the educational investigations of urban statistical societies, Lord Kerry's educational returns of 1835, the early commissioner-like reports of inspectors of schools, factories and prisons, they form part of a swelling interest in popular education which was so marked a feature of the 1830s and 1840s.[13]

The second group of reports, those of the 1850s and 1860s, appear more professional and more thorough and certainly focussed more closely on administrative and legislative issues. The Newcastle Commission's terms of reference were wide enough: 'to inquire into the present state of popular education in England and Wales'. In practice, as the commissioners acknowledged, they concentrated their attention upon a pre-existing apparatus, especially the grant system, now greatly grown in scope and expense, upon legislation dealing with attendance and upon the work of the Charity Commission.[14] They were more careful too, aided by innovations in law, to distinguish categories of working-class children. Children were parcelled into bundles for appropriately assorted treatment: children of the 'independent' or 'self-supporting' working class for ordinary elementary schooling, pauper children for 'separate' or 'district' schools, vagrant or destitute children for industrial or ragged schools, children who had fallen foul of the law for reformatories. After Newcastle, the collection of documents splits, one series dealing with 'ordinary' children, the other with 'exceptions'. The concern with classifying exceptions can be seen still more obsessively in the 1861 Select Committee.[15]

The last group of reports, occupying the period after Forster's Education Act of 1870, were essentially concerned with the operation and revision of existing law and departmental practice. Cross was charged 'to inquire into the working of the elementary education acts'; the 1896 Departmental Committee dealt with the whole poor law inheritance as it had affected pauper children in London.[16]

The Reports and the working class

The most obvious fact about the volumes is that they are full of middle-class people and the gentry puzzling about the schooling of children of the working class. The children were defined with varying degrees of imprecision and there were also changes in the kinds of people who did the talking, notably the growing contingents of civil servants and the emphatic arrival of the elementary school-teachers before Cross in 1886. The objects of inquiry, however, were rarely agents of it. A careful combing reveals only a scattering of examples of working-class witnesses. The education series is less revealing in this respect than contemporary inquiries into conditions of work or trade unionism. These often found room for working-class testimony, even for the testimony of children. It is true that Francis Place contributed to the Brougham and Roebuck Select Committees. He was a major witness before the latter. An ex-Jacobin, journeyman-tailor and secretary of several trade clubs, he was in his own words 'an observer of the habits, manners and intelligence of the working people'.[17] His evidence was certainly distinctive both for his educational secularism and for his championing of working-class respectability and 'improvement'. But he was detached from the radical culture of the artisans by his Benthamism and by his association with middle-class politics and educational schemes. His view of the working class was that of a man who had risen out of it.[18]

Even so, there was a dearth of similarly derived evidence until 1887 when three 'representatives of the working classes' appeared before Cross. They are listed rather incongruously among the more normal run of witnesses – civil servants, HMIs, clerics, members of school boards, voluntary school managers and teachers. The label is of doubtful accuracy for two out of the three. Thomas Ekford Powell, once apprentice bookbinder, was union secretary of this decidedly aristocratic trade and also a minor salaried official of the London School Board.[19] Henry Williams was a small jobbing printer working at home and employing youthful labour on his own account.[20] Only Thomas Smyth, a plasterer and, with Powell, a delegate of the London trades council, was an unambiguously working-class witness.[21] All three distinguished themselves from the very poor, Williams with a snobbish pride, Smyth with a radically egalitarian emphasis, wanting to erode the differences. Smyth also advocated unpalatable policies: more democratic control of board schools, finance through progressive taxation, the abolition of fees and an end to class privileges in education. Like his Chartist predecessors thirty or forty years earlier he saw 'this question of educating the people, as a lever by which I hope they will raise themselves from their present degraded position'. The commissioners were not a uniformly conservative group but some received these opinions with evident hostility. They bullied him with official statistics, equated his views with 'communism' and attempted to convert him. He was pointedly asked by one commissioner 'whether you have any special advantages with regard to the mastery of this subject of the education as given in schools'.[22] Readers of the Cross Commission may judge the force of his reply and the general value of his testimony. But certainly all three token working-men spoke as parents with children at elementary schools – a unique perspective before educational inquiries. That they differed a great deal only adds to the value of their evidence; parenthood in elementary education was by no means a monolithic interest.

The reports are nearly barren, then, of testimony directly out of working-class circumstance. But wholesale omission is not the end of possible distortions. After all, if something important is obviously missing from a source there is every incentive to look for it elsewhere. This is not quite the case: the users of the schools *are* encountered in the reports observed through the eyes of the providers. The danger lies in uncritically accepting externally derived images.

Parents and children figure in the reports mainly in the context of three kinds of argument. They appear as objects of educational 'need', as sufferers from various species of 'ignorance'. They are seen as recipients of a service in arguments about the *effects* of education. Finally they are examined as more or less haphazard users of the schools in the context of the problem of attendance.

Questions about educational 'needs' and effects were most prominent in the early reports. There were two main reasons for this. It had to do with the general chronology of the educational movement or, more correctly, the drive for schooling. The statistical series compiled at the time and recent local studies strongly suggest that the really sustained boom in public elementary schooling (that is of schools provided by philanthropy) was delayed until the 1830s, possibly until the 1840s.[23] Earlier growth was fluctuating and uncertain, probably with a marked plateau in the early 1820s. Until the mid-century the main pre-occupations of educational enthusiasts were how to accelerate and sustain philanthropic energies (with or without state interference), how to multiply schools and, as important, how to enhance their quality. Of course, there is some discussion of attendance in the early reports[24] but the problem of how to get the children to the schools, once provided and approaching efficiency, was a more central concern of the 1850s and early 1860s. Hence the emphasis in the early reports on both coverage and educational method and the need to establish a case for extension and sophistication through exposing the extent of 'ignorance' and the power of better kinds of teachers and schools to remove it.[25] Disclosures about the deplorable behaviour of working-class adults and adolescents, about children running wild in the streets and about their petty stocks of knowledge provided the ammunition of educational activism.

Allied to this was anxiety about a range of social problems. Education was linked with pauperism, crime, public order and economic and social discipline in general. These were all issues which orthodox opinion designated 'moral' and with which, therefore, education could deal.[26] So attention was directed to popular culture and behaviour especially at times and in places of crisis. The chronology of the reports illustrates the connection. A bunch of early inquiries to which Brougham's committee belonged occupied the post-war years of distress and turbulence. A further bigger cluster marked the decade of Reform Bill crisis, new Poor Law, the mushrooming of the unstamped press from 1830 to 1836 and the first Chartist upsurge. By contrast, the 1820s, relatively a peaceful and prosperous decade, produced no major educational inquiry. As significant were the places chosen for study: the Brougham Select Committee paid particular attention to the poorest, most riotous parts of London including Spitalfields, Bethnal Green and St Giles; the 1838 Committee concentrated on raw and radical cities of the North: Wales was the home of Rebecca and of Chartist insurrection.[27]

In the quieter mid-century years the problem of attendance was the Achilles heel of provided schooling. It undercut the commitment of the 1830s – to remoralize a whole class. Financially, because of dependence upon fees, it was disastrous. Children, it was found on recurrent investigation, attended very irregularly, changed school often, were withdrawn from schooling early (commonly at the ages of ten or eleven) while a substantial minority escaped school entirely.[28] One inspector of schools called this 'the mockery of education'; it seemed to undermine the whole massive growth of voluntary schools, state aid and teacher training.[29] To explain this aberration people began to look more closely than before at the attitudes of parents and children. For this reason the period from 1850 to the gradual introduction of general compulsion between 1870 and 1880 is particularly rich in observation. By the time Cross reported, the problem had changed; effective enforcement replaced concern with parental motivation, except perhaps in the matter of fees.[30] It is the Newcastle Commission with its distinctive attitude to parental aspiration that is potentially the most useful source.

The volume of evidence produced by these concerns is so large it is hard to summarize even typical deficiencies. Not all biases of perception were systematic, class-related. Individuals varied in their sympathy or perspicuity and, ideally, individual witness should be related to individual biography. But some points may be made about uniformities leaving reservations till later.

Readers of the reports should first try to gauge the gulf between observer and observed in nineteenth-century conditions. There is a glimpse of this in exchanges between Smyth and the Cross Commissioners but essential nuances of speech and tone elude the printed word. Most witnesses, schoolteachers apart perhaps, were removed from the working class in almost every conceivable aspect of life and culture – income, education, habitation, dress, language and, not least, family circumstance. Understanding required rare gifts of mental translation. They encountered working people as their social inferiors, as masters to men, as broadcloth to fustian, often literally as riches to rags. If encounter was more than casual – and often a whole view of the working-class child was shaped on the streets –[31] it occurred through a business or professional or philanthropic capacity. This may, in one respect alone, have allowed an observer to pierce the opacity of another culture. Few of the people who reported were 'professional' investigators of the poor. The nearest contemporary equivalent to the ubiquitous social scientist were statistical society experts and the assistant commissioners. These men were also commonly members of professions, very commonly clerics.[32] More usually knowledge of the poor was built up from some kind of work among them. Role was superimposed on class: clergyman to 'flock', manufacturer to 'hand', giver to recipient (the philanthropic nexus), master or mistress to servant, magistrate to criminal, teacher and school manager to child and parent. Role and class shaped perception but also the information the observed might yield. In all these relationships, moreover, the stronger party took the active part. It was teachers, clergymen and magistrates that did all the talking. A Mayhew-like ability to listen was rare.[33] A sense of the normality of one-way communication is caught in one exchange before the 1834 Committee. Henry Althans, inspector of British and Foreign schools, was asked, 'Are you consulted by the parents of the children?' He answered, 'I very frequently call the parents together and examine the children in their presence, and address the parents on the advantages of education.'[34] In the complicated sociology of school, teachers, managers, parents and children might each have had their definitions of what school was for but parents and children may well have known more of the dominant definitions than teachers and managers knew of theirs. Very authoritarian teaching regimes must have strengthened a tendency still observable in the modern school.[35]

The reports provide many examples of such obscurity. In extreme instances whole areas of existence, physical or cultural, were simply shut out from view. Witnesses to Brougham's Select Committee noted the unwillingness of businessmen-philanthropists and even doctors to penetrate the inner regions of areas like St Giles because of disease or fear of 'annoyance' – 'those who undertook to visit that district got cool upon it.'[36] The reports of the commissioners of 1847 resemble travellers' tales from darkest Wales. The language, object of official attack, also obscured an underlying culture despite the aid of bilingual school-teacher assistants. Commissioner Lingen, later secretary of the Education Department (and of whom much more later), made strenuous attempts to comprehend 'the phenomenon of a peculiar language isolating the mass from the upper portion of society' though he was inclined to see the loss as all Welsh.[37] Symons, his colleague and a moralistic anti-Radical, made a virtue of his incomprehension.[38] His sneers at 'Welsh screech', Welsh immorality and Welsh sedition rebounded forcefully on the whole commission, stigmatized by the Welsh popular media as 'the treason of the Blue Books'.[39] A study of Symons' method, on which at least he was especially explicit, shows some of the sources of his bias. Welsh parents at sunday schools were suspicious of his note-book; Welsh children in day schools had to be bribed out of silence. He relied heavily on the evidence of Anglican clergymen and of an anglicized elite.[40] Here a class barrier was heightened by linguistic difference and something akin to racial arrogance. More commonly, superficial observation produced stereotypes. The problem of attendance evoked two such – the poverty and the apathy arguments. Rarely found apart, they were often employed in broken-backed combination. But the poverty argument was the dominant explanation before Brougham's Select Committee declining in force thereafter. The commonest explanation overall was the weakness of will to benefit from schooling. The Brougham findings are early, interesting and untypical. The Committee's third report declared, 'there is most unquestionable evidence that the anxiety of the poor for education continues not only unabated, but daily increasing'.[41] This should be read in the light of the educational politics of the post-war period. A part of Brougham's own strategy was to use popular demand to break down the opposition of the 1790s to education of all kinds. It can be seen best in his rôle within the mechanics' institute movement as rhetorician of educational progress.[42] But the evidence of his report tended to support his conclusion. Most witnesses found that parents wanted schooling for their children and were prevented from acquiring it by lack of resources – lack of schools or commonly lack of clothes or shoes. The parochial returns tell a similar story though sometimes in suspiciously stereotyped language. Of the various formulae adopted, the optimistic ones – 'the poor are without sufficient means of education, but are desirous of possessing them' – greatly outweigh the more jaundiced and sometimes more revealing versions – 'At present, in many cases, it appears as if the poor thought they were laying the subscribers under an obligation, by permitting their children to attend the charity school.' (Egremont, Cumberland).[43] Evidence given in person by London philanthropists was all the more telling since the parents in question were usually labourers, 'casual poor' and frequently Irish.[44]

Brougham revealed a large unsatisfied demand, but does not show why so many parents were 'desirous', nor, in depth, how poverty limited the use of existing facilities. The 'poor' emerge as one would expect from the philanthropic vision: dreadfully dirty and dissolute, easily tempted by drink, crime and fornication, but malleable under superior influence, 'grateful' and even 'civil'. Gratefulness was often illustrated by anecdote:

Is there any indisposition on the part of parents to send their children? – I believe not: as far as my experience goes, there is a great desire to send them, even among the lower orders. With the permission of the Committee, I would mention an anecdote: an old Irish barrow-woman, with a pipe in her mouth, came into the girls' school one day, and said to the mistress, 'good madam, God Almighty has got a place for you in Heaven, for your kindness to my child.'[45]

In the same anecdotal way poverty or 'distress' were reduced to discrete phenomena that happened to come to attention – typically to 'the pardonable pride' of parents about sending children to school in rags.[46] The portrayal of poverty as a crushing, permanent and total way of life was rarer, though Edward Wakefield and his allies on the progressive wing of the British and Foreign School Society got nearest to it, their house-by-house inquiries anticipating the thoroughness of the statistical societies:

> In the course of my visits, I witnessed great misery; wretchedness which appeared to me very permanent . . .the unhealthy appearance of the majority of the children was too apparent. It would seem that they came into the world to exist during a few years in a state of torture, since by no other name can I call sickness, and dirt and ignorance.[47]

The dominant stereotype emerged in the reports of the 1830s, carrying over into the average run of assistant commissioners' reports for Newcastle, especially those of Hedley, Hare, Wilkinson and Hodgson. Attitudes hardened. Doubts expressed by early witnesses about the genuineness of parental interest – 'they profess so' – crystallized into dogma. Parental reasons became 'excuses'.[48] The force of poverty was minimised, or seen to affect only a separate working-class stratum. Sometimes it was argued that high wages or booms of economic activity increased indifference.[49] Witnesses stressed 'apathy', 'carelessness', 'refractoriness' and an ignorance of the benefits of what was on offer. 'Want of will' as one assistant commissioner put it, 'much exceeds the want of power'.[50] The opinion of Dr Kay, soon to move from Poor Law to Education Department, and star witness in 1838, was typical:

> As far as the pecuniary resources of the population are concerned, with the exception of hand-loom weavers, and some of the inferior paid operatives . . . I do not think there is any deficiency of funds, if they are properly applied to the education of the poor in Manchester.[51]

Most witnesses in the 1830s favoured the charging of a realistic fee for schooling, for if poverty was not a cause of non-attendance parents might value what they paid for.[52] A number favoured compulsion, usually an 'educational test' legally prohibiting employment of the illiterate and thereby placing the onus on the parent.[53] A pervasive anti-Radicalism caused observers to dismiss as 'seditious' forms of popular self-activity whose indigenous self-image was educational. The wide circulation of the *Poor Man's Guardian* was deplored for example, despite the markedly educational stance of this, the most intellectually impressive of the unstamped journals.[54] More often, popular opinion was seen as inert, needing stimulus from without. As Professor West has suggested, educators denied the existence of a legitimate and indigenous educational demand and looked to 'temporary imposed choice' as a solution to parental perversions.[55] The problem of perception, the moralism of conclusions (and the eccentricity of the man they called 'the Baby Professor') are caught in a statement of Samuel Wilderspin, leading proponent of infant schools in the 1830s:

> To the state of morals generally I have paid some attention. I have put on various disguises and gone in among them, and I have seen them as they are and not as they appear to be. If you go in dressed respectably they put on a reserve, and you do not see them as they are, but if you go in with a dirty face and with a long beard and a jacket on, you see them as they are, and you find their conversation generally consists in immoral language, and language of an obscene nature.... They may dabble a little in politics, but generally there is a lamentable want of general information; and young creatures of both sexes may be seen in the public houses hearing all this, pledging each other in their glasses, and the boys with a pipe stuck in their mouths smoking.[56]

Correcting the bias of the reports

It is not intended to examine in detail how school appeared to parents and children or to replace stereotypes with more complete versions. But a closer approximation to completeness is possible and it is worth discussing how it might be achieved.

The most important need is for sources that express a more indigenous view of educational process. Searching for these involves questioning common assumptions of educational history which the official sources encourage: notably, a belief in working-class passivity and the assumption that only managed and sponsored forms of education were (are) worth the name. The notion that learning occurs mainly in school or college is, after all, a very modern one. In England (though not in Scotland) the ambition of mass schooling – of getting all the children into schools – was a nineteenth-century innovation. To equate school and education is to disguise the most significant historical development of all: the drive to supplant spontaneous, indigenous and haphazard forms of learning by supervised, controlled and routinized ones. It is also necessarily to represent hostility or apathy to schooling as opposition to education or learning itself.

The schools need placing in a wider educational context. The types with which the reports mainly deal – sunday and monitorial schools, the infant schools of the 1820s and 1830s, the state-aided voluntary schools of the mid-century and their board school successors – formed part of the total resources for learning available to children. They certainly encountered many rivals. Some of these, like private schooling, education in family or at work or some forms of apprenticeship, were customary, though sometimes persisting with surprising vitality. Others, like the educational improvisations of Jacobins, Radicals, Owenites and Chartists, were deliberate attempts at substitution.[57] Achieving hegemony of school and college was a long process. And this history of educational 'advance' is as much to do with monopoly, engrossment and even the destruction of alternatives as with filling gaps. Recreating indigenous networks of learning poses great difficulties. It is akin to (or a part of) the retrieval of the popular cultural forms of the past. It is easier to study the cultural aggressions of nineteenth-century authority (including aggression directed towards children in schools) than to discover the more normal patterns by which children acquired skills and a view of their social world. Two kinds of source, however, are especially valuable. The networks used by individuals can be studied from working-class autobiography, a genre obsessed with the pursuit of knowledge.[58] It is possible to examine the (often peripheral) place of schooling, alongside family, neighbourhood, friends and forms of companionship in learning. Secondly, the popular radical press shows how the most politically-committed section of the working class viewed provided schooling, how its educational goals differed from those of philanthropy and how education was sought independently. These sources are especially rich between the 1790s and the 1850s because of the vitality of counter-culture.[59] Both pose problems of use and representativeness – but that is a different story. Certainly they supply a startlingly different picture from that of the reports.

A second resource is to read the reports in a certain way, using the information which they sometimes provide but not succumbing to the implied definitions of its significance. The reader can often translate observation into a working class milieu for himself, drawing on knowledge derived from other sources. He is helped in this by the fact that not all observations fit the favoured meanings. It was often observed, for instance, that parental attitudes to schooling were utilitarian. Progress in reading, writing and arithmetic were the main tests of the efficiency of a school. These skills once acquired, children were withdrawn.[60] To providers this indicated an unwillingness to make further sacrifices. But perhaps this instrumental attitude to schooling was a rational adjustment to circumstance. Perhaps parents took from school what they valued, rejecting as soon as possible the petty regulation and the large measure of indoctrination which schooling always entailed. This matches much observed behaviour and also the very explicit recognition of the ideological content of schooling informing the whole radical tradition.[61] The 'moral' training of school, central for the educator, was detested by the radicals, and perhaps regarded as dispensable by many more in the struggle for economic security. A somewhat similar explanation may account for the surprising persistence of private schooling despite its expense and the drive to replace it. Schools wholly financed from fees were at least subject to parental control. As one assistant commissioner put it, disapprovingly, 'Parents may dictate their own programme'.[62]

Again, not all witnesses in the reports showed the same, or the same degree of, bias. Where special thoroughness or perspicuity is plain, evidence should be given a disproportionate weight. The evidence of James Ridall Wood in 1838 is a case in point. Wood was personally responsible for a set of reports on urban school provision published in the 1830s mainly under the auspices of the Manchester Statistical Society. His precise and accurate work produced more reliable counts of different kinds of schools than the governmental series, especially of the ephemeral private sector.[63] His data was collected on the ground by tramping round the streets of cities like Birmingham, 'leaving not even a court that was inhabited, to the best of my belief, unexplored'.[64] He was also a man of independent judgement though not exempt from every philanthropic bias. He was one of the few witnesses of the 1830s to stress the force of poverty in unambiguous language – 'It appears to me, in fact, that the only way in which general education can obtain must be by an advance in the wages of the adult population.'[65] Compared with all the circumlocution on this absolutely central issue and all the piecemeal and peripheral schemes to encourage attendance, this was exceptionally honest and clear-headed.

Some of the Newcastle assistant commissioners' reports are also especially valuable. The commissioners themselves, in their instructions, showed a novel interest in popular opinion. The heading 'the supply and demand of education' introduced a comprehensive set of questions about non-attendance and irregular attendance, many phrased to encourage curiosity about parental choice.[66] Assistant commissioners were told 'you should attempt to collect trustworthy evidence as to the general level of intellectual power amongst the class in question'.[67] They were to 'remember the importance of taking the evidence of the parents of the school children, as well as that of the patrons and managers of schools'.[68] The advantage (but also the difficulty) of 'personal acquaintance with persons of the labouring classes' was stressed.[69]

This prospectus was not uniformly followed, even in spirit. Dr Hodgson's report on London was full of familiar prejudice – parental 'excuses', 'self-caused' poverty and denunciation of 'claptrap about the oppression of the workmen'.[70] But a few assistant commissioners took this part of their brief very seriously. Here, for example, is Patrick Cumin (another future secretary of the Education Department) describing his procedure at Bristol:

I thought it expedient to examine some of the working classes themselves – the fathers and the mothers of the children who attend the National and the British schools. For this purpose I got the schoolmasters to invite a certain number of the parents to meet me. I visited others at their houses; I walked through the most degraded part of Bristol under the guidance of a police superintendent. By the kind permission of merchants and manufacturers, I went into the great works, and saw the men, women, and boys at work, and I put to them . . . questions . . . . Moreover, I visited public libraries and places of popular resort at all times of the day. . . . The opinions and feelings of the working men . . .are important matters in this inquiry, and . . .the only satisfactory method of ascertaining their opinions and their feelings, is to come directly in contact with the labouring man at his work, or after he has finished his daily task . . .I confess that I attach more weight to the evidence derived from the workpeople themselves than from any other source.[71]

This was hardly random sampling, nor talking in conditions of equality, but at least Cumin allowed working people to speak for themselves. He collected pithy comments from colliers and carpenters, labourers and errand boys, often reporting them with a mild surprise.[72] Other reports in the series have, in whole or in part, similar virtues: Fraser's report on the South Western agricultural counties, Foster's section on Pennine leadminers, some of Winder's material on Lancashire and Yorkshire.[73] It is as though they were discovering for the first time what Jenkins found in Wales: 'It is not a vice or moral delinquency that we have to deal with, but a state of opinion.'[74] It is the recognition of this dimension that is so often missing from the poverty and apathy stereotypes.

These findings influenced the commissioners' treatment of the problem of attendance.[75] They concluded that most parents appreciated education, that they chose to withdraw their children once literate and that the standard of satisfactory attendance should indeed be 'the standard which the respectable part of the [working] class set up by their conduct.'[76] On these grounds and a more doctrinaire respect for 'the natural demands for labour' they opposed a general compulsion. The usual moralistic censure was reserved for 'the most degraded part of the population'.[77]

It is important not to romanticize these conclusions. It could be argued, with much truth, that the commission's measure of parental aspiration was used to lower the threshold of educational ambition and to justify a conception of elementary education as class-bound and even more limited than that of the 1830s. The more 'democratic' tone of the report and the typical mid-Victorian discovery of a 'respectable' working class should be set beside the unwillingness to intervene in the economy or to recognize continuing economic insecurities. The commission also over-looked the idealistic in favour of the pragmatic elements in working-class educational opinion.[78] Even so, the report is unique in the collection in taking popular opinion at all seriously. In later discussions, including those of Cross, popular opinion, despite its contribution to 1870, disappears from view or re-assumes a stereotypical pattern. As a recent historian of policy in the 1870s and 1880s has put it, 'almost everyone assumed the apathy or active hostility of parents and children.'[79]

The reports and policy-making

We have attempted to show how unsatisfactory the reports are as documents about getting knowledge and about working people as educational actors. This was because inquiry belonged essentially to the providing classes and because the control of schooling, certainly up to 1870, very faithfully reflected the class distributions of economic power and of access to political influence. We would also insist that resulting biases are central to understanding the contents of reports, that a closer study of popular attitudes is feasible though difficult and that it must of necessity change understanding of a more familiar story.

Obversely, the reports say a great deal about giving knowledge, or selling it, or administering it by main force. They introduce the worlds of managers, administrators and even teachers. They trace the growth of schooling and of its cumbrous infra-structures – educational theory, teacher training, state finance and control, national and, later, local administration, educational law. But even here there should be some reservations or warnings. Much depends on the questions asked, the use to which the sources are put. In what follows three such uses will be discussed: the reports as a source for educational policy-making; as a way of examining the configuration of educational opinion; as a mine of general information abut the schooling enterprise.

Historians of government policy may wish to disentangle the steps by which state power in education grew and to explain why government action took the forms it did. The reports seem especially germane to this theme. After all, they seem to record policy-making process. With a few exceptions, they make recommendations or were designed to do so. But a closer examination is needed of the reports as would-be policy-making activities and of the policies actually pursued by government.

Again the reports fall into three or four groups corresponding to phases in policy-making. Before the Education Department was created in 1839 there was no real focus for national policy. Decisions were taken locally, often influenced by metropolitan innovators. The two largest voluntary societies – the National and the British and Foreign – exercised some central control, though neither was as capable or as willing to direct operations as the general histories sometimes imply. Certainly the Church of England had a massive ecclesiastical apparatus which was increasingly put to educational uses, but the Anglican policy of engrossment, so successful from the 1830s to the 1870s,[80] was always opposed by Dissent, by all kinds of radicals and, not least, by liberal-minded politicians. Respect for religious liberty was partly the cause but the National Society was also rightly seen as a vehicle of social and political conservatism.[81]

Even so, attempts were made to make national policy. The main drive came in the 1830s from loosely-connected groups of enthusiasts, middle-class, often professional, involved in philanthropy or statistical inquiry, interested in educational method at home and abroad, influenced by the doctrines of economic and political liberalism and sometimes already active as public servants in fields related to education. Many of the witnesses of the 1830s were of this kind, giving evidence alongside the officials of the societies.[82] Many were, like Professor Pillans, James Simpson and Dorsey, from Scotland; many more, like Kay and Henry Brougham, were educated there. They often had allies in parliament, active members of the reformed House of Commons like Thomas Wyse, Roebuck and Slaney. Some had connections with Whig magnate families which had lately come to power, especially with Lord John Russell and Lord Lansdowne.[83]

In other fields of government, innovative policies can be traced directly to men like these.[84] Their main instrument was the Royal Commission of Inquiry. In the Poor Law, in factory legislation and in matters of police and local government the impetus generated by commission often proved decisive. An examination of the reports themselves often throws a direct light on policy-making. Recommendation tended to pass into law.

In education it was different. The inquiries of 1816-18, 1834-35 and 1838 were failures in the special sense that they did not determine the direction of policy. Of the four main items of the Brougham plan, two failed entirely (an educational commission of inquiry and the plan for parochial schools on the Scottish model), one passed only in an emasculated form (the Charity Commission) and the fourth was delayed fifteen years (building grants for schools resuscitated by Brougham and the Whig ministry in 1833).[85] The 1834-35 Committee failed to report anything of substance except its evidence.[86] Slaney's draft report of 1838, itself a modest version of a bigger plan, was whittled down to platitudes by the opposing High Church group on the committee.[87] Slaney's intervention certainly influenced the creation of the Committee of Council in 1839, but was just one of the accumulating pressures that forced the Whig ministers to act. The form of action owed little to previous public debate. Though the plan for a state normal school was on the lines approved by educational experts, it was soon scotched by Anglican opposition. Though the favoured inspection of schools was also adopted, it took a curious hybrid form, most inspectors also being clerics of the Church of England. In all this, and in the constitutional shape of the Committee of Council itself, the *real politik* of Church and State was more immediately influential than the ideas busily canvassed since 1818.[88]

If public inquiry was peripheral to policy up to 1839, it was still more marginal in the decade of Kay's secretaryship. Some of the great inquiries of the 1840s bore on educational matters, especially the Commissions on Children's Employment and Handloom Weaving. Despite its title the latter became very much an investigation into education and the surrounding penumbra of 'moral' issues.[89] The Children's Employment Commission may have provided some of the impetus for Sir James Graham's ill-fated educational clauses of 1843.[90] More typically policy was secreted in the Council Office and inquiry was systematically connected to this departmental activity. The Welsh Commission was typical of this phase. Although it derived from a parliamentary motion, Kay used the commissioners very much as he sought to use his early inspectors – to publicize educational deficiencies and to hammer away at the need for civilizing schools and missionary teachers. The Minutes of 1846, the next big step in educational policy, owed little to public inquiry and report and almost all to Kay and the inspectorate. The secretary learned by trial and error, using the political space won by seven years of tact and collaboration.[91]

Kay's removal from office in 1849 marked the beginning of a third phase which lasted until the 1860s. The department ceased to be a source of major initiatives, while attempts by pressure groups and individual members of Parliament to make policy by other routes were frustrated. This impasse mainly affected the education of the 'independent' working class. In other areas, especially technical education or the treatment of criminal and destitute children, there were important innovations.[92] But in elementary education, thus defined, lines of policy remained essentially those of 1846, undercut in 1862 by the Revised Code.

The causes of this situation were complex and have been discussed elsewhere.[93] They had to do both with a tendency towards bureaucracy in the department itself and the unwillingness of politicians, scarred from previous battles, to make war on the religious denominations. In this situation, the Newcastle Commission was uniquely placed to make a major contribution.

In some ways, it was indeed the most influential educational inquiry of the century. But it was influential in a peculiar way. In large part the familiar pattern of frustration was repeated. Few recommendations passed into practice. The schemes for borough and county rates and boards fell flat. The very emphatic proposals about amalgamating the work of Education Department and Charity Commission remained dead letters until the creation of the Board of Education 1899-1903.[94] Even sensible minor proposals like those dealing with the education of outdoor paupers were neglected.[95] Instead the commissions more general findings were used to justify policies of restriction towards which political and departmental opinion was moving anyway. The commission provided educational arguments in favour of payment by results and the reduction of the grant-aid system and paved the way for the Revised Code. It provided a set of excuses for policies that were prepared in the office and which were heavily influenced by the Gladstonian climate of financial retrenchment.[96]

The major change of the mid-1860s was that politicians replaced administrators as the effective policy-makers. More accurately, the climate of educational opinion changed so as to allow the department's political leadership to
exercise a responsibility it had always, in theory, possessed. As legislation
became thinkable, initiative passed from the permanent officials to those
involved in parliamentary and general politics. Most of the major changes in
educational policy from 1870 onwards can be ascribed to particular politicians. Forster was very much the author of the 1870 Act while recent work
has shown the key roles of Sandon, Salisbury, Acland and Mundella in the
years that followed.[97]

The Cross Commission has to be viewed in this context. It originated in the
desire of the Conservative government to do something to aid voluntary
schools, and its membership was heavily weighted in that direction.[98] But
once again, its influence on subsequent policy is doubtful, partly because it
was so deeply divided in its recommendations, partly because decisions were
taken by the politicians in the light of educational propriety and political
advantage. The commission was most influential, perhaps, in hastening the
dismantling of payment by results, an issue on which the commissioners and
the bulk of the witnesses were unanimous.[99]

Unlike the great commissions of the 1830s, the reports in this collection
were not central to the policy-making process. Policy-making in education
was more clandestine; before Forster's Act even parliament was often by-
passed by the department's un-parliamentary constitution and its ability to
'legislate' by minute. In terms of historical sources, this puts a premium on
the records of the Education Department and other departments concerned
with education (printed and unprinted),[100] upon sources which reveal negoti-
ation between government and interested parties, and above all upon the
private and political correspondence between Kay and Lingen and their
political superiors and among the politicians themselves.[101]

Against this, it could be argued that the reports contain the public interrogation of policy-makers, especially of the civil servants. Kay gave evidence
to Slaney's committee shortly before he became secretary and also to Newcastle. Lingen was a Welsh Commissioner and a witness before Newcastle,
Argyll, the Select Committee of 1861 and at least two other select committees. He appeared before Cross, eighteen years after he had left the Education Department for the Treasury. Lingen's successor, Francis Sandford,
was himself a Cross Commissioner; Cumin, who followed him, gave voluminous evidence. Many inspectors of schools and other minor officials gave
public testimony.[102]

This is often useful. In 1838 Kay sketched out his ideal policy including rate
aid and teacher training before it was modified by the controversies of 1839-40
and Whig caution.[103] Lingen's Welsh report provides a unique insight into his

views on education as opposed to the administration of it.[104] More often, however, accounts of policy-making are retrospective, usually recollected at some distance. They are often disappointing. Kay's account of 1839-49 to Newcastle was positively misleading, partly because it was so self-effacing. We learn little about his role in the normal school plan of 1839, in the educational clauses of 1843, or the major though abortive initiative of the Aberdeen Coalition in 1853, for which, though no longer secretary, he was largely responsible.[105] His account of the creation of the Committee of Council in 1839 was confused and in obvious matters of fact, incorrect.[106] As in his *Autobiography* he was misleading too in his account of the origins of the Minutes of 1846.[107] Only in his general characterization of policy-making as a tentative and gradual process of learning by mistakes is his evidence really useful.[108]

Lingen's evidence is also disappointing but for different reasons. He was too much the civil servant and too conscious of the explosiveness of educational issues to give more away than was necessary to make his point. Checked against contemporary evidence, his statement that the Revised Code derived mainly from Newcastle is too simplified to be convincing.[109] Nor, from his public evidence, do we get the full flavour of his personal distaste for the denominational system and its voluntary organization and his wish that it should be done away with as soon as something more rational could have a hope of working. It would have been suicidal to declare himself a 'secularist', though this was what, in contemporary jargon, he really was.[110] His caution before Newcastle can be compared with the candour of Frederick Temple. Having left the Education Department for the headmastership of Rugby, Temple was quite prepared to enlarge upon a policy of secularization.[111] Just as the volatility of educational politics cramped policy itself, so it inhibited revelations before public inquiries.

There are, however, two useful exceptions — the Select Committees of 1864 (Inspector's Reports) and of 1865-66 (Constitution of the Committee of Council on Education).[112] Neither have been reprinted in the IUP series but they are interesting examples of Commons' inquiry in a probing, quasi-judicial mood. They operated against the recent background of the unpopularity of the Revised Code, an inspectoral revolt against Lowe's and Lingen's policies and even a whiff of departmental scandal over the censoring of inspectors' reports. Members included unrepentant opponents of the department, especially Lord Robert Cecil, who were quite prepared to grill witnesses. This proved especially revealing since the committee (unlike the education series) interrogated politicians as well as civil servants. The reports allow us to recreate the distribution of authority within the department and they throw more light on the origins of the Revised Code than any other public source.[113]

The reports and educational opinion

There is a danger of taking too narrow a view of policy-making or of seeing 'influence' in too mechanical or too biographical a way. Those directly responsible for decisions, on a national plane, worked within a context. In education this context was especially wide. It was difficult for officials or politicians to create for themselves areas of immunity, more difficult than in relatively technical matters like the control of pollution of the air, the prevention of accidents in factories, or even the curing of disease.[114] Education belonged rather to a class of public questions (like the relief of poverty) where ideology was most intrusive and aspirations to science largely specious. Kay and Lingen, of course, attempted to define areas of special authority, Kay by stressing a pedagogic expertise, Lingen by concentrating on his administrative and bureaucratic imperatives.[115] But though they defended themselves to some extent from controversy, they could not remove its causes. The basic condition of policy-making was the divisiveness of issues and their capacity to create passion, polemic and struggle.

It has become customary to ascribe this to 'the religious difficulty', as though religion was, as A.V. Dicey might have classed it, a kind of 'cross-current' affecting a more normal pattern of 'law-making opinion'.[116] No-one, especially having read the reports that spend so much time on it, could deny the importance of religious division in English education. But religion was neither a unique nor an autonomous influence; it was often the vehicle of other basic differences. The secularization of society has not, after all, led to a decline in educational controversy.

Another way of analyzing nineteenth-century educational problems is in terms of the tension of contradictory impulses. Most educators wished to Christianize the working class, identifying Christian morality with secular virtue. But they could not agree in what true Christianity lay. Could it be captured in formularies or secured by allegiance to a particular church? Or did it spring, through grace, from access to the scriptures? Or did it repose in some frame of mind, the beliefs common to all Christians, or in an ethical practice?[117] Education was seen, especially in the 1830s but recurrently thereafter, as a source of social and political stability. School-teachers could anticipate the work of Radicals, Socialists or Trade Unions.[118] But educators were not entirely agreed on the form that society or politics should take. They were pulled between more or less conservative and liberal ideals.[119] Conservatives feared, indeed, that certain kinds of knowledge too lavishly bestowed without controlling guarantees might actually foster agitation, or artificially raise expectations that could never be satisfied. Liberals repeatedly celebrated the death of these attitudes, but they none-the-less persisted.[120] Some believed that education would intellectually equip an industrial work-force; many more saw it as a source of work-discipline, time-thrift or rational economic behaviour.[121] At the same time both agriculture and the industrial economy rested on a base of child, female and adolescent labour, placing school and work in competition.[122] Moreover, though industrialization eventually supplied the means to erode mass poverty, the labour of children was long required to supplement family incomes. When seen from below this created a paradox that was stark indeed. As the *Poor Man's Guardian* put it, reflecting on the phenomenon of the charity school:

> You have starved the father and the mother, and then take the babe to rescue it from want, crime, ignorance, and nakedness, consequent on living at home.[123]

Then again, launching the schooling enterprise and still more achieving a general coverage, required massive finance. But taxing the propertied to supply it long remained unthinkable.[124] A central control of education was feared as a threat to Anglican prerogatives, or for its secularizing tendencies, or from a long, rich libertarian tradition. But the obvious, Lingenesque solution of 'decentralization on to really responsible shoulders' (i.e. secular local authorities) was resisted till 1870 from a similar tangle of motives.[125] Again, from the 1820s to the 1880s fees were very generally charged for schooling and educators stressed the moral value, to the parent, of payment. They also emphasized ('exceptions' apart) the duty of parent to child, censuring it in the neglect. Yet the parent was denied a direct say in the content of schooling which, even after 1870, was reserved to more 'responsible' parties.[126]

Throughout the period, the treatment of children deemed 'exceptional' was less controversial. Few disagreed that the state or philanthropy stood *in loco parentis* for orphaned, destitute, criminal, pauper or (an ill-defined category) vagrant children. Even the Newcastle minority conceded the principle.[127] But even here there were differences of approach. Some favoured a deterrent or quasi-penal treatment, stressing 'less-eligibility', usually favouring law and state institutions; others, commonly the philanthropists, stressed rehabilitation and moral rescue. The Select Committee of 1861 revolved around this disagreement with particular reference to the ragged school child, and resolved it in favour of the hard men.[128] A more humane programme, for pauper children at least, had to await the Departmental Committee of 1896. It abandoned belief in empauperization, less-eligibility and a separate treatment in favour of treating pauper children more like ordinary children and outside the barracks of the district schools.[129]

Concerted action would have been impossible without some broad areas of agreement. For most of the century it was accepted (by all but working-class Radicals and a few 'eccentrics' like Robert Owen and the phrenologist James Simpson)[130] that elementary education equalled working-class education and that it should be confined to narrow limits. After the post-war thaw, reading, writing and simple arithmetic were admitted to the curriculum of the elementary school together with an essential ingredient usually associated with religion ('religion and morals') and concerned with the shaping of behaviour and the child's affective nature. More progressive educators always tried to push beyond this limit and by the end of the century were achieving some successes,[131] but beyond literacy and 'morals' controversy was liable to break out. The typical recurring charges were those of 'over-education' and the neglect of elementary subjects.[132] Most educators also saw schooling as essentially regulative, though they differed on the best source of restraint. Secularists favoured a knowledge of natural or economic law.[133] Churchmen and many dissenters stressed theologically-derived sanctions.[134] Some educators favoured punishment, others reward, others 'emulation'. The educational experts of the 1830s looked to a kindly but 'civilizing' relationship between teacher and children.[135] But for celebrations of learning as secular liberation or as the development of hidden potentialities we have to look outside the reported orthodoxies.

The greatest value of the reports is in disentangling opinion on issues like these and charting areas of consensus. This is relevant to the study of policy-making and even of 'administrative history'. But the reports could also be used to study, say, attitudes to children, to poverty or to class. Schooling touched so many salient dilemmas and was so fertile in points of principle and prejudice that it provides an excellent vehicle for the study of ideology. Here the selectivity of the reports and their social enclosed-ness is more of an asset than a disadvantage. Speaking to their own kind on uncontroverted issues, wearing biases on their sleeves in a Romantic, pre-Marxian, pre-Freudian era, witnesses before the early inquiries can be astonishingly self-revealing. What on earth (raising twentieth-century children on Spock and play-groups) are we to make of another of Wilderspin's statements?!

I have had many instances where I have had to correct a child of only 12 months old; and in Wigan there was a little creature that could not speak, and yet domineered over the child that carried it about, and when it came to school it would not sit by itself; it wanted always to be on the back of the other, and I saw at once that I must enforce obedience. I had to whip it twice. It was only 15 months old; and then I had that very child at a public examination, before at least 350 auditors, and the child put out its arms to me and kissed me, and every person present was astonished. It only proved you cannot begin too early to train a human being.[136]

Other uses
The reports are most likely to be used for the light they throw on national or local aspects of schooling. Someone studying education in a particular locality, for example, may find it covered by an assistant commissioner, or may wish to use the statistical series compiled by Brougham, Newcastle, Argyll or

the Welsh Commission. He may find that some local activist gave evidence before a select committee or wrote in to a commission. The really big surveys — Newcastle, Argyll or Cross — are especially useful in these respects and it is always worth searching indexes.
There is no substitute for the close examination of local educational sources even though, in the voluntary era especially, they are scattered and fragmentary. Nor can these blue books supply the necessary material on regional economies and societies. But it is still possible to underutilize these stock sources for educational historians. This is especially true of the statistical material. An overall chronology of the spread of schooling, especially before 1870, is badly needed and it is surprising that educational history has not supplied it. We should know more too about the regional distributions of schooling or the relative strengths of different kinds of schools as between, for example, agricultural and industrial counties, metropolitan areas and those more distant from London, well-provided regions like the far North and those where provided schooling was relatively weak like Wales. We need more studies of the social and economic geography of schooling and of school use. The contemporary estimates, not only Brougham and Newcastle, but also the Kerry returns of 1835, Mann's educational census of 1851 and, where relevant, the statistical society series, are a useful point of departure. It is true they are full of technical pitfalls and that there is nothing in a statistical series that makes it exempt from bias.[137] It is probable, for instance, that the quality of returns from local agents is very uneven. The clerical returns of the Brougham series (useful incidentally in all kinds of more literary ways) certainly under-estimate the extent of non-Anglican provision in large urban parishes, partly because of antipathy to Dissent, partly because a clergyman might be ignorant of many forms of provision in a teeming population.[138] There are difficulties in the definition of different kinds of schools, in the definition of a 'school' itself, in different criteria of 'attendance' and in incompatibility between different series on these and other scores. But use for relatively modest purposes is certainly possible. One approach, in local studies, is to start from the general series, mapping some major educational variables, the overall chronology of growth, differences within the region and its typicality or otherwise compared with a national pattern. Results can then be compared with the findings of research on local sources which may give some measure of the inadequacies of the general series, especially their tendency to under-record.[139] This would certainly be an advance on present tendencies either to make ambitious global calculations with tricky data, or to eschew use altogether through excessive scepticism.[140]
    Perhaps, in the last resort, the opposite vice is more alluring — regarding the reports as compendia of educational information, carrying a special authority. Certainly the reports themselves often encourage this attitude.

They breathe the Victorian faith in 'fact', a rather naîve assumption of objectivity and a belief that truth most often emerges from the infinite accumulation of instances. Assistant commissioners were told to concentrate on 'fact' and avoid 'opinion'.[141] Assistant Commissioner Wilkinson's formulation was characteristic:

I have endeavoured simply to investigate facts. I have neither permitted my mind to be influenced by any controversial bias, nor have I adopted any theory whatever upon any question relating to popular education.[142]

Stances of impartiality like this were often betrayed on every following page. On the contrary, of course, the reports were emphatically political documents. The educational politics of class was always present, together with a politics derived more from the internal divisions of orthodoxy. The reports were designed as much to persuade as to discover. They were also, in the opinions recorded, biased towards the active portions of middle and upper class opinion. They were forums of the committed, the philanthropic and the anxious and do not necessarily represent the whole range of even propertied opinion.

This ordering and marshalling of 'fact' was not confined to the substantive reports themselves, to the actual recommendations and their supporting arguments, though it is here that the political intent is easiest to detect. The Newcastle Commission, for instance, received in its written evidence, a large volume of support for the continuation or even extension of something like the existing grant aid system.[143] But its conclusions were informed by the reports of untypical assistant commissioners like Fraser and by Lingen's formidable case about administrative complication.[144] The political dimension is plain too where the inquiring body was itself divided. Slaney's Select Committee, for instance, split along the liberal-Tory Anglican rift. The chairman, by calling a class of expert witness dominated the proceedings of the inquiry itself, but conservative obstruction prevented this evidence from being embodied in recommendations.[145] The Committee of 1861 canvassed rival reports and recorded patterns of voting on the issue of state aid to ragged schools.[146] But political intent extended to every aspect of inquiry, including the choice of investigators. The Education Department in 1858, for example, was determined that Newcastle should contain no pronounced friend of the existing system and to judge from the final membership (including the exclusion of Sir John Pakington from whose parliamentary motion the commission derived) Lingen's advice was followed.[147] Even the choice of witnesses and the actual processes of interrogation were, in part, manipulative. It is an interesting exercise, where the names of questioners are given, to identify cases for defence and prosecution as it were, in sessions with particular witnesses.

This is not to suggest that members of inquiries never changed their minds,

0353424

nor, as has been stressed throughout, that biases prevent any use whatever. The internal and external politics of the inquiries are an important part of the whole educational story. But neglect of this dimension can produce a large effect on the historiography. The Senior-Chadwick view of the old Poor Law presented in the Poor Law Commission Report of 1832 had a profound effect on poor law history. It is only quite recently that the report has been set in its ideological and political context and its findings and evidence more closely scrutinized.[148] One result of this has been a more accurate and sometimes more favourable view of the pre-1834 systems in all their variety.

No one report on education carried this kind of authority. The historical dominance of a single version, compelling, coherent but incomplete, should be easier to avoid.

Footnotes

1 *Third Report of the Royal Commission appointed to inquire into the Working of the Elementary Education Acts,* HC 1887 [C.5158] XXX, q.52,630 IUP series Education: General 36, p.392. Hereafter cited as *Cross Commission.*

2 For the origins of the inquiry see Hansard, *Parliamentary Debates* (3rd Series), LXXXIV, cols.845-65 & *Reports of the Commissioners on the State of Education in Wales,* HC 1847 [C.870] XXVII-Part I, p.iii IUP Series Education: General 1. Hereafter cited as *Welsh Commission.*

3 They also, of course, sometimes received written memoranda from witnesses and others, though rarely on a large scale.

4 Newcastle despatched Matthew Arnold to France, Holland and Switzerland and Mark Pattison to Germany. For Argyll and the Schools Inquiry Commission jointly, Rev. James Fraser (also a Newcastle Assistant Commissioner) reported on the common schools of the USA and Canada. These reports have been ignored in what follows but for Arnold see the valuable study by W. F. Connell, *The Educational Thought and Influence of Matthew Arnold,* (London 1950).

5 For a full list see *Cross Commission: Digest of the Evidence,* 1888, HC 1888 [C.5329]XXXVII, pp.iii-v. IUP series Education: General 37, pp.541-43.

6 [*First*] *Report from the Select Committee on the Education of the Lower Orders in the Metropolis* 1816, HC 1816 (498) IV,p.1. IUP series Education: Poorer Classes 1. Hereafter cited as *Brougham Select Committee.*

7 e.g. *Select Committee on Police in the Metropolis* 1816-18, *First Report,* HC 1816 (510)V.IUP series Crime & Punishment: Police 1 & *Select Committee on Mendicity in the Metropolis* 1814-16, *First Report,* HC 1814-15(473) III.

8 *Brougham Select Committee: Third Report* 1818, HC 1818(426)IV, pp.55-59. IUP series Education: Poorer Classes 2. For the background see Chester W. New, *The Life of Henry Brougham to 1830* (Oxford 1961), pp. 209-25.

9 [*First*] *Report from the Select Committee on the State of Education* 1834, HC 1834 (572) IX, p.iii. IUP series Education: Poorer Classes 6, p.11. Hereafter cited as *Roebuck Select Committee.*

10 *Report from the Select Committee on the Education of the Poorer Classes* 1838, HC 1837-38 (589) VII, p.iii. IUP series Education: Poorer Classes 6, p.515. Hereafter cited as *Slaney Select Committee*. The attention of both committees was directed to more specific questions, but like Brougham, both interpreted their briefs with the maximum of width.

11 *Welsh Commission: Instructions,* HC 1847 [C.870] XXVII – Part I, p.iii. IUP series Education: General 1.

12 The Welsh Commissioners' reports were, indeed, minutely detailed, including school by school descriptions and even details of the interrogation of children.

13 For a discussion of the nature of this interest see Richard Johnson, 'Educational Policy and Social Control in Early Victorian England', *Past & Present,* No. 49 (Nov. 1970), pp.96-119.

14 *Report of the Commissioners appointed to inquire into the State of Popular Education in England,* HC 1861 [C.2794] XXI – Part I, p.542. IUP series Education: General 3. Hereafter cited as *Newcastle Commission.*

15 The fact that the early reports — Brougham, Roebuck and Slaney — do not systematically distinguish categories of children or strata of the working class has posed a problem of classification for IUP too. Since these reports deal with all sections of the working class, readers might be wise to regard them as part of the Education: General set and treat only volumes 7, 8 & 9 of the series as belonging to the Education: Poorer Classes set.

16 *Cross Commission: Final Report,* HC 1888 [C.5485] XXXV, p.xxii. IUP series Education: General 37, p.30. *Report of the Departmental Committee appointed by the Local Government Board to inquire into the existing systems for the maintenance and education of children under the charge of managers of districts schools and Boards of Guardians in the Metropolis,* HC 1896 [C.8027] XLII, p.iv. IUP series Education: Poorer Classes 8, p.11. Hereafter cited as *Departmental Committee of 1896.*

17 *Roebuck Select Committee,* HC 1835 (465) VII, q.779. IUP series Education: General 6, p.341.

18 For his career and interests see Graham Wallas, *The Life of Francis Place* 1771-1854, (London 1898). His involvement with the West London Lancasterian Association can be traced in *Place Papers,* BM Add MSS 27,823. For some shrewd judgements on the man see E. P. Thompson, *The Making of the English Working Class* (London 1963).

19 *Cross Commission: Third Report,* HC 1887 [C.5158] XXX, qq.52,792-52,802. IUP series Education: General 36, p.397.

20 *ibid.,* qq.48,508-11 & 48,546.

21 *ibid.,* qq.52,554 & 52,603.

22 *ibid.,* q.52,719.

23 This statement is based on the author's research on the following sources: *Brougham Select Committee: A Digest of Parochial Returns,* HC 1819 (224) IX – Part III, esp. p.1171. IUP series Education: Poorer Classes 5. *A Return of the Number of Schools in Each Town, Parish* . . . (Lord Kerry's Returns), HC 1835 XLIII, esp. pp.1330-31. *Census 1851 – Education,* HC 1852-53 XC. Also the reports of various statistical societies, for one of which see *Roebuck Select Committee,* HC 1835 (465) VII, pp.101-20. IUP series Education: Poorer Classes 6, pp.375-94. See also the local studies list in the bibliography to this commentary. I am grateful to Michael Frost and Jacqueline Grayson for material on Birmingham and Worcestershire.

24 *Roebuck Select Committee,* HC 1835 (465) VII, evidence of Rev. J. C. Wigram, qq.1-20. IUP series Education: Poorer Classes 6, pp.275-83. But many other examples could be given.

25 These were the leading themes of the Slaney and Roebuck Committees and of the Welsh Commission.

26 For the distinction of 'moral' and 'physical' used by Dr Kay among others see Johnson 'Educational Policy and Social Control', esp. pp.101-103.

27 For treatment of the relevant areas in Wales see J. C. Symons on Monmouthshire, Rev. H. V. Johnson on Llanidloes and Lingen on South Wales, esp. HC 1847 [C.871] XXVII – Part II, pp.291-94; HC 1847 [C.872] XXVII – Part III, p.67; HC 1847 [C.870] XXVII – Part I, pp.2-3. IUP series Education: General 1 & 2.

28 For a useful summary of these problems see Nancy Ball, 'Elementary School Attendance and Voluntary Effort before 1870', *History of Education*, II (January 1973), pp.19-34.

29 *Minutes of the Committee of Council on Education* (octavo edn.), 1850-51, pp. 264-67.

30 Parental attitudes to fees were the commonest focus for reflection on working-class opinion on the Cross Commission.

31 See, for example, Lingen's limited experience — 'Every day, as I walk from my home to the office, if I had nothing else to do, I could march off three or four little beggars whom I see as I come through the Parks.' *Select Committee on the Education of Destitute Children*, HC 1861 (460) VII, q.3782. IUP series Education: Poorer Classes 7, p.217. But some of the evidence to this committee was more sympathetic, notably Mary Carpenter's, *ibid.*, qq.2277-78. Many other examples of the street encounter could be given.

32 It is not intended to imply that modern sociological observation is without bias. Professionalizing the activity creates its own biases.

33 For a modern assessment of Mayhew's method see E. P. Thompson & Eileen Yeo (ed.), *The Unknown Mayhew* (London 1971).

34 The quotation continues — 'Do you find that your visits are well received by the parents? — Yes, we generally get a large attendance.' HC 1834 (572) IX, qq.1579-80. IUP series Education: Poorer Classes 6, p.129.

35 I owe these thoughts and much else in this commentary to discussions with friends in Birmingham about 'alternative education', especially with Dick Atkinson and Anita Halliday.

36 *Brougham Select Committee: First Report*, HC 1816 (427) IV, p.7. *Third Report*, HC 1816 (495) IV, p.254. IUP series Education: Poorer Classes 1.

37 *Welsh Commission*, HC 1847 [C.870] XXVII – Part 1, p.2. IUP series Education: General 1.

38 e.g. 'There is no Welsh literature worthy of the name.' HC 1847 [C.871] XXVII-Part II, p.66. IUP series Education: General 2.

39 This episode is not well covered in the secondary sources, probably because most of the protesting literature is in Welsh. I am grateful to Miss Anne Davies, who has the language, for her study of the 1847 Report and its reception in an undergraduate dissertation for the University of Birmingham.

40 *Welsh Commission*, HC 1847 [C.871] XXVII – Part II, pp.4-5. IUP series Education: General 2.

41 *Brougham Select Committee: Third Report*, HC 1818 (426) IV, p.56. IUP series Education: Poorer Classes 2.

42 For this see New, *Henry Brougham*, pp.330-46.

43 For the drawing up of the returns see *Brougham Select Committee: A Digest of Parochial Returns*, HC 1819 (224) IX-Part III pp.i-ii. IUP series Education: Poorer

Classes 5. The returns themselves, on a sample of which this passage is based, occupy three whole volumes: IUP series Education: Poorer Classes 3-5.

44 The committee was especially interested in the education of the Catholic poor and interrogated a number of priests and laymen.

45 HC 1816 (427) IV, p.30. IUP series Education: Poorer Classes 1.

46 *ibid.*, p.256.

47 *ibid.*, p.41. Wakefield, with Place and some other witnesses, were leading members of the West London Lancasterian Association.

48 e.g. *Roebuck Select Committee*, HC 1835 (465) VII, q.21. IUP series Education: Poorer Classes 6, p.280. *Newcastle Commission*, HC 1861 [C.2794] XXI-Part III, pp.517-20. IUP series Education: General 5.

49 e.g. 'The parents become high in their manners and difficult to manage, when wages are very good.' *Roebuck Select Committee*, HC 1835 (465) VII, q.14. IUP series Education: Poorer Classes 6, p.278.

50 *Newcastle Commission*, HC 1861 [C.2794] XXI – Part III, P.353. IUP series Education: General 5.

51 *Slaney Select Committee*, HC 1837-38 (589) VII, q.58. IUP series Education: Poorer Classes 6, p.536.

52 *ibid.*, qq.78-81.

53 *ibid.*, qq.60-61 & evidence of Braidley, *Roebuck Select Committee*, HC 1834 (572) IX q.2348. IUP series Education: Poorer Classes 6, p.190.

54 e.g. *ibid.*, q.2406 & HC 1835 (465) VII, qq.83-85. IUP series Education: Poorer Classes 6, pp.196 & 286.

55 E. G. West 'Resource Allocation and Growth in Early Nineteenth-Century British Education', *Economic History Review*, XXII (April 1970), esp. p.89.

56 *Roebuck Select Committee*, HC 1835 (465) VII, q.393. IUP series Education: Poorer Classes 6, p.309.

57 The most useful published introduction to this tradition remains Brian Simon, *Studies in the History of Education 1780-1870*, (London 1960). For a deeper study of the Owenite contribution see Harold Silver, *The Concept of Popular Education* (London 1965). See also the criticisms of Simon, explicit and implicit, in the excellent essay by Eileen Yeo, 'Robert Owen and Radical Culture' in *Robert Owen: Prophet of the Poor*, ed. Sidney Polland and John Salt (London 1971). For earlier phases see Thompson, *Making of the English Working Class*.

58 A full list would be very long. It would include the famous pursuits of knowledge of William Lovett, Thomas Cooper and Samuel Bamford. For a fuller list see the working-class entries in Mathews, *British Diaries* and the same author's *British Autobiographies*. Though not himself a working man, the educational writing of William Cobbett is a primary source for early popular attitudes to school and learning.

59 Especially useful for their education emphasis are *The Black Dwarf, The Gorgon, Cobbett's Political Register, The Republican* in the early period; later, the whole of the Owenite press especially *Crisis, Pioneer* and *The New Moral World*, and, for a more political orientation, *The Poor Man's Guardian*. Later still the *Northern Star* is invaluable for its coverage of Chartist ideas and events. But most of the political unstamped and the movement literature of the 1830s, 1840s and early 1850s are deeply concerned with education and educational policies.

60 For an early observation see *Brougham Select Committee: Second Report*, HC 1816 (469) IV p.147. IUP Education: Poorer Classes 1. Later examples include *Roebuck Select Committee*, HC 1834 (572) IX q.814. IUP series Education: Poorer Classes 6, p.80. *ibid.*, HC 1835 (456) VII qq.14-17. IUP series Education: Poorer Classes 6, p.280. *Slaney Select Committee*, HC 1837-38 (589) VII, qq.747-51. IUP

series Education: Poorer Classes 6, p.605. There are many examples in the reports of Newcastle Assistant Commissioners.

61 For an especially trenchant example see William Cobbett, *Cottage Economy* (London, 1850 edn.), pp.10-11. And compare later versions in the *Poor Man's Guardian* (which disagreed with Cobbett on some essentials) e.g. 13 August 1831, (Leader).

62 *Newcastle Commission*, HC 1861 [C.2794] XXI – Part II, p.196. IUP series Education: General 4.

63 See the use and appraisal of the reports (without mention of their author) in the recent Hurt-West controversy: West, 'Resource Allocation and Growth'; J. S. Hurt, 'Professor West on Early Nineteenth-Century Education', *Economic History Review*, XXIV (November .1971), pp.624-32. E. G. West, 'The Interpretation of Early Nineteenth-Century Educational Statistics', *ibid.*, pp.633-42.

64 *Slaney Select Committee*, HC 1837-38 (589) VII, q.1228. IUP series Education: Poorer Classes 6, p.641.

65 *ibid.*, q.1151.

66 HC 1861 [C.2794] XXI – Part II, pp.10-13. IUP series Education: General 4.

67 *ibid.*, p.18.

68 *ibid.*, p.12.

69 *ibid.*, p.19.

70 HC 1861 [C.2794] XXI – Part III, pp.517-24 & 563. IUP series Education: General 5.

71 *ibid.*, pp.25-26.

72 e.g. *ibid.*, p.27.

73 e.g. Winder on autodidacts and co-operative societies, HC 1861 [C.2794] XXI – Part II, pp.240-42. IUP series Education: General 4.

74 *ibid.*, p.474.

75 Cumin and Fraser were especially cited in support.

76 HC 1861 [C.2794] XXI – Part I, p.190. IUP series Education: General 3.

77 Identified as those who never sent their children to school at all, *ibid.*, p.179.

78 That this idealism survived the decline of Chartism is evident from Simon, *Studies*, pp.340-67.

79 Gillian Sutherland, *Policy-Making in Elementary Education 1870-1895* (Oxford 1973), p.160.

80 For an interesting local study see Michael Sanderson, 'The National and British School Societies in Lancashire 1803-1839: the roots of Anglican supremacy in English Education' in *History of Education Society: Local Studies and the History of Education*, ed. T. G. Cook (London 1972) pp.1-36.

81 The classic contemporary statement is John Morley, *The Struggle for National Education* (London 1873, reprinted with introduction by Asa Briggs, Brighton 1972).

82 i.e. Pillans, Julius, Brougham and perhaps Braidley in 1834; Wilderspin, Simpson, Dorsey and possibly Place (an 'expert' of earlier vintage perhaps without Brougham's ability to keep up to date) in 1835; Kay, Wood, Caldwell, Corrie, Buxton and Ashworth in 1838. All these were involved in the statistical movement in Manchester, Birmingham or London, and dominated the 1838 Committee.

83 For connections between Russell and Kay before 1839 see J. R. B. Johnson 'The Education Department 1839-1864: A Study in Social Policy and the Growth of Government', (Unpublished Ph.D. thesis, Cambridge 1968), pp.55 & 62. Hereafter cited as Johnson 'Education Department'.

84 For an early identification of the type see O. R. MacGregor, 'Social Research and

Social Policy in the Nineteenth Century', *British Journal of Sociology*, VII (1957). For examples of such groups at work see S. E. Finer, *The Life and Times of Edwin Chadwick* (London 1952, reprinted 1970) & the same author's 'The Transmission of Benthamite Ideas 1820-50' in *Studies in the Growth of Nineteenth-Century Government*, Gillian Sutherland, ed., (London 1972).

85 New, *Brougham*, pp.213-21 & 324-31. For his role in 1833 (a retrospective account) see *Brougham Papers* (University College London) 10,378, Russell to Brougham, 4 August 1853.

86 HC 1834 (572) IX, p.iii & HC 1835 (465) VII, p.iii. IUP series Education: Poorer Classes 6, pp.11 & 273.

87 HC 1837-38 (589) VII, pp.iii-xv. IUP series Education: Poorer Classes 6, pp.515-27. For the bigger plan see Johnson, 'Education Department', p.50 note 1.

88 This is a very superficial summary based on *ibid.*, pp.40-84.

89 See especially HC 1841 [C.296] X, pp.398-402. IUP Series Industrial Revolution: Textiles 10.

90 The Children's Employment Commission is reprinted in full in the IUP series Industrial Revolution: Children's Employment, 6-11.

91 This paragraph is mainly based on Johnson 'Education Department', Chs. II, III & IV.

92 Especially a string of Acts dealing with reformatories and industrial schools.

93 Johnson 'Education Department', Chs. VII & VIII. For Lingen's role see A. S. Bishop, 'Ralph Lingen, Secretary to the Education Department 1849-1870', *British Journal of Educational Studies*, XVI (June 1968), pp.138-65 & Richard Johnson, 'Administrators in Education before 1870: Patronage, Social Position and Role', in *Studies in the Growth of Nineteenth-Century Government*, Gillian Sutherland, ed. pp.110-38.

94 A. A. Bishop, *The Rise of a Central Authority for English Education* (Cambridge 1971) pp.259-69.

95 Until 1873.

96 This interpretation is based on correspondence in the *Granville Papers*, PRO 30 29. See also the sources cited in note 93 above.

97 Sutherland, *Policy-Making in Education*, pp.345-46.

98 *ibid.*, pp.265-66.

99 *ibid.*, pp.266-84.

100 The unprinted records in the PRO are disappointingly thin before 1870, but records of the Treasury, the Poor Law Commission, the Council Office and the Home Office sometimes supply useful information. *The Minutes/Reports of the Committee of Council on Education* (1839-) are invaluable and contain the reports of HMIs. They were published in two forms — as ordinary Parliamentary Papers and in an octavo edition for more general circulation. Contents of the two series sometimes differ.

101 For some of the most useful collections before 1870 see Johnson, 'Education Department', p.511; for the later period see Sutherland, *Policy-Making in Education*, p.365.

102 Especially before Newcastle and Cross.

103 HC 1837-38 (589) VII, pp.1-26 & 31-42. IUP series Education: Poorer Classes 6, pp.529-54 & 559-70.

104 HC 1847 [C.870] XXVII– Part 1, pp.1-42. IUP series Education: General 1.

105 The most useful published account of Kay's contribution remains Frank Smith, *The Life and Work of Sir James Kay-Shuttleworth* (London 1923). But see also Johnson

'Education Department', Chs. I, III. IV & VIII and Nancy Ball, *Her Majesty's Inspectorate 1839-1849* (Birmingham 1963). Compare these with *Newcastle Commission*, HC 1861 [C.2794] XXL – Part VI, qq.2306-2455 & 2986-3129. IUP series Education: General 8, pp.311-37 & 380-402.

106 According to Kay the creation of the Committee of Council and the normal school plan derived from the report of a select committee chaired by Lord Brougham in 1835. He seems to have confused the 1816-18, 1834-35 and 1838 committees. *ibid.*, qq.2308-10.

107 Johnson, 'Education Department', pp.170-90 (where this is argued at length).

108 HC 1861 [C.2794] XXI – Part VI, esp. q.2368. IUP series Education: General 8, p.322.

109 *Cross Commission: Third Report*, HC 1887 [C.5158] XXX, qq.56,207-10.

110 *Newcastle Commission: Minutes of Evidence*, HC 1861 [C.2794] XXI-Part VI, esp. q.506. IUP series Education: General 8, p.81 & cp. the account of Lingen's views in Johnson 'Education Department', pp.416-28.

111 *ibid.*, qq.2456-2985. This is also an interesting example of an espousal of the case for a parental say in school management.

112 *Select Committee on the Committee of Council on Education: Inspectors' Reports*, HC 1864 (468) IX; *Select Committee on the Constitution of the Committee of Council on Education*, HC 1865 (403) VI & 1866, VII.

113 e.g. HC 1865 (403) VI, qq.380-86.

114 The career of Sir John Simon illustrates the power of, in this case, a medical expertise in policy-making. See Royston Lambert, *Sir John Simon 1816-1904 and English Social Administration* (London 1963).

115 For their contrasting styles of administration see Johnson, 'Administrators in Education' in *Studies in the Growth of Nineteenth-Century Government*.

116 A. V. Dicey, *Law and Public Opinion in England during the Nineteenth Century* (2nd Edn., London 1962), pp.311-60.

117 These questions are recurrent themes in the reports, underlying differences between High Church Anglicans, the British and Foreign School Society and more latitudinarian Christians. The emphasis on an ethical Christianity is characteristic of working-class radicalism where the ethic is turned against existing institutions and the religion of the churches.

118 For a late example see *Cross Commission: Second Report*, HC 1887 [C.5056] XXIX, qq.31,843-46.

119 For examples of how alternative social ideals were reflected in the nature of schooling see J. M. Goldstrom, *The Social Content of Education 1808-1870*, (Shannon 1972). Or compare the educational ideals of secularists like Place or James Mill with those of their anglican contemporaries.

120 For a late, crusty, example of gentry conservatism see evidence of Sir Charles Alderson to Newcastle, HC 1861 [C.2794] XXI – Part V, pp.9-14; IUP series Education: General 7.

121 There is an unresolved debate running through the reports on whether elementary schools should include industrial training and, if so, whether it was valuable mainly for 'habits' or for skills.

122 All the Newcastle Assistant Commissioners produced massive evidence on the extent of child labour.

123 *Poor Man's Guardian*, 16 June 1832, reprinting an article from *The Ballot*.

124 This remained a vexed question before Cross and was connected with the payment

of fees. Fee-paying in elementary education was greatly reduced between 1892 and 1895. See Sutherland, *Policy-Making in Education*, esp. pp.324-30.

125 The Lingen quotation is from *Select Committee on the Constitution of the Committee of Council on Education*, HC 1865 (403) VI, q.138.

126. But studies of the popular(?) politics of school boards are needed. For the debate about parents as voluntary school managers see *Cross Commission: Final Report*, HC 1888 [C.5485] XXXV, p.67. IUP series Education: General 37,p.99. One remains sceptical about the effectiveness of parental representation and notes that most of the parents on management boards seem not to have been working class. See the Cross statistics in this, HC 1888 [C.5485] XXXVI – Part II, Return A. IUP series Education: General 38, pp.403-63.

127 HC 1861 [C.2794] XXI – Part I, pp.297-98 IUP series Education: General 3.

128 Compare the rival draft reports, HC 1861 (460) VII pp.viii-xii. IUP series Education: Poorer Classes 7, pp.16-20.

129 HC 1896 [C.8027] XLIII, pp.170-72. IUP series Education: Poorer Classes 8, pp.184-86.

130 For Owen's very muted evidence see *Brougham Select Committee: Third Report*, HC 1816 (495) pp.238-42. IUP series Education: Poorer Classes 1. For Simpson's interesting brand of secularism, with its almost egalitarian emphasis, see *Roebuck Select Committee*, HC 1835 (465) VII, Appendix 3. IUP series Education: Poorer Classes 6, pp.395-480.

131 Especially with the decline of payment by results.

132 e.g. *Newcastle Commission*, HC 1861 [C.2794] XXI – Part I, pp.242-66.

133 e.g. Francis Place before *Roebuck Select Committee*, HC 1835 (465) VII esp. qq.821-1019. IUP series Education: Poorer Classes 6, pp.347-64.

134 e.g. Rev. Daniel Wilson before *Brougham Select Committee: Fourth Report*, HC 1816 (497) IV, esp. p.279. IUP series Education: Poorer Classes 1.

135 e.g. Kay to *Slaney Select Committee*, HC 1837-38 (589) VII, qq.17-20. IUP series Education: Poorer Classes 6, pp.530-31.

136 *Roebuck Select Committee* HC 1835 (465) VII, q.167. IUP series Education: Poorer Classes 6, p.29.

137 For some of the pitfalls see assessments of sources in the Hurt-West controversy (cited note 63 above).

138 Compare, for example, the list of places with British schools given by William Allen in 1816 (HC 1816 IV, pp.118-19) with the relevant parochial returns. Schools listed by Allen are sometimes missing.

139 I am grateful to Jacqueline Grayson for discussions on these lines about the methodology of local studies.

140 As in the Hurt-West controversy. West tends to global uses; Hurt to scepticism.

141 e.g. *Welsh Commission*, HC 1847 [C.870] XXVII – Part I, p.iv. IUP series Education: General 1, or *Newcastle Commission*, HC 1861 [C.2794] XXI – Part II, p.7. IUP series Education: General 4.

142 HC 1861 [C.2794] XXI – Part III, p.321. IUP series Education: General 5.

143 Only a handful of respondents were opposed to the grant system. HC 1861 [C.2794], XXI – Part V, answers to questions 12 a, b & c. IUP series Education: General 7.

144 Fraser's report was 'repeatedly canvassed by the commissioners'. *Newcastle Commission Files*, PRO,T 74/2D, Fraser to secretary of commission, 21 March 1861.

145 The crucial vote was on Slaney's fourth resolution. HC 1837-38 (589) VII, p.xii. IUP series Education: Poorer Classes 6, p.525.

146 HC 1861 (460), VII, pp.viii-xvi. IUP series Education: Poorer Classes 7, pp.16-24.

147 *Granville Papers*, PRO 30 29 Box 22 a, Bundle marked '1858', Lingen to Granville, 14 February 1858.

148 Especially important in this modern re-assessment are: Mark Blaug, 'The Myth of the Old Poor Law and the Making of the New', *Journal of Economic History*, XXII (1963) & 'The Poor Law Report Re-examined', *Journal of Economic History*, XXIV, (1964).

Bibliography

There are many outline histories of education in the nineteenth century. Familiar to readers of this commentary, they record, besides, a story grown stale from repetition, failing to connect education with other historical themes. But Frank Smith's two volumes — *The Life and Work of Sir James Kay-Shuttleworth*, (London: J. Murray, 1932) and *A History of English Elementary Education 1760-1870*, (London University Press, 1931) — are still worth consulting, the former as an important source book using items in the Kay-Shuttleworth collection that are not longer extant. A. E. Dobbs, *Education and Social Movements 1700-1850*, (London: Longmans, Green & Co., 1919) remains valuable for a different reasons — as an attempt to view educational growth against a wider scene of material and cultural change. Reading it now for its fertility of ideas prompts the thought that the separatist tendencies of educational history derived from neglect of this, the Hammond-Tawney generation of social historians. Of recent general studies Mary Sturt, *The Education of the People*, (London: Routledge and Kegan Paul, 1967) is the freshest.

The history of education has been so flabby conceptually that contributions from sociologists ought to be welcomed. Michalina Vaughan and Margaret S. Archer, *Social Conflict and Educational Change in England and France 1789-1848*, (Cambridge University Press, 1971) test rival models of educational and institutional change. Historically the research is rather thin and their version of Marxism is crude. Individual theorists or spokesmen stand in for complex educational traditions. But their conclusions, especially on the relationship of educational change and industrialization, are stimulating, often validated by a closer look at the sources. Similar in intention but narrower in scope and less convincing in conclusions is John McLeish, *Evangelical Religion and Popular Education: A Modern Interpretation*, (London: Methuen, 1969). N. J. Smelser, *Social Change in the Industrial Revolution*, (London: Routledge and Kegan Paul, 1959) is sociologically more sectarian, but this study of factory and family in nineteenth-century Lancashire bears closely on educational themes. It is not to be neglected despite the jargon and the determination to fit complex historical circumstance into a pre-arranged functionalist schema. It is a pity that Michael Anderson, *Family Structure in Nineteenth-Century Lancashire*, (Cambridge: Cambridge University Press 1971) missed the chance to fit school into the context of family and neighbourhood. Does this reflect the genuinely peripheral role of schooling in the communities examined? Brian Simon, *Studies in the History of Education 1780-1870*, (London: Lawrence and Wishart, 1960) and *Education and the Labour Movement 1870-1920*, (London: Lawrence and Wishart, 1965) are historical in method but proceed on some firm theoretical premises. They draw attention, albeit episodically, to combative working-class educational traditions, but avoid assessing the popular representativeness of these radical voices. The same problem underlies his useful collection of documents — *The Radical Tradition in Education in Britain*, (London: Lawrence and Wishart, 1972).

A more systematic study of nineteenth-century government has involved a closer look at educational administration and policy-making. The most impressive contribution is Gillian Sutherland, *Policy-Making in Elementary Education 1870-1895*, (Oxford University Press, 1973). Here the full range of sources for policy-making is employed and the author has a wide (but wide enough?) view of the context of central decision-making. The civil servants have been examined in two essays in *Studies in the Growth of Nineteenth-Century Government*, (London: Routledge and Kegan Paul, 1972) edited by the same author — Richard Johnson, 'Administrators in Education before 1870: Patronage, Social Position and Rôle' and Gillian Sutherland 'Administrators in Education after 1870: Patronage, Professionalism and Expertise'. J. S. Hurt, *Education in Evolution: Church, State, Society and Popular Education 1800-1870*, (London: Hart Davis, 1971) is especially useful on the Revised Code but is more narrowly governmental in approach than the title suggests. A. S. Bishop, *The Rise of a Central Authority for English Education*, (Cambridge: Cambridge University Press, 1971) traces the development of three government departments concerned with education to their junction at the turn of the century as the Board of Education. Neither of these books, nor P. H. J. H. Gosden, *The Development of Educational Administration in England and Wales*, (Oxford University Press 1966), innovate in their use of sources and make only small inroads into what is quite a traditional way of writing educational history. Studies of individual policy-makers or particular episodes include: A. S. Bishop, 'Ralph Lingen, Secretary to the Education Department 1849-1870', *British Journal of Educational Studies*, XVI (June 1968); W. H. C. Armytage, 'A. J. Mundella as Vice-President of the Privy Council, and the Schools Question, 1880-85', *English Historical Review*, LXIII (1948); D. W. Sylvester, *Robert Lowe and Education* (Cambridge, 1974); Henry Roper, 'Toward an Elementary Education Act for England and Wales, 1865-68', *British Journal of Educational Studies*, XXIII, (June 1975); W. P. McCann, 'Elementary Education in England and Wales on the Eve of the 1870 Education Act', *Journal of Educational Administration and History*, II (Dec. 1969). Nancy Ball, *Her Majesty's Inspectorate 1839-49*, (Birmingham Institute of Education, 1963) is by far the best of a number of studies of the corps; W. F. Connell, *The Educational Thought and Influence of Matthew Arnold* (London: Routledge, 1950) is by far the best biography of an individual inspector and is useful for much else besides. Eric E. Rich, *The Education Act 1870* (London: Longmans, 1970) is based on a useful thesis long unpublished and is the best of a spate of books commemorating the Forster Act.

Economic and social historians have rarely repaired the defects of educational history. For a survey of how education has been treated in the general economic histories (i.e. cursorily) see the useful essay in R. M. Hartwell, *The Industrial Revolution and Economic Growth*, (London: Methuen, 1971). The staples of research in economic history — studies of industries, regions, towns or individual firms — commonly have something to say on educational provision, but usually in a piecemeal, descriptive way. One exception is C. J. Hunt, *The Leadminers of the Northern Pennines in the Eighteenth and Nineteenth Centuries*, (Manchester University Press, 1958) which has an intriguing discussion of the schooling strategies of leadmining companies. Also useful are W. G. Rimmer, *Marshalls of Leeds: Flax Spinners 1788-1856*, (Cambridge: Cambridge University Press 1960) and Rhodes Boyson, *The Ashworth Cotton Enterprise*, (Oxford University Press 1970). Sidney Pollard's two articles on factory discipline provide essential background to the educational philanthropy of the factory master. See 'Factory Discipline in the Industrial Revolution', *Economic History Review*, XVI (1963-64) and 'The Factory Village', *English Historical Review*, LXXIX (1964).

Local educational histories are uneven in quality and serve the voluntary era better than the school boards. Some attempt to relate school provision and school use to the economic and social structure of the region, but they rarely employ the full range of techniques and sources increasingly used by economic and social-structural historians. They are, however, essential reading and where sufficiently systematic at the very least help to build the regional chronology of schooling. The most useful are: James Murphy, 'The Rise of Public Elementary Education in Liverpool: Part I & II', *Transactions of the Historic Society of Lancashire and Cheshire*, CXVI & CXVIII (1964 & 1967); Marion Johnson, *Derbyshire Village Schools in the Nineteenth Century*, (Newton Abbot: David and Charles, 1970); Leslie Wynn Evans, *Education in Industrial Wales 1700-1900: A History of the Works Schools System in Wales during the Industrial Revolution*, (Cardiff: Avalon Books, 1971); David Wardle, *Education and Society in Nineteenth-Century Nottingham*, (Cambridge: Cambridge University Press 1971); R. R. Sellman, *Devon Village Schools in the Nineteenth Century*, (Newton Abbot: David and Charles, 1967); T. W. Bamford, *The Evolution of Rural Education: Three Studies of the East Riding of Yorkshire*, (Research Monograph No. 1, Institute of Education, University of Hull, 1965). This last is especially good, innovatory in technique and approach. A. P. Wadsworth, 'The First Manchester Sunday Schools', *Bulletin of the John Rylands Library*, XXXIII (1950-51) remains the liveliest introduction to the movement.

Educational documents, locally collected, are invaluable source material. See especially the series edited by Rex C. Russell under the title *A History of Schools and Education in Lindsey and Lincolnshire 1800-1902*, (Lincoln, 1965) and Surrey Educational Research Association, *Extracts from Records Illustrating the History of Education in Surrey*, (2nd Edn., Surrey County Council 1962). These supplement collections with a national scope: John Stuart Maclure (ed.), *Educational Documents England and Wales 1816-1967*, (London: 2nd Edn., Chapman and Hall, 1968); G. M. Goldstrom (ed.), *Elementary Education 1780-1900*, (Newton Abbot: David and Charles, 1972).

On the school board era see the older works — H. B. Philpott, *London at School: The Story of the School Board 1870-1904*, (London: T. Fisher Unwin, 1904) and J. H. Bingham, *The Period of the Sheffield School Board 1870-*

1903, (Sheffield: J. W. Northend, 1949). More recent works include David Rubinstein, *School Attendance in London 1870-1904,* (University of Hull 1969) and Angela Gill, 'The Leicester School Board 1871-1903' in *Education in Leicestershire 1540-1940,* ed. Brian Simon, (Leicester University Press 1969).

There are signs that the isolation of educational history is breaking down. One connecting route is via the redefinition of labour history. Especially since the publication of *The Making of the English Working Class* attention has shifted from labour institutions to working-class culture and experience. Edward Thompson's massive re-appraisal has significant implications for educational history. Since learning both by children and by adults is an integral part of patterns of popular culture, an educational and a labour or social history must in time mesh, to the benefit of both but especially the former. There are already signs of this occurring, though most work to date has concentrated upon working-class political articulacy and the pursuits of knowledge that underlay it. If educational historians fail to take note of all the excellent work in this field, they will be unable to take it further. Especially important are the studies of Owenism, so centrally an educational or counter-educational movement. See J. F. C. Harrison, *Robert Owen and Owenites in Britain and America,* (London: Routledge and Kegan Paul, 1969); Harold Silver, *The Concept of Popular Education,* (London: MacGibbon and Kee, 1965); and the very stimulating article by Eileen Yeo on 'Robert Owen and Radical Culture' in *Robert Owen: Prophet of the Poor,* ed., Sidney Pollard and John Salt, (London: Macmillan, 1971). For the similar educational emphases of Chartism see the older but still useful study by H. V. Faulkner, *Chartism and the Churches,* (Columbia University Press, 1916) and the collection of documents edited by Dorothy Thompson — *The Early Chartists,* (London: Macmillan, 1971). Many of the local studies of Chartism are also relevant, not to say the whole factory movement.

An allied interest is in the development of a mass reading public. Here too educational and wider themes are necessarily related. Three general works are essential starting points. Raymond Williams, *The Long Revolution,* (London: Chatto and Windus, 1961) puts nineteenth-century developments in a perspective that is broad as well as long. R. D. Altick, *The English Common Reader: A Social History of the Mass Reading Public,* (London and Chicago: University of Chicago Press, 1957) is sometimes bitty and impressionistic but none the less a pioneer. R. K. Webb, *The British Working Class Reader 1790-1848: Literacy and Social Tension,* (London: Allen and Unwin, 1955) is rather slight in research but contains an important argument that might well be applied to schooling too. More substantial are two recent studies of the unstamped press of 1830-36 which bridge the themes of Radicalism, counter-education, readership and responses of authority — Joel H. Wiener, *The War of the Unstamped: The Movement to Repeal the British Newspaper Tax 1830-36,* (Cornell University Press 1969) and Patricia Hollis, *The Pauper Press: A Study in Working-class Radicalism in the 1830s,* (Oxford University Press 1970).

Another way of pulling education off the historical periphery is by exploring linkages between educational expansion and industrial revolution or the sources of retardation in each. Work on the critical period up to 1850 seems to yield mainly negative results, suggesting that connections were complex, mediated by social and political concerns. Michael Sanderson's work, concentrating on the Lancashire test case, is outstanding. See his three important articles: 'Education and the Factory in Industrial Lancashire 1780-1840', *Economic History Review*, XX (1967); 'Social Change and Elementary Education in Industrial Lancashire 1780-1840', *Northern History*, III (1968); 'Literacy and Social Mobility in the Industrial Revolution in England', *Past and Present*, No. 56 (August 1972); and the debate sparked off by the last: Thomas W. Laqueur & M. Sanderson, 'Literacy and Social Mobility' & 'A Rejoinder', *Past & Present*, No. 64 (August 1974). Less soundly based empirically, stretching nineteenth-century statistical series to breaking point to demonstrate a modern argument, E. G. West's work has none the less highlighted the important contribution of private schooling up to 1870 and revealed significant areas of debate within an older school of political economy. See especially: E. G. West, *Education and the State: A Study in Political Economy*, (London: 2nd revised edn., Institute of Economic Affairs, 1970) and 'Resource Allocation and Educational Growth in Early Nineteenth-Century Britain', *Economic History Review*, XXX 1970. His most recent book — *Education and the Industrial Revolution* (London: Batsford, 1975) — continues his campaign against social-democratic historians and educationalists but fails to produce much of substance on its avowed theme: 'the relationship between education and the process of industrialization during the nineteenth century'. If, as both authors in different ways suggest, educational expansion followed no clear economic logic, the argument that schooling was to do with social and political control (including discipline for work) may grow in strength. On this see Richard Johnson, 'Educational Policy and Social Control in Early Victorian England', *Past and Present*, No. 49 (December 1970).

The approaches outlined above necessarily focus attention upon literacy. It will receive increasing attention as the most measurable educational 'effect'. It would be a pity, however, if the other intended effects of schooling (central in the minds of contemporaries) were lost sight of in the hot pursuit of quantification, valuable though precision here will be. For discussions of the methodologies involved (in assessing school use as well as literacy) see B. I. Coleman, 'The Incidence of Education in Mid-Century' in *The Study of Nineteenth-Century Society*, ed., E. A. Wrigley, (Cambridge: Cambridge University Press 1972) and R. S. Schofield, 'The Measurement of Literacy in Pre-Industrial England' in *Literacy in Traditional Societies*, ed., Jack Goody, (Cambridge: Cambridge University Press 1968). For a survey of some contemporary estimates see R. K. Webb, 'Working-Class Readers in Early Victorian England', *English Historical Review*, LXV (1950). For an introduction to regional differences from the county series see G. R. Lucas, 'The Diffusion of Literacy in England and Wales in the Nineteenth Century', *Studies in Education: Journal of the Hull Institute of Education*, III (1961). For some local results see W. P. Baker, *Parish Registers and Illiteracy in East Yorkshire*, (East Yorkshire Local History Society, 1961) and Roger Smith, 'Education, Society and Literacy: Nottingham in the Mid Nineteenth Century', *University of Birmingham Historical Journal*, XII (1969). And for a stimulating if premature attempt to pull it all together with suggestions on causation see Lawrence Stone, 'Literacy and Education 1640-1900', *Past and Present*, No. 42 (February 1969).

Another obvious route of integration is with education's nineteenth-century twin — religion. Unfortunately modern studies have often remained captive to nineteenth-century religious allegiances. Example of the genre are H. B. Binns, *A Century of Education, being the Centenary History of the British and Foreign School Society,* (London: Dent, 1908), H. J. Burgess, *Enterprise in Education: the Story of the Work of the Anglican Church in the Education of the People prior to 1870,* (London: S.P.C.K., 1958), H. F. Mathews, *Methodism and the Education of the People 1791-1851,* (London: Epworth Press, 1949). Studies of the Anglican Church commonly deal with education. Geoffrey Best, *Temporal Pillars: Queen Anne's Bounty, The Ecclesiastical Commission and the Church of England,* (Cambridge: Cambridge University Press 1964) and G. Kitson Clark, *Churchmen and the Condition of England,* 1832-1885 (London: Methuen 1973) are useful on the general Anglican strategy. Michael Sanderson, 'The National and British School Societies in Lancashire 1803-1839' in *Local Studies and the History of Education,* ed. T. G. Cook for the History of Education Society, (London: Methuen, 1972) and Diana McClatchey, *Oxfordshire Clergy 1777-1869,* (Oxford: Clarendon Press 1960) are good local studies. James Murphy, *The Religious Problem in English Education: The Crucial Experiment,* (Liverpool University Press 1956) is the best discussion of 'the religious difficulty' at least in its early form but is also good on the educational politics of the 1830s.

There has been less work on the distinctive social and political characteristics of denominational education, on, for example, Anglicanism as a form of educational conservatism. Useful on this and on allied themes, however, is G. M. Goldstrom, *The Social Content of Education 1808-1870: A Study of the Working-Class School Reader in England and Ireland,* (Shannon: Irish University Press, 1972). The study of the social geography of nineteenth-century religions, now a booming research area, has yet to produce significant published results on education. For a promise of things to come, however, see Alan Everitt, 'Non-conformity in the Victorian Countryside˜ in *Local Studies and the History of Education* (cited above) and the sources given there.

Older studies of special aspects of education are often better than the outline histories and some remain 'standards'. These include R. W. Rich, *The Training of Teachers in England and Wales in the Nineteenth Century,* (Cambridge: Cambridge University Press, 1933) and A. H. Robson, *The Education of Children Engaged in Industry in England 1833-1876,* (London: Kegan Paul and Co., 1931). Asher Tropp, *The Schoolteachers: The Growth of the Teaching Profession in England and Wales,* (London: Heineman, 1957) is more sociological in approach than the earlier study. On contemporary educational theory see Hugh Pollard, *Pioneers of Popular Education 1760-1850),* (London: Heineman, 1957) which, however, is actually a rather uncritical study of educators who were central to the liberal orthodoxies of the period. For more genuine heterodoxies see W. A. C. Stewart and W. P. McCann, *The Educational Innovators 1750-1880,* (London: Macmillan, 1967). But perhaps the most interesting and resourceful book on contemporary method to appear recently has been Malcolm Seaborne, *The English School: Its Architecture and Organisation 1370-1870,* (London: Routledge and Kegan Paul, 1971) which portrays school as a physical entity, but is alive to its social purposes and to the need for an agreed chronology of change. Peter Gordon, *The Victorian School Manager* (London: Woburn Press, 1975) works a similar neglected vein, is full of fascinating detail from unfamiliar primary sources, but fails to illuminate the sources of local educational philanthropy.

THE DOCUMENTS

ELEMENTARY EDUCATION

Poorer Classes Volume 1

REPORT FROM THE SELECT COMMITTEE ON THE EDUCATION OF THE LOWER ORDERS IN THE METROPOLIS WITH MINUTES OF EVIDENCE AND APPENDIX, 1816

336 pp

Despite general apathy and often outright opposition, parliamentary intervention in the cause of popular education found successive champions in Samuel Whitbread and Henry (afterwards Lord) Brougham. In 1816 Brougham procured the appointment of a Select Committee to examine the education of London's lower orders and to see what could be done for the education of the poor. At the committee's request the scope of inquiry was later extended to include England and Wales generally. The specific interest of the committee was in the pauper children who roamed the streets of London but they did not attempt to dissociate this from the general question of education. (The inquiry took place to the background of the Lancaster Bell dispute and the fragmented voluntary educational movements of the time). In their short report the committee pointed to the large numbers of neglected children, to the desire of the poor for education and to the beneficial effects produced by the voluntary movements, as powerful arguments for parliamentary intervention. However, they also mentioned that any proposed measures would have to concur with the prevailing dispositions of the community. The volume has a large body of evidence from witnesses connected with education of the poor, including Robert Owen, originator of the infant school system and one of the founders of British socialism. It gives a vivid description of the condition of destitute children in London and of the institutions which attempted to cater for them, and provides much valuable information on the finances of schools, the administration of charities and other related matters.

Original references

1816	(498) IV	Education of the lower orders in the Metropolis, Sel. Cttee. Rep.
1816	(427) IV	Education of the lower orders in the Metropolis, Sel. Cttee. 1st Rep., mins. of ev.
	(469)	Education of the lower orders in the Metropolis, Sel. Cttee. 2nd Rep., mins. of ev.

Poorer Classes Volume 2

FIRST TO FIFTH REPORTS FROM THE SELECT COMMITTEE ON THE EDUCA-
TION OF THE LOWER ORDERS WITH MINUTES OF EVIDENCE, APPENDICES
AND AN ADDITIONAL REPORT, 1817–1818

464 pp

The inquiries of Brougham's committee into the misapplication of
charitable funds excited much discussion and controversy. Meanwhile the scope of the inquiry was extended to cover England, Wales
and Scotland as well as London. These reports were concerned with
many general aspects of education for the lower classes, but more
particularly with further inquiry into the abuse of charitable funds.
They took evidence on the management of financial administration
of Croydon and Wellingborough charities, Eton College, and the
schools of St. Bees, Winchester, Highgate, Pocklington, Brentwood,
Mere, Spital, Yeovil and Huntingdon. (These institutions had
originally been intended for the education of the poor). As there
were endowments for the education of the poor attached to the
universities of Oxford and Cambridge, the committee also examined these. The evidence and appendices have extracts from
financial accounts and other documents relating to the colleges and
universities, some of which had never been made public before. Of
special interest are the statutes of Eton College and of St. John's and
Trinity Colleges, Cambridge, reprinted in full in the fourth and fifth
reports. The committee's inquiries resulted in the appointment, in
1819, of commissioners to examine the administration of charities.

Original references

1817	(479) III	Education of the lower orders, Sel. Cttee. Rep.
1818	(136) IV	Education of the lower orders, Sel. Cttee. 1st Rep.
	(356)	Education of the lower orders, Sel. Cttee. 2nd Rep.
	(426)	Education of the lower orders, Sel. Cttee. 3rd Rep., mins. of ev.
	(427)	Education of the lower orders, Sel. Cttee. 4th Rep., appendix (A) documents.
	(428)	Education of the lower orders, Sel. Cttee. 5th Rep., appendix (B) documents.

Poorer Classes Volume 3

DIGEST OF PAROCHIAL RETURNS MADE TO THE SELECT COMMITTEE ON
EDUCATION OF THE LOWER ORDERS (PART I ENGLAND), 1819

584 pp

These returns constitute the most extensive and compact factual survey of British education in the early nineteenth century. They were obtained in reply to a circular questionnaire sent to the parochial clergy, and the digests were compiled by the committee with the assistance of two barristers. The digests are arranged in alphabetical order by county and parish and a summary table is provided for every county. The statistics given for each parish include population, number of poor, number of schools (endowed and unendowed) and the number of children attending each category of school. The clergymen's comments on the state of education are also given. This volume covers the counties from Bedford to Monmouth.

Original reference
1819 (224) IX Pt. I   Education of the lower orders, digest of parochial returns, Part I.

Poorer Classes Volume 4

DIGEST OF PAROCHIAL RETURNS MADE TO THE SELECT COMMITTEE ON EDUCATION OF THE LOWER ORDERS (PART II ENGLAND), 1819

604 pp

This is a continuation of Poorer Classes volume 3 and covers the counties from Norfolk to York. In addition to enumerating the endowments and schools the digests provide information on the history of endowments, on their value, on the sources of finance for unendowed schools, on salaries of teachers and on the systems of teaching used. The clergymen's comments indicate that the voluntary movements had not succeeded in providing adequately for the education of the poor and that poor parents everywhere were anxious to have their children educated. These were the main considerations put forward by the committee when they recommended state intervention.

Original reference
1819 (224) IX. Pt. II   Education of the lower orders, digest of parochial returns, Part II.

Poorer Classes Volume 5

DIGEST OF PAROCHIAL RETURNS MADE TO THE SELECT COMMITTEE ON EDUCATION OF THE LOWER ORDERS (PART III WALES, SCOTLAND AND BRITISH ISLES), 1819

356 pp

The third and final volume of the digest contains the returns for

Wales, Scotland and the British islands (Alderney, Guernsey, Jersey, Man, Sark and the Scilly Isles) together with supplemental returns for England and summary tables for the three countries. The digests for both Wales and Scotland contain more detailed information than those for England (Poorer Classes 3 and 4). A comparative glance at the information shows that Scotland was better provided with schools than either England or Wales. In Wales there were many parishes without a school of any kind.

Original reference
1819   (224) IX Pt. III   Education of the lower orders, digest of parochial
                                returns, Part III.

Poorer Classes Volume 6

REPORTS FROM SELECT COMMITTEES ON POPULAR EDUCATION IN ENGLAND AND WALES, WITH APPENDICES AND INDICES, 1834–1838

704 pp

Although the 1832 Reform Act was an important victory for liberal opinion in the British Parliament, in educational matters it did little more than intensify demands for concerted government action. Parliament as a whole remained indifferent to pleas for a national system of popular education and was still content merely to stimulate voluntary effort and to intervene only where voluntary effort could not reach. Accordingly, in 1833, Roebuck's proposals for a national system were rejected and instead £20,000 was voted as a grant to stimulate educational development. In the following year a select committee was appointed to examine the state of education of the people of England and Wales, the application and effects of the grants and the expediency of further grants. This committee was reappointed in the following year and in 1837 another committee was set up this time to consider the best means of providing useful education for the children of the poorer classes in the large cities of England and Wales. The committees included such notable proponents of a progressive educational policy as Roebuck and Russell, and are exceptionally important because they span the years when parliamentary intervention was taking shape. The evidence taken by them is an important source of information on the educational facilities of the time, on the impact of new ideas and developments on British educationalists, and on the nature of the impasse which was retarding progress. Among the organizations whose activities were described in detail were the National, and British and Foreign School Societies, the Sunday School movement and the infant schools. Views on and proposals foɪ solution of the religious question took up a large part of the evidence but many witnesses saw this merely as an excuse for the failure to implement a universal system of popular education. What these witnesses considered to be the real issues were: state finance and organization, compulsory education and competent inspection. The progressive viewpoint is excellently summarized in the evidence of James Simpson taken before the 1835 committee on Irish education and reprinted in the appendix to the 1835 report in the present volume. Simpson's thesis was that 'education could elevate the moral and intellectual state of the working classes' and his evidence attempts both to prove this and to delineate education as he conceived it. His conception involved education financed by equitable taxation, education for both sexes, co-education of the different ranks of society and many other elements which seem well before their time.

Original references

1834	(572) IX	State of education, Sel. Cttee. Rep., mins. of ev., appendices, index.
1835	(465) VII	Education in England and Wales, Sel. Cttee. Rep., mins. of ev., appendices, index.
1837–38	(589) VII	Education of the poorer classes in England and Wales, Sel. Cttee. Rep., mins. of ev., appendices, index.

Poorer Classes Volume 7

REPORTS ON THE EDUCATION OF DESTITUTE AND NEGLECTED CHILDREN, 1841–1878

488 pp

The 1837–38 inquiries on the Poor Law (see Irish University Press Poor Law set) scrutinized the whole field of public provision for the under-privileged classes. These committees took considerable evidence on education for both the destitute and working classes and in this area as in others were strongly influenced by ideas derived from Benthamite utilitarianism—the working classes should be made as self-supporting as possible and only the genuinely destitute should receive public assistance. These ideas constituted the basis of educational policy from the establishment of the committee of the Privy Council for education in 1839 until the Newcastle Commission reaffirmed it in 1861 (see Irish University Press Education: General set). In 1861, a select committee on education for destitute and neglected children was appointed with terms of reference strikingly like those of the Newcastle Commission: 'to examine how education for destitute and neglected children can be most economically and efficiently assisted from public funds'. The committee included Sir Stafford Northcote, Robert Lowe and John Pakington. The emphasis on economy ruled out any attempt to bring about sweeping changes but the committee's report is a valuable survey of the condition of pauper children, the facilities for their education and the effectiveness of government aid. Particular attention was paid to the relationship between poverty and juvenile deliquency in the towns and cities and the financing and organization of workhouse, industrial and ragged schools were thoroughly examined. The committee's recommendations reaffirmed the general principles of parliamentary policy but made several suggestions for improvement. The witnesses included Ralph Lingen and Patrick Cumin. This volume contains two further papers: reports by poor law inspectors (1826) defending workhouse education against allegations made before the Newcastle Commission and a report on new methods of catering for pauper children (1878). The first of these has extensive information on workhouse education, and on its effects on the lives of pupils while the second examined and approved the idea of training pauper children in 'family units' rather than in large institutions.

Original references

1861	(460) VII	Education of destitute and neglected children, Sel. Cttee. Rep., mins. of ev., appendices.
	(460–I)	Education of destitute and neglected children, Sel. Cttee. Rep., index.
1862	(510) XLIX	Education of pauper children; W. H. T. Hawley, R. Weale, J. Walsham, A. Doyle, Poor Law Inspectors; Reps.
1878	(285) LX	The home and cottage system of training and educating children of the poor; F. J. Mouat, Local Government Board Inspector, Capt. J. D. Bowley; Rep.

Poorer Classes Volumes 8 and 9

REPORT FROM THE DEPARTMENTAL COMMITTEE ON THE EDUCATION AND MAINTENANCE OF PAUPER CHILDREN IN THE METROPOLIS WITH MINUTES OF EVIDENCE, APPENDICES AND INDEX, 1896

Volume 8   616 pp
Volume 9   520 pp   40 folding tables

The harsh approach to the poor marked by the 1834 Poor Law and subsequent official reports gradually lost support during the second half of the nineteenth century with the growth of more enlightened attitudes. This is strikingly illustrated by the 1896 committee on education and maintenance of pauper children which took as its guiding principle the provision for these children of individual care and a life as similar as possible to that of more privileged children. This was the underlying idea in the 180-page report which examined and made recommendations on the problem under the headings: the effects of aggregation of children in large communities, the condition of existing institutions (cubic space, food, etc.), the prevalence of ophthalmia, education and training (finance, facilities, inspection, religious instruction, industrial training), apprenticeship and employment, defective children, associations for the care of neglected children after leaving school, emigration, legal aspects of the control and custody of children, etc. The report emphasized the advantages of the natural environment provided either by foster parents or in the home and cottage system and discussed at length proposed reforms. It was accompanied by 800 pages of oral evidence and a long appendix of replies to questionnaires from officials administering the poor law and education systems—boards of guardians and managers, superintendents, matrons, head teachers, medical officers, etc., connected with the district, separate and Roman Catholic certified schools. These appendices give full statistics on number of children, teaching staff, provisions for instruction, etc. Volume 8 has the report and first section of evidence; volume 9 has the remainder of the evidence, the appendices and indices.

Original references

Volume 8

1896	[C.8027] XLIII	Education and maintenance of pauper children in the Metropolis, Dept. Cttee. Vol I Rep.
	[C.8032]	Education and maintenance of pauper children in the metropolis, Dept. Cttee. Vol II Pt. I, mins. of ev.

Volume 9

1896	[C.8032] XLIII	Education and maintenance of pauper children in the Metropolis, Dept. Cttee. Vol II Pt. II, mins. of ev., index.
	[C.8033]	Education and maintenance of pauper children in the Metropolis, Dept. Cttee. Vol III, mins. of ev., appendices.

Education: General Volume 1

PART I OF THE REPORT FROM THE ROYAL COMMISSION APPOINTED TO INQUIRE INTO THE MEANS OF EDUCATION AVAILABLE IN WALES, 1847

568 pp   2 folding charts

The polarization of Welsh Society with the growth of Methodism, and the educational and literary revivals of the late eighteenth and early nineteenth centuries form the back-drop to the 1847 Royal Commission report. In their terms of reference the commission were required to consider especially the means for teaching the English language to Welsh children and this requirement provides a key to the timbre of the reports. The commissioners saw a culturally isolated community nurtured on the theology-orientated Sunday schools, with a character and pride in it which was specifically Welsh, but needing 'salvation' from the more pragmatic culture of England.

The first part of the report deals with the southern counties of Carmarthen, Glamorgan and Pembroke. It has a large body of statistical information on education facilities for the lower orders (the inquiry was confined to education for the lower orders). Schools, day, evening and Sunday, are enumerated; the number of pupils and teachers, the cost of running the school and a variety of similar details are given.

Special attention is paid to describing the poor condition of the schools and the deficiencies of the teachers, and to evaluating the education given in each school. The commissioners' comments amounted to an endictment of the whole system, an endictment Welshmen were not to be very happy about.

Original reference
1847   [870] XXVII   Education in Wales, R. Com. Reps. Part I,
              Pt. I   Carmarthen, Glamorgan and Pembroke.

Education: General Volume 2

PARTS II AND III OF THE REPORT FROM THE ROYAL COMMISSION APPOINTED TO INQUIRE INTO THE MEANS OF EDUCATION AVAILABLE IN WALES, 1847

784 pp

Parts II and III of the Royal Commission report complete the survey of Welsh education, dealing with north and central Wales and with Monmouthshire. Coal mining was extensive in many of the areas discussed and was causing fundamental changes in Welsh society. The coal mine or the factory had in many cases usurped the place of the parish church as the community centre. Factory and mine schools were often more important sources of education than ordinary day schools—the majority of the children worked with their parents. Indeed the commissioners found that to depict Welsh education as it was, it was necessary to go outside the schools altogether and examine the structure of society and the mode of life. As in Part I of the report, there was general criticism of the educational system. The condition of school buildings in north Wales, and the standard of teachers and teaching generally were discredited. Many teachers were in the profession because they were unfit for any other occupation and in many cases their knowledge was scanty and their acquaintance with the art of teaching was negligible. The reports are liberally strewn with instances of failure to accept that Welsh culture had an inherent value. The commissioners were at one in recommending that means should be taken to expedite the demise of the Welsh language though some of them recognized that there were elements of imagination and poetry in the rough Welsh spoken ways. On the same theme, one commissioner felt that the Welsh were too prone to mythical and metaphysical research; the same commissioner mentioned 'as a matter of satisfaction to all friends of Wales that not a single day school in his area taught Welsh'.

Part II of the report has several references to the agrarian disputes known as the 'Rebecca Riots'.

Original references

1847	[871]	XXVII	Education in Wales, R. Com. Reps. Part II,
		Pt. II	Brecknock, Cardigan, Radmor and Monmouth.
	[872]	Pt. III	Education in Wales, R. Com. Reps. Part III,
			Anglesea, Carnarvon, Denbeigh, Flint, Merioneth
			and Montgomery.

Education: General Volume 3

REPORT FROM THE ROYAL COMMISSION APPOINTED TO INQUIRE INTO THE STATE OF POPULAR EDUCATION IN ENGLAND AND TO CONSIDER WHAT MEASURES WERE REQUIRED FOR THE EXTENSION OF SOUND AND CHEAP INSTRUCTION TO ALL CLASSES, WITH INDEX, 1861

728 pp   2 folding charts

By 1857 many Englishmen thought that the £541,000 parliamentary grant for education was excessive. With this in view the Newcastle Commission on 'popular education' was set up. It was partly on the recommendations of the commission's report that Robert Lowe's system of 'payment by results' was introduced in 1862. 'Payment by results' in the view of many historians retarded the development of British elementary education for the remainder of the century. The report was based on five volumes of oral evidence, reports from assistant commissioners and letters from people of many different shades of opinion. In general it was favourable in its criticisms of the systems though it pointed out that much better use could be made of existing educational facilities especially those catering for the destitute poor. All the questions disputed in educational controversies at the time were examined in the report. Among the most hotly debated of these was the part played by religion in the schools. Despite the growing strength of the 'secularist movement', the commission recommended that there be no interference with religious instruction. Poor school attendance was highlighted as the most serious fault in elementary education, this was attributed to poverty and lack of understanding on the part of parents. An interesting observation in this respect was that poverty and pauperism were hereditary. Other than its proposal for reorganizing the grants system, the main recommendations of the commission were that county and borough boards should be set up to regulate education, that better use should be made of educational charities, that improvements should be made in teacher training colleges and that the education of children working in factories should be better provided for.

Original reference
1861   [2794–I] XXI   State of popular education in England, R. Com.
                Pt. I   Rep., Vol. I, index.

Education: General Volume 4

REPORTS FROM ASSISTANT COMMISSIONERS ON POPULAR EDUCATION IN REPRESENTATIVE AGRICULTURAL, INDUSTRIAL AND MINING DISTRICTS, 1861

648 pp

Districts were selected for specialized examination by the Newcastle Commission so as to present as complete a picture as possible of the state of popular education. The assistant commissioners were asked to dismiss all theories and ideas which they might have gleaned from the public controversies which raged at the time and to concentrate on providing the inquiry with extensive factual information. This series of reports deals with agricultural areas in the south and east, textile manufacturing districts in Lancashire and Yorkshire and centres of the iron, coal and pottery industries in Warwickshire and Staffordshire. Comprehensive statistical information on elementary schools in each district is presented together with the opinions of the assistant commissioners on the overall result and the deficiencies of the education provided.

Special attention is paid to the operation of the parliamentary grant and to inefficient use of other finances. The educational problems varied with the nature of the district. In rural areas schools were largely denominational, and non-sectarian schools would be unacceptable; town populations on the other hand were not so definite in their religious preferences. In large industrial centres the demand for children's labour, both at home (while the mother was working) and in the factories, made successful education very difficult. In spite of the numerous defects mentioned, the assistant commissioners found the machinery which provided education for the masses to be generally satisfactory. J. S. Wander for example observed the 'great results' of education in Rochdale and in Bradford, while Rev. Thomas Hedley described education in the eastern agricultural counties as 'voluntary in spirit and national in extent'. Recommendations put forward constituted a little improvement here and there for the machine rather than a complete overhaul.

Original reference
1861   [2794–II] XXI   State of popular education in England; education
             Pt. II   in rural and other districts, J. Fraser, etc. Reps.
                       R. Com. Vol. II, Rep.

Education: General Volume 5

REPORTS FROM ASSISTANT COMMISSIONERS ON POPULAR EDUCATION IN REPRESENTATIVE MARITIME AND METROPOLITAN DISTRICTS, 1861

608 pp

These constitute the remainder of the reports on selected districts. They cover the maritime areas around Bristol, Plymouth, Hull, Yarmouth and Ipswich, and several parishes in London. The reports provide detailed information under all the headings specified by the instructions to the assistant commissioners (size, cost, condition, quality of education, etc. for all public, private, Sunday, evening and factory schools). In his report on Bristol, Patrick Cumin (later to be secretary of the Education Department) made a plea for a better system of education, especially for the poor. The people of Bristol were engaged in a great variety of occupations from naval to agricultural and there was widespread poverty in the area. Mr. Cumin devoted a large section of his report to 'ragged' and other schools for the poor. He condemned the idea that only children of the upper classes were entitled to a liberal education and proposed that 'school pence' for pauper children should be paid out of the rates. The report on Hull denied that there was unhealthy competition between private and public schools and stressed the need in that particular area for an education which was both technical and general. The reports on parishes in London examined many of the problems specifically associated with schools in a large metropolis e.g. pupil-teacher ratios, extremely poor attendance, etc. Among the aspects of the system especially criticized were the petty snobbishness of some schools and the subjects taught in girls' schools.

Original reference
1861   [2794–III] XXI   State of popular education, education in the
          Pt. III   metropolis and other districts, J. Wilkinson, W. B.
                Hodgson, etc., Reps., R. Com. Vol. III, Rep.

Education: General Volume 6

REPORTS FROM ASSISTANT COMMISSIONERS ON POPULAR EDUCATION IN CONTINENTAL EUROPE TOGETHER WITH SPECIAL REPORTS ON EDUCATIONAL CHARITIES, TEACHER TRAINING COLLEGES AND EDUCATION IN LIVERPOOL, 1861

432 pp

Rev. Mark Pattison and Matthew Arnold were instructed by the Newcastle Commission to study the broad principles underlying popular education systems in European countries and to find out how these principles were put into practice. Arnold's reports dealt with France, Holland and Switzerland and Pattison's dealt with Germany. As Arnold was a strong advocate of sweeping changes in Britain's educational system some doubts have been expressed as to why he was chosen for this particular mission. His reports reviewed the origins and traditions of education in each of the three counties and then proceeded to compare and contrast Britain's system with its continental counterparts. The reports are well argued and written. They give the information sought by the commission but interpret and measure every facet against the author's ideas on education. Arnold found much that pleased him in the French system and took particular note of the operation of compulsory attendance there. Aspects of the Dutch and Swiss systems also impressed him, e.g. the thorough inspection of schools and teachers in Holland. Many of his comments on British education were extremely critical—he was not one to believe that a 'cheap' education could also be 'sound'. His report was later reprinted in book form. The most striking feature of Pattison's report are its analysis of the church-state issue in German education and its account of the German seminary system of teacher training. Pattison concluded that the latter produced teachers rather than men of liberal education.

The special reports surveyed two important aspects of British elementary education, the endowments and charities which financed many of the schools, and the teacher training colleges. The administration of charities was found to be inefficient; Mr. Cumin, the assistant commissioner, suggested plans for the systematic reorganization and co-ordination of funds available from these sources. The main faults attributed to the teacher training system were that it failed to develop the mind and did not provide adequate training in teacher methodology.

Original reference

1861   [2794–IV] XXI State of popular education, education in central
             Pt. IV   Europe, M. Arnold, M. Pattison, etc. Reps., R.
                           Com. Vol. IV, Rep.

Education: General Volume 7

ANSWERS TO CIRCULAR OF QUESTIONS SENT BY THE ROYAL COM-
MISSION ON POPULAR EDUCATION TO PEOPLE OF ALL SHADES OF
OPINION, 1861

488 pp

The commissioners avoided direct conflict with radical views on education by sending a circular of questions to people who were close to the real forum of learning, the parish and the classroom. The questionnaire was used to obtain the views of the 'silent masses' on the education system as it affected them. The information requested comprised the type and standard of education desired, the advantages of the various systems of schools, the need for industrial and domestic training, the effectiveness of prize schemes, competitive examinations for minor state appointments, libraries, the mechanics' institutes and a host of other topics relating to the efficiency of the educational system. The questionnaire sought especially to establish the views of parish clergy, teachers, etc. on the grant system and on the results of the education being provided for the poor.

The replies to the circular, without being radical in their approach, provided a broad spectrum of views on the educational needs of the country. They were generally in favour of redoubled efforts to educate the poor. They were critical of the quality of teaching, the duration of schooling and the inadequate finances available. The lack of parental interest and the value of child labour were given as reasons for the poor standards of education. Some of the replies gave the views of minorities (e.g. Roman Catholics) on the educational system.

Original reference
1861   [2794–V] XXI   State of popular education in England, answers to
            Pt. V   circular of questions, R. Com. Vol. V, Rep.

Education: General Volume 8

MINUTES OF EVIDENCE TAKEN BY THE ROYAL COMMISSION ON POPULAR EDUCATION TOGETHER WITH MISCELLANEOUS REPORTS AND LETTERS TO THE COMMISSION, 1861–1862

848 pp   1 coloured map   4 folding charts

The oral evidence was taken from Ralph Lingen, secretary, and other officers of the Committee of the Privy Council on Education, school inspectors, principals of training colleges and teachers. The evidence examined the principle on which state aid for education was based, i.e. the encouragement of voluntary effort. Witnesses assessed the efficiency of the grant system in the light of this principle and provided information on how money was being spent in education. No fundamental criticisms were voiced but the evidence is a guide to parliamentary policy of stimulating rather than controlling education. It also provides extensive information on the training colleges, the state of the denominational controversy and the inspection system.

The shorter papers give the views of H. S. Tremenheere, J. K. Shuttleworth and E. Chadwick on a number of aspects of the commission's inquiry. Tremenheere claimed that the required stimulus had been given to education and that consequently government aid should be phased out. Shuttleworth pointed out that, if the financing of education were transferred to local authorities, control of schools would also be exercised at local level and he felt that this would leave the way open for religious discrimination. Chadwick's paper explained his recommendation that

manual work and physical training should be introduced into the
schools.

Original references

1861	[2794–VI] XXI	State of popular education, mins. of ev., R. Com.
	Pt. VI	Vol. VI, Rep.
1861	(231) XLVIII	State of popular education, letter by J. K. Shuttleworth on Rep. of the commission.
	(354)	State of popular education, paper by H. S. Tremenheere.
	(410)	Enumeration of dissenting schools, Cttee. Rep. to the commission.
1862	(120) XLIII	State of popular education, half-time teaching and military and naval drill and on the time and cost of popular education on a large and small scale, E. Chadwick.
	(120–I)	State of popular education, letter to N. Senior explanatory of the former paper.

Education: General Volume 13

FIRST REPORT FROM THE ROYAL COMMISSION APPOINTED TO INQUIRE
INTO SCHOOLS IN SCOTLAND WITH MINUTES OF EVIDENCE,
APPENDICES, 1865–1867

568 pp

Education in Scotland did not suffer from the same degree of
class distinction as in England nor did it have the same clear-cut
divisions between elementary and secondary levels. Furthermore,
it had adapted itself with greater facility to the demands of an
industrialized society. However, by 1864 the system was considered to be in need of reorganization. As well, there was strong
opposition in Scotland to the 'revised code' introduced in 1862
as a result of the Newcastle Commission inquiry (IUP volumes
Education : General 3–8). Consequently, a commission was appointed, under the chairmanship of the Duke of Argyle, to examine
all levels of Scottish education and to ascertain whether 'a plan
of national character' would be more suitable than the existing
parochial system and grant scheme.

With their first report, the commissioners submitted the evidence
taken up to March 1865 and an appendix which gives extensive
information on the educational operations of the Church of
Scotland, educational facilities in the North Western Highlands,
the number of teachers trained at institutions in Glasgow and
Edinburgh, financially-aided schools in Scotland and the overall
standard and result of Scottish education. The oral evidence

describes the general school system, covering endowed and unendowed schools. One of its major themes was the effectiveness of the denominational school system.

Witnesses in general expressed dissatisfaction with the famous 'revised code' which made payment of parliamentary grants dependent on the efficiency of the schools. The code was expected to 'reduce Scottish education to the rudiments' and to create social distinctions between those who could pay for education and those who could not. The grant system, even as it was, was considered to be militating against poorer areas. Also included in this volume is an appendix to the first report which was not submitted until 1867. The appendix is made up mainly of replies from university professors, clergymen and others to a list of questions on the main features of Scottish education. The replies indicated a preference for a national rather than parochial education system, provided the state undertook to sponsor religious instruction.

Original references

| 1865 | [3483] XVII | Schools in Scotland, R. Com. Rep., mins. of ev., appendix. |
| 1867 | [3858] XXV | Schools in Scotland, appendix to R. Com., 1st Rep. |

Education: General Volume 14

SECOND REPORT FROM THE ROYAL COMMISSION APPOINTED TO INQUIRE INTO SCHOOLS IN SCOTLAND, TOGETHER WITH REPORTS OF ASSISTANT COMMISSIONERS, 1867

984 pp   2 folding maps (1 coloured)   12 illustrations

This volume has an eight-chapter report on Scottish elementary education together with a statistical survey of the lowland country districts and assistant commissioners' reports on education in Glasgow, rural Scotland and the Hebrides. The main report was a thorough study of the elementary school system, it examined the facilities and requirements of each region and of the country in a scientific and sympathetic way. There was considerable variation in the standard of education from place to place. The average ratio between the number of students and the total population was satisfactory but in some parishes it was as low as 1 in 20. In areas of the lowlands 35 per cent of the children were not provided with school places. These facts indicated that the poorer sections of the population were worst provided for and least interested in education. In the Highlands, education was hampered by the remoteness and ruggedness of the country and the grant system had done little to improve matters. The commission reviewed the defects of the parochial system and the likely effects of the 'revised code' on Scottish elementary education. In their recommendations they attempted to suggest a parliamentary policy which, while retaining the advantages of the traditional system, would remove its defects. They proposed the judicious introduction of a national scheme incorporating all existing voluntary schools and avoiding sectarian character where possible. They further suggested that a Board of Education be set up in conjunction with the Education Department to supervise the organization of the national system and to see that sufficient school buildings and teachers were provided.

The assistant commissioners' reports are valuable sources of information on every aspect of Scottish education at the time. They provided the analysis of the systems in different socio-economic regions on which the main reports were based.

Original references

1867	[3845] XXV	Schools in Scotland, elementary schools, R. Com. 2nd Rep., appendix.
	[3845–I]	Schools in Scotland, lowland country districts, Col. Maxwell, A. C. Sellar, Rep.
	[3845–II]	Schools in Scotland, Glasgow, J. Greig, T. Harvey, Rep.
	[3845–III]	Schools in Scotland, country districts, Col. Maxwell, A. C. Sellar, Rep.
	[3845–IV]	Schools in Scotland, Hebrides, A. Nicholson, Rep.

Education: General Volume 15

STATISTICS ON SCOTTISH SCHOOLS TOGETHER WITH A REPORT ON THE COMMON SCHOOL SYSTEM IN THE UNITED STATES AND CANADA, 1867

736 pp   14 plans and illustrations

The statistics were collected by the registrars of births and deaths on the instructions of the commission. The country was divided into counties and parishes and all schools in each parish were enumerated together with their type, number of teachers and pupils, denominations, physical condition, etc. There is a comment on the total school accommodation of each parish.

Rev. James Fraser's report on the common school system of the United States and Canada was submitted to both the Argyle and Taunton Commissions (see IUP volumes Education : General 17–32). Rev. Fraser was, among other things, required to examine the legislative approach to education in the United States and Canada especially with respect to compulsory attendance, the financing of education, the relations between central and local government in controlling education, the external and internal organization of the schools, the part played by the churches in education and the teaching of religion. His report is not only a source of extensive information; it is an interesting attempt to compare Britain's culture with that of her colonial offshoots. Fraser doubted, for example, if American taste was founded on the best models; 'they would' he reported 'consider Milton better than Shakespeare, Johnson better than Addison.' He found this cultural bluntness and lack of suppleness in other areas also— Americans did not appreciate the softer virtues of womanhood as did the British. On the other hand he credited the Americans with great energy and willingness to provide education and to embibe knowledge, which he felt, if directed with more insight and perspicacity could be very valuable. He recommended that several elements of the organization of education in the United States and Canada could be copied with profit in Britain.

Original references
1867   [3845–V] XXVI Schools in Scotland, statistics.
        [3857]   Schools in Scotland, common school system in
                          U.S. and Canada, J. Fraser, Rep.

Education: General Volume 16

THIRD REPORT FROM THE ROYAL COMMISSION APPOINTED TO INQUIRE INTO SCHOOLS IN SCOTLAND WITH AN APPENDIX, TOGETHER WITH GENERAL AND SPECIAL REPORTS OF ASSISTANT COMMISSIONERS, 1867–68

736 pp

The third report of the commission and the assistant commissioners' reports deal with middle-class schools (these were for people 'between' the labouring classes and the wealthy professional and commercial classes). The schools were of three types: Burgh schools (managed by the town councils); academies and institutions (founded by subscription) and private schools. They catered for pupils up to 16 years of age. The reports described the history, organization, finances, management, curricula, etc. of each type of school and commented on the efficiency of middle-class education. They made a number of recommendations of lesser importance but were generally satisfied that Scottish middle-class education was more extensive and more modern than most. The ratio between those receiving post elementary education and those not was much higher in Scotland than in England and elsewhere. This was particularly attributable to the insistence by the Knox religious reformers that every child should have the opportunity of university education. The commissioners urged that this equality of opportunity be allowed to continue. Their most important recommendations dealt with the establishment of an efficient examination system and with the physical condition of the schools.

Original references

1867–68 [4011] XXIX   Schools in Scotland, Burgh and middle-class schools, R. Com. 3rd Rep., Vol. I, assistant commissioner's general and special reps.

[4011–I]   Schools in Scotland, R. Com., 3rd Rep., Vol. II, assistant commissioner's special reps.

Education: General Volume 34

FIRST REPORT FROM THE ROYAL COMMISSION APPOINTED TO INQUIRE INTO THE WORKING OF THE ELEMENTARY EDUCATION ACTS WITH MINUTES OF EVIDENCE AND APPENDIX, 1886

560 pp

Despite controversy and opposition, William Edward Forster's Elementary Education Bill became law in 1870. Further Acts in 1876 and 1880 achieved minor improvements in Forster's scheme. During this period the number of elementary schools increased rapidly as did the cost of maintaining them. In 1886 a commission under the chairmanship of Richard Assheton Cross was set up to inquire into the general state of elementary education and especially to review the operation of the recent legislation.

The commission's first report contains oral evidence taken from Patrick Cumin, secretary of the Education Department, school inspectors including Matthew Arnold, principals of training colleges and several educational associations which represented denominational interests. The interrogation of witnesses followed a pre-arranged scheme designed to elicit information and opinion on the educational state of the population, the growth of educational legislation, the efficiency of the existing system, the denominational question and so on. Mr. Cumin gave a detailed account of the finances and administration of the system and commented on the constitution of the education department (returns and other data relating to his evidence are included in the appendices). Many witnesses raised questions of grievances and discrimination inherent in the system—non-conformists still held that public money should not be used to support denominational teaching.

Original reference
1886   [C. 4863] XXV Elementary Education Acts (England and Wales),
                       R. Com. 1st Rep., mins. of ev., appendices.

Education: General Volume 35

SECOND REPORT OF THE ROYAL COMMISSION APPOINTED TO INQUIRE INTO THE WORKING OF THE ELEMENTARY ACTS WITH MINUTES OF EVIDENCE AND APPENDICES, 1887

1,120 pp

The commissioners submitted evidence taken from over seventy witnesses in 1887. The witnesses represented a lower level of educational administration than those of the first report: headmasters, clergymen, chairman of school boards, etc. A notable exception was J. G. Fitch, chief inspector of schools. The evidence followed the scheme adopted in the previous report but highlighted many new questions such as the pupil-teacher system, the half-time system, the effectiveness of the conscience clause, the value of scientific and technical instruction in junior schools and the desirable age for termination of schooling. Witnesses were asked for their opinions on the total educational result of the present system and this provided an opportunity for the expression of some interesting views. 'Payment by results' was generally condemned while conflicting criticisms of the pupil-teacher and half-time systems were advanced. Suggestions included the selection of inspectors from elementary teachers and the introduction of pension schemes for teachers.

Original reference
                       R. Com. 2nd Rep., mins. of ev., appendices.
1887   [C. 5056]XXIX Elementary Education Acts (England and Wales),

Education: General Volume 36

THIRD REPORT OF THE ROYAL COMMISSION APPOINTED TO INQUIRE INTO THE WORKING OF THE ELEMENTARY EDUCATION ACTS WITH

MINUTES OF EVIDENCE AND APPENDICES, 1887

776 pp

The third report contains further oral evidence together with appendices of returns giving extensive information on the population density and school attendance density, the illiteracy rate, and the employment of children.

The evidence was taken from witnesses ranging from the secretary (Patrick Cumin) and former secretary (Ralph Lingen) of the Education Department to a representative of the working class. Many of the witnesses represented non-conformist and Roman Catholic schools; others were deputed by their organizations to raise specific points, e.g. the employment of children in the theatre. University professors, headmasters and school inspectors complemented and clarified points of evidence taken earlier.

Among the issues discussed by witnesses were the quality of teacher training, social distinction between board and voluntary schools, compulsory attendance and technical instruction. The details of school expenditure (cost of upkeep, teaching materials, etc.) and also the difficulties of teaching religion in mixed schools were examined. A number of witnesses testified that Mundella's code (1880) had improved the operation of the grant scheme.

Original reference
1887   [C. 5158] XXX Elementary Education Acts (England and Wales), R. Com. 3rd Rep., mins. of ev., appendices.

Education: General Volume 37

FINAL REPORT OF THE ROYAL COMMISSION ON THE WORKING OF THE ELEMENTARY EDUCATION ACTS WITH FURTHER MINUTES OF EVIDENCE AND AN INDEX, 1888

1,128 pp

The final report of the commission was splintered by disagreements. The main point of contention was the position of the denominational schools. A majority report (fifteen commissioners) recommended strong enforcement of the conscience clause while at the same time suggesting that state aid should be given to denominational schools and that where possible children should have the option of attending a school of their own religious persuasion. The minority report (eight commissioners) saw in such a policy an opportunity for renewed denominational disputes, and a retrograde step in the whole parliamentary approach to education. Not only on the denominational question but on almost every important issue there was dissent and reservation. One or more of the commissioners disagreed with the majority recommendations on 'payment by results', the pupil-teacher system, religious instruction, etc. The minority report goes so far as to accuse the majority of giving a slanted and polished account of the history of British education from 1839 to 1870.

The majority report lists among the witnesses on whose evidence it is based thirteen teachers, nine managers of public elementary schools, chief inspectors and inspectors, representatives of school boards and of voluntary schools, six of the leading advocates of secular education and Mr. Cumin and Lord Lingen (a digest of the evidence is appended to the report). Such extensive evidence was calculated to lend authority to the report. It has seven sections devoted to: existing law on education; the state of elementary education and the machinery for carrying it on; public elementary schools; the examination system; the parliamentary grant; income and expenditure of schools; the work of local educational authorities and finally a summary of conclusions and recommendations. Extensive recommendations were made on every aspect of the subject. Apart from those already mentioned the most important dealt with the provision of sufficient teachers and with the school curricula. An interesting feature of the minority report is its liberal almost socialist tone—while condemning state aid for schools run on a religious basis it demands a strong and purposeful government approach towards providing efficient elementary education not only for the lower classes but for the upper classes as well.

Original references

1888	[C. 5485]	Elementary Education Acts, R. Com., final Rep.
	XXXV	
1888	[C. 5329]	Elementary Education Acts, R. Com., mins. of
	XXXVII	ev.
	[C. 5329–I]	Elementary Education Acts, index to R. Com. Rep.

Education: General Volume 38

STATISTICAL REPORTS OF THE ROYAL COMMISSION ON THE ELEMENTARY EDUCATION ACTS TOGETHER WITH INFORMATION COLLECTED FROM FOREIGN AND COLONIAL COUNTRIES, 1888

840 pp

The statistical reports are summaries of information collected by
sending circulars to the school boards, school managers and headmasters in areas selected so as to give returns representative of the
country at large. The returns are tabulated and arranged for ease of
reference and comparison and in some cases the comparisons are
actually drawn, e.g. one table sets statistics for different towns,
counties and districts side by side. In addition to giving factual
statistics the school authorities were asked to comment on the
system and to make suggestions for improvement. Comments
ranged over the effects of the Acts, the revised code, the administration of the system, compulsory education, etc. There were in particular numerous complaints about the 'code' in general and about
the tension and pressure occasioned by the examinations for grants.
The process of obtaining remission of fees through the Poor Law
Guardians was considered disagreeable in many of the returns,
and to be deterring poor people from applying. A modern note in
some of the replies is the desire for an emphasis on environmental
studies (local industries, etc.). The information on education in
colonial and foreign countries relates to: free education, state and
voluntary effort, compulsory attendance, religious teaching, night
schools and special training schools. Most of the British colonies,
most of the American states and twelve European countries are
represented in the information.

Original references
1888   [C. 5485–I]   Elementary Education Acts, R. Com. Rep., foreign
                    XXXV   and colonial information.
1888   [C. 5485–II]   Elementary Education Acts, R. Com., Statistical
                    XXXVI Rep.

Education: General Volume 39

INFORMATION COLLECTED BY THE ROYAL COMMISSION ON THE
ELEMENTARY EDUCATION ACTS FROM PRINCIPALS OF TRAINING
COLLEGES TOGETHER WITH THE APPENDIX TO THE FINAL REPORT OF
THE COMMISSION, 1888

736 pp

The information on training colleges was obtained by sending a
circular questionnaire to the principals of the colleges throughout
England and Wales. The questions covered the time devoted to

study, classes, practice teaching and religion, the conditions of admission to the colleges (particularly religious requirements), the educational standards of students, examinations, expenses of the colleges and the ease with which students obtained appointments. The principals were also asked to make suggestions for improvement. The appendix to the final report contains several interesting documents submitted to the commission. A letter from Patrick Cumin (see IUP volumes Education: General 34 and 36) complained that he was the only representative of the Education Department to give evidence before the commission. Several memorials on almost every aspect of the inquiry depict the range and amplitude of opinion on education outside of the official centres of control. A return of the by-laws and regulations on religious instruction and scripture reading in force in each school board district in England is included together with schemes and syllabuses for religious teaching (this return had been ordered by the House of Lords in May 1888).

Original references
1888   [C. 5485–III]   Elementary Education Acts, R. Com. Rep.,
                XXXVI information from principals of training colleges.
        [C. 5485–IV]   Elementary Education Acts, appendix to R. Com.,
                final Rep.

EDUCATION:
FINE ARTS & DESIGN

Celina Fox

Commentary

For George Godwin, in 1841, when speaking as secretary of the Art Union of London:

> The influence of the fine arts in humanising and refining, in purifying the thoughts and raising the sources of gratification in man, is so universally felt and admitted that it is hardly necessary now to urge it. By abstracting him from the gratification of the senses, teaching him to appreciate physical beauty and to find delight in the contemplation of the admirable accordance of nature, the mind is carried forward to higher aims, and becomes insensibly opened to a conviction of the force of moral worth and the harmony of virtue. By assisting works of fine art . . .all may rest assured that they are forwarding the best interests of humanity and entitling themselves eminently to the applause of the high-minded.[1]

The parliamentary papers devoted to the fine arts and design in nineteenth century England reflect a very deep and specific conviction about the moral benefits bestowed through their cultivation. The theory was scarcely new.[2] What was, was its scale and the importance it took on when not merely applied to a single academy, but to an entire nation, as an adjunct to their general education and a suitable recreation for their leisure. Moreover, in common with other aspects of Victorian educational theory, the moral can rarely be separated from a more practical, materialist side. Montesquieu and eighteenth century mercantilist theory had underlined the intimate connection between commerce, industry and the arts. Money from trade created a surplus which could be spent on luxury goods and art patronage.[3] Nor was this an unequal partnership. It was also important to encourage art in its 'loftier attributes':

> since it is admitted that the cultivation of the more exalted branches of design tends to advance the humblest pursuits of industry, while the connexion of art with manufacture has often developed the genius of the greatest masters in design.[4]

The relationship between art and industry, the necessity of encouraging both the 'highest branches of poetical design' and the 'lowest connexion between design and manufactures' was first brought to public notice in the Select Committee on Arts and Manufactures of 1835-36. It was appointed to inquire into 'the best means of extending a knowledge of the ARTS and of the PRINCIPLES of DESIGN among the People (especially the Manufacturing Population) of the Country', as well as to examine the existing institutions connected with the Arts, namely the National Gallery and the Royal Academy. It stated for the first time themes which were to be endlessly explored in other government reports and minutes of evidence compiled in the cause of art and design, and which for the most part, were never satisfactorily resolved.

The committee exposed a lack of faith in the products and designs of British manufacturers compared with those of the French, and a low standard of taste in the community at large, which needed to be remedied. What was required was art education for the whole country 'from the prince to the mechanic'. The rot began at the highest level with indiscriminate private patronage, and the exclusion of art from the minds of the aristocracy in their public schools and universities. This was seen to be matched by an equal want of study and education in the arts amongst manufacturers who produced fabrics and goods requiring applied design. Finally, there existed a total lack of discrimination throughout the general public. Thus the designs in demand would, 'in the nature of things, always be of the least tasteful description; that is to say, till the bulk of mankind are much more cultivated than they now are, or are likely soon to be'.[5]

The remedy to this absence of art and design from the supply-demand cycle was seen by the committee to take the shape of a general diffusion process. Education of a specifically practical nature would increase the means of applying art to the manufactures of the country, while elementary art education would increase the demand for goods which exhibited a high level of quality in design. The employment of people would be extended by enabling them to use faculties which they were not able to use at that moment and to work with precious materials rarely handled. Similarly, exhibitions would through good practice and emulation lead to 'improved taste in the public and an improved capability on the part of the working man', stimulating invention. Casts, paintings, works of proportion and beauty – for scientific improvements in machinery it was thought depended on the perfection of form in construction – 'everything in short which exhibits in combination the efforts of the artist and workman' – should be shown in free galleries, or perhaps in rooms connected with factories. One class of mechanics always knew others and improvements would spread swiftly from one department to another. Thus, the supply of art would create a demand for art, and the demand for art would in its turn create a supply of art. Finally, to seal the contract, this creation of a new taste would greatly improve the morals of the country.[6] Despite the traditionally pessimistic view of manufacture taken by the Royal Academy, as represented by Shee and Cockerell,[7] it was clear, the committee believed, that the government should intervene and aim at the 'development and extension of art', though neither control its action nor force its cultivation. State patronage would serve the end of national status, under pressure from economic necessity:

> Our national greatness rests on the skilled industry of our people; it must be a part of sound domestic policy to foster, by every means within our reach, the talent which gives currency and importance to our indigenous products, and draws within the vortex of British manufacture the raw material of other climes, to be spread again over the world, enhanced in value by the labour, skill and taste of British artisans.[8]

The committee report recommended the establishment of a Normal School of Design, the formation of open Public Galleries or Museums of Art, and that the principles of design should be part of any permanent system of elementary education. It made recommendations on the copyright laws and fiscal duties. It drew attention to the German Kunst-Vereine system of art patronage, and summarized the evidence on the National Gallery and Royal Academy.

The fulfilment of these suggestions took place in such a vacuum, lacking both coherent theory and practical expertise, that the administrative instruments employed needed much tempering and adaptation before they could, by any standards, be described as adequate. The Select Committees and Royal Commissions expose the high spots of disaster, of not only theoretical, but principally of administrative confusion. They do not form part of an open public policy, but more often seem like torchlit journeys into shadowy private basement reserves, which otherwise would have lain hidden from view. Without them we would be left for instance, in the case of the National Gallery, only with the slovenly minutes and attendance record of the Trustees meetings,[9] while the Royal Academy persistently refused to divulge its affairs to Parliament.[10] Neither institution started to issue an annual report until after the middle of the century, the Gallery in 1856, the Academy from 1860.

The parliamentary papers constantly provoke the question: who was competent to make judgements concerning the arts on a national scale? For the National Gallery, this involved consideration of the qualifications of the Trustees. Were the 'gentlemen of taste' who had been delegated the task suitable for making decisions over purchases or conservation?[11] Yet their presence is a natural corollary to the fact that before 1853, of the ninety-one pictures added to the collection since its foundation, two thirds had been donated by private owners, and indeed in the Gallery's first century less than a quarter of the pictures were purchased with funds voted by Parliament. However, individual connoisseurship carried with it an aura of privacy and exclusivity. One owner had refused to sell a painting to the Gallery on the grounds that a favourite work of art and he himself would be exposed to unfavourable publicity, to 'the rude tustle of newspaper recrimination'.[12] If private patrons were uneasy about exposure to public view, so too were the artists themselves. The guarded behaviour of the Royal Academy before the 1863 Royal Commission was largely provoked by the threat of lay judgement. As the Academy's 'Observations' pointed out, the views of the Commissioners themselves were, however honest and impartial, 'after all, those of unprofessional men'.[13] Similarly, the composition of the Royal Commission on the decoration of the Palace of Westminster was criticized for not having an artist on it, apart from Eastlake. One assailant went so far as to see such 'amateurs' as the bane of British Art, who 'rule it, constraint it, enslave it, making use of the artists as mere mechanical means, as mere slaves of their wills'.[14] Yet this denigration does not take account of the private patron like Sir Robert Peel, who was willing to spend his time in numerous public inquiries concerning the arts,[15] or those like John Sheepshanks, the Leeds cloth manufacturer, who bought contemporary British art 'off the peg' and then left his collection to the nation.[16] The presence of such individuals was vital for a government which intended to carry out a programme, if it can be so dignified, of art education on the cheap.

The government could afford to be stingy because it expected the support of private generosity or the self-support of the institution in question, whether it be a national or provincial museum, local art school or country-wide elementary art education. Government aid for the arts was not a popular issue: no party won votes on it. The only time it became anything like a party question was when Joseph Hume led the radical attack on the 'close corporation' of the Royal Academy in 1839 and 1844. A group of the most prominent exponents of art and design education – Hume, William Ewart M.P. and Sir Thomas Wyse M.P. – did set up the Society for Promoting Practical Design, spurred on by Haydon, in 1837, but they were not held together by any united political standpoint to make them consistently effective as a group.[17] During the 1840s, Ewart, Henry Cole, John Bowring and Thomas Potter were all involved in the Anti-Corn Law League, which organized an important free trade bazaar to display British manufactures at the Covent Garden Theatre in March 1845. Judging from contemporary reports, it is clear that this event anticipated and helped to provide the rationale for the Great Exhibition of 1851, as much as the more publicized annual exhibitions of arts manufactures, arranged by the Society of Arts at the end of the 1840s.[18] Yet despite the fact that these men of a common free trade connection had a vested interest in improving the standards of taste and design in the country, in many ways their position was an ambivalent one. Although they were prepared to attack such bastions of outdated 'privilege' as the Royal Academy, they did not relish the thought of government interference with free market forces. After all, if anything is stressed by Henry Cole in his preface to the catalogue of the Great Exhibition, it is the fact that it was the result of British private enterprise and owed a great part of its success to its independence of the government.[19] Similarly, the Report from the Select Committee on the South Kensington museum in 1860, unfortunately absent from this collection, repeatedly emphasized the role of private liberality in the growth of the museum's collections, which had been almost wholly built up 'without cost to the State.'[20] Cole concentrated on developing the principle of self support in elementary art education rather than getting involved in the vexed question as to who was responsible for training designers for industry: the manufacturers or the state. Felicitous quotations from Adam Smith were used to support 'manuring the country with elementary drawing power,' and producing a general sweetening effect, rather than to encourage first-hand experience in practical cultivation or encounters with the open market.[21] The only opposition he took on, risking the charge of government monopoly, were small fry like the wood engravers in the 1840s, or the photographers in the 1850s, craftsmen and artists rather than large-scale industrialists.[22] However, even while Cole was rallying private individuals for donations or encouraging the adoption of the principle of payment by results in the Department of Science and Art, his autobiography reveals his constant battle with the Treasury for money to take examples of British art and manufactures abroad, to seize the opportunity of purchasing unique collections for the museum, and to improve the buildings at South Kensington.[23] It was not without a certain rueful appreciation that he quoted Gladstone in a letter to *The Times* in 1872 on the state of public architecture, 'Vacillation, uncertainty, costliness, extravagance, meanness, and all the conflicting vices that could be enumerated are united in our present system'.[24]

Controversy was started by individuals in the newspapers rather than in the House. Haydon's manoeuvres behind the scenes provided background noise to both the Select Committees of 1835-36 and of 1841, while his letter to *The Times* in 1845 brought into the open the state of the Schools of Design.[25] Similarly, it was an anonymous letter to the *Morning Herald* which sparked off the whole controversy over the legality of the Art Unions, and Morris Moore's vituperative pamphlets which exposed the cleaning and purchasing blunders at the National Gallery.[26] Samuel Carter Hall's *Art-Union* journal prided itself on revealing the trade in fraudulent 'old masters' and illustrating the application of art to industry.[27] The *Journal of Design and Manufactures* was Henry Cole's chief weapon for waging war on the structure of the Schools of Design as it existed in the late 1840s.[28] The larger outside pressure groups to emerge and to petition public representatives were the textile manufacturers over the copyright laws and the print dealers over the Art Unions, but both groups were split internally on the question of how to reconcile good taste with mass production. In the face of such cross-tensions, it is not surprising that the men who made a permanent mark once some system had been established in the fifties were administrators like Sir Charles Eastlake or Cole himself, managers rather than idealists. For the rest, the relationship between private generosity and public parsimony, between amateur connoisseurs, artists and pressure groups provides neither a consistent narrative nor a coherent development. What perhaps is clear is that so long as many of the protagonists scarcely seemed to know what they were about, the public could not be expected to know either.

I

It is useful to examine the project concerning the decoration of the Palace of Westminster first, for it expressed most clearly the remnants of the ideology concerned with high art. Academic theory from Alberti to Reynolds was based on a hierarchical view of art, the foremost place being allotted to history painting in its most idealized, decorous and timeless form.[29] The effect of such work had been amply illustrated in the recent frescos undertaken at Munich. The highest classes had the opportunity of judging the propriety of the classic illustrations, while the Tyrolean peasants held up their children and explained to them the scenes from Bavarian history. As Cornelius had said, it was difficult to impress on the minds of a nation at large a general love of art, unless by means of painting on a large scale. The lower classes could not be expected to have a just appreciation of the delicacies and finer characteristics of painting in oil; they required large and simple forms, very direct action and in some instances, exaggerated expression.[30]

The evidence presented to the Select Committee of 1841, and running through the reports of the Royal Commission, constantly stressed the role of large scale history painting, and its importance is reflected in the appointment of the historian Hallam, and later Macaulay, to serve on the commission.[31] History painting was to be the chief means of decorating the 'palace of the senatorial body', and cannot be separated from what was, sometimes, an extreme concern with national prestige. Prince Albert's working presence added lustre to the enterprise although some doubt has been expressed as to whether he did not at first favour the employment of foreign artists.[32] Not only do the Select Committee and commission reports emphasize a patriotic support for British artists,[33] but they also display a certain chauvinism over subject matter. Viscount Mahon rebuked Hallam's vague suggestion that foreign scenes could be used with the words, 'I would no more consent to admit foreign scenes to decorate a British House of Parliament, than I would

an alien to sit among its members.' Hallam's idea stemmed from his conviction as to the paucity of subject matter in British history fit for the grand style
of history painting, for such subjects must at least be 'nationally honourable.
There are facts of great interest to a reader, over which we ought to draw a
veil'.[34]

If the ideal subject matter could not quite be lived up to in reality, the ideal
medium of fresco presented obstacles in practice, not least of which was the
fact that no English artist knew much about the medium. A great deal of
evidence and appendices to the Royal Commission reports centres on discussion as to the best means of carrying out fresco painting. Certain advantages
were agreed on: fresco was more durable, did not need varnish and therefore
was not shiny and difficult to see, that it absorbed less light and was more
easily cleaned. Above all, because of the speed required before the paint
dried into the plaster, the argument was that the artist only had time to
concentrate on the higher qualities of art: correct drawing and design, elevation of character and dramatic effect. Fresco would encourage composition,
drawing and grandeur of design; it would raise the character of art and elevate
public taste, in an area where private patronage was quite inadequate, there
being not sufficient space in private houses for the purpose.[35]

The hankering after some replacement for the patronage of high art remained in the 1840s one of the main ostensible reasons for new initiatives in
the field. Since the Reformation, according to many experts, the patronage of
religious art had been forgotten, with a subsequent decline in all other
branches of historical painting. The most profound question asked at the
hearings of the 1845 Select Committee was whether the Art Unions had
furthered the cause of high art. For some witnesses, the Art Unions were
partially responsible for the betterment of taste since the 1830s, along with the
British Museum, the National Gallery and exhibitions like the display of
cartoons at Westminster. For others, however, they had had no visible effect.
Etty believed that the Unions simply provided a temporary excitement,
rather like dram-drinking, compared with the natural nourishment flowing
from the highest sources that Church and Government alone were in a
position to offer.[36] Whatever subsidiary assistance might be rendered by the
unions, there was a feeling at many points in the debate that somehow the
ideals of high art had been sullied. To fall foul of the Lottery Acts proved that
the methods used by the Art Unions were 'not exactly in consonance with
the highest scale of morals.' The example of Italy was used to show the 'very
degraded and distressing effects of lotteries.' Etty spoke of union prizes being
raffled in public or put up for sale in a broker's shop.[37]

Again high art theory was tied down to practical issues with the National
Gallery. In the Select Committee of 1835-36, the specific connection was
made between artistic and moral education in relation to the Gallery. Many

witnesses agreed that Sunday opening would undoubtedly have as good a moral effect as it had done in France. One ornamental sculptor believed the class of workmen who had forsaken the gin shop for the coffee house and penny periodicals would be further encouraged in their search for respectability and refinement by opening museums and art galleries to the public.[38] Similarly, the report from the Select Committee on National Monuments and Works of Art in 1841 pointed out the gratifying results of free admission. The behaviour of the people, especially compared with fifty years previously, was exemplary. They 'cease to be a mob when they get a taste'. They were drawn in to consideration not only of the building, but, especially in the case of a religious edifice, of its purpose.[39] There were some dissenters who remarked on the idle people who brought their children into the National Gallery 'cracked nuts, and wore jackets which smelt of smoke and dirt'.[40] However, it is a tribute to a more generous sentiment that the Gallery still remains equally accessible to both east and west ends, despite the South Kensington lobby of the 1850s. Hopefully, it fulfilled Peel's promise when it was first built, that 'placed in the centre, and in the full stream of London industry, persons of various classes would all meet in mutual good will'.[41]

Writing in 1853 on Tom Taylor's 'Life of Benjamin Robert Haydon', J.W. Croker questioned the necessity for high art, doubted the improvement of public taste on subjects of art and was sceptical of the utility of decorating public edifices like the new Houses of Parliament. Though he condescended to suspend judgement until it was finished, he wondered whether, 'when the first novelty is over, these works will appear deserving of the – we may call it – eternity for which they are destined'. He continued:

We do not think that the climate of our country, the capacity of our public edifices, or the genius of our people, is favourable to this style of decoration, and we fear that the greatest advantage to be hoped from it – the employment of a dozen artists practising a style incompatible with domestic decoration, and therefore incapable of supplying an adequate personal livelihood to its professors – will not at all fulfil the expectations that are formed from it.[42]

II

Taking Reynold's dictum that if the higher arts flourished, the inferior ends would also be answered, many witnesses before the 1841 Select Committee on the Promotion of Fine Arts furthered the view that the middle class of artists, with skill as ornamentalists in encaustic, porcelain and glass painting or wood and metal carving, would flourish, create new objects of industry and employment and encourage exports.[43] The whole scheme for the decoration of the Palace of Westminster would in short combine to forward moral elevation and industry in the country. It would illustrate a determination by the House to take the opportunity of:

> encouraging the Arts, and of associating them with our Public Architecture, our Legislation, our Commerce, and our History, would alone stimulate and raise their character and quality, and extend their beneficial influence over a still wider circle.[44]

Such hyperbole fell rather flat when the frescos began to decay,[45] but more realistic attempts were being made to relate 'fine' and 'applied' art, newly made urgent in the face of a mass market and mass taste. Many witnesses – architectural sculptors, modellers, manufacturers and artists – before the 1835-36 Select Committee implied that the want of protection for inventions was responsible for the lack of originality in design. The Acts in existence were ambiguous and to take a case to court cost too much. Bowring, who described the French system, suggested the need for a cheap and accessible tribunal: a council of arbitration composed of master manufacturers and workmen to decide on the priority of invention, which would work with a system of registration. The varying degree of protection would depend on the different manufacturers, but a comprehensive measure was worthy of the serious attention of the government.[46]

The 1840 Select Committee on Copyright of Designs resolved that it was expedient to extend copyright. However, the evidence presented varied and there was a serious division of opinion. The anti-protection band based their arguments first, on an ostensible lack of uniqueness in the concept of design, second on a belief generally in the benefits of free trade, and third on an optimism as to the help it gave to a mass lower class market. These men were mainly forward looking, free trade manufacturers, notably, Brooks, Lee and Kershaw, who catered for a mass market. As Brooks said, copying 'exalts our name.' Protection was tyrannical and thus injurious to trade; copying reduced prices. Basically, for him there was no such thing as the unique art object, 'I say there are no original patterns . . .they are all designs, taken from other patterns, put together'.[47] Similarly, Kershaw argued, 'every man is a copier . . .my invariable instructions to our pattern designers are, to copy no man's patterns, but to improve upon other men's ideas'. He wanted no protection beyond that which merit and genius, and fair and open competition would give him. The extent of pattern copying was exaggerated; the majority of the trade agreed that protection was an injury.[48] For Lee also, there was no objection to being copied, for he produced a constant succession of new prints and sales were not affected. To produce and sell at a moderate profit was better protection than Parliament; besides, government interference would injure the lower classes at that point. In the present state of distress in the cotton districts, it would be better not to experiment and risk alteration which would reduce the call for labour.[49]

As Lee pointed out, those who wanted protection were in general fine printers catering for the middle classes. Potter, a calico printer from Manchester, agreed that those who produced the richest, most complicated and most original designs were for the protection bill; those who produced a lower style of work by means of the machine were against.[50] Clarkson argued that copying produced inferior work, being worked on inferior cloth in an inferior style of execution. Copies such as these were not purchased by the upper classes, 'Your pattern becomes plebeian, and the patrician character of the original is thus impaired.' – it made the pattern vulgar and lost its repute among the higher classes.[51] Therefore, the case for new laws was based on the uniqueness and quality of the original design, backed by an argument that copyright, by bringing about a greater variety between cheap and expensive goods, would help exports.[52]

The history of the Art Unions present a rather more complex example of the problems of reconciling art with mass markets. The role of the Art Unions was essentially that of the popularizer, the first instrument designed to provide mass art for a mass public. Despite the establishment hierarchy of the London Art Union headed by the Duke of Cambridge as first President, middle class ignorance was the gap it sought to fill. It achieved this through its prizes in paintings, sculpture, medals and ceramics which were chosen by the prize-winner, through the earliest free exhibitions and through the distribution of free engravings. During the seventy-five years of its existence, it distributed over a million engravings, including 15,000 of Frith's 'Ramsgate Sands', and 20,000 prints each of Maclise's 'The Death of Nelson' and 'The Meeting of Wellington and Blucher'. Through the use of electrotype processes, the unions could produce what was technically a limitless supply of art. Not surprisingly, some of the leading opponents of the scheme in both Select Committees were the print publishers and dealers who feared an oversupply of cheap engravings.[53]

Thus, the Art Unions implicitly brought into question the whole theory of art as understood in eighteenth-century terms. High art was being replaced by a commodity which could be bargained over and mass produced like any manufactured article; it catered for a middle brow taste unconcerned with the connoisseurship surrounding the unique art object. The industrial revolution and its economics struck at the very doors of art itself and begged the question as to whether quantity was to replace quality. This in essence is what the two Select Committees on the Art Unions were all about. For a detailed account of the setting up and the history of the London Art Union, and especially its leading spirit George Godwin, Anthony King's article in *Victorian Studies* is excellent.[54] However, perhaps a more typical union is that of Birmingham, for London never was the subject of attacks to the same degree as any of the others. Mason's evidence as secretary of the Birmingham Art Union in 1845 reveals the ambivalence of a provincial union's role, in an area which was a focus of the manufacturing trades and a centre of a large population, to reconcile the tenets of high art with the needs of a mass public. Was the union to support expensive works of art, in other words of established metropolitan artists, or to encourage local artists in the provinces, which might be described as 'a nursery of talent'? Or was it to encourage the application of art to the special purposes of its own local industry, perhaps in collaboration with the Schools of Design? Mason believed in making high art instrumental to the commercial prosperity of England. His Art Union he hoped would act as a link, for good feeling bound high art and design alike and artisans would benefit from contemplating works of art.[55]

III

The optimism of such hypotheses, designed to foster at one and the same time the elevating effect of high art and the progress of design for mass manufactures, received a rude jolt whenever administrative machinery was knocked together to put it into practice. The two besetting problems were first, who was in charge; second, where was the money coming from. In the case of the decoration of the Palace of Westminster, despite stress being laid on the necessity for harmony between architect and artists in 1841,[56] friction existed between Sir Charles Barry and the Royal Commissioners, neither of whom had clear briefs as to where their responsibilities ended. In the twelfth report, for instance, reference is made to the difficulties with the architect, who proposed 'a far greater amount of decoration ... than we considered it advisable to recommend,' and restated the second appendix of the sixth report which said that Barry was given sole responsibility only for decorative work.[57] Furthermore, the filtering of all information through the Royal Commission and its conscientious sifting by Eastlake (who took the opportunity to produce some of his most important pieces of art criticism, to be found buried in the appendices[58]), was matched by a delay in the building. Parliament only finally approved the scheme in 1847 and three years later, the Treasury voted a grant of £4,000 a year. The enterprise had been prolonged beyond the interest, let alone the enthusiasm of the mass public and beyond the lives of its main protagonists.

By the 1860s, the Art Unions were not only seen 'to foster the love of chance and speculation rather than to encourage high art',[59] but also to have provoked administrative anomalies. As a result of inadequate government supervision, the Lottery Laws had been set at defiance by many societies pretending to be Art Unions, but not so constituted by the Board of Trade. Exemption from these laws was the business of the Board of Trade; prosecution for violation, however, came under the Home Office. In addition, the Board of Trade was uncertain of the powers it had been granted, so a man like Godwin could get his way in any squabble.[60] For Henry Cole, the whole

business only confirmed the words of St Paul on the dangers of tampering with the law, 'you must not sin that grace may abound'.[61]
However, perhaps the history of the National Gallery until the middle of the century is the prime example of administrative bungling in relation to the arts. As the report of the 'bulky'[62] 1853 Select Committee found, there were fundamental defects and anomalies in the system itself, 'in the want, more especially, of any clear definition of the powers or responsibilities of the managing body of the Institution, and in the absence of specific regulations for their guidance in the performance of their duties.' Only scanty documentation existed, framed by the Treasury at the time of its origin and there had been nothing since.[63] The double responsibility of the Keeper, to the Trustees and to the Treasury, is ineloquently but revealingly displayed in the testimony of Seguier in 1836.[64] Nearly twenty five years later, Lord Aberdeen, the only remaining member of the original Trustees, spoke of the Trustees' lack of clear purpose and want of defined responsibility as to the buying, cleaning and management. According to George Foggo, the historical painter and author of the first critical catalogue of the collection, the National Gallery found itself between two influences, both of which had had an injurious effect, namely that of the Treasury and that of the Royal Academy, 'a private and secret society'. For William Coningham, M.P. for Brighton and an art collector of rare distinction, 'you will never have the administration of the fine arts in this country placed on a sound or solid foundation, until some Minister is made politically responsible in his place in Parliament for it.'[65]

Several problems recur in the debate centred on the Gallery, all of which were aggravated, if not initiated by administrative confusion. For a start, what sort of painting was a national collection to hold? An idea was put over in the 1835-36 report that some portion of the Gallery ought to be devoted to the best examples of modern British masters, especially those on a large scale which would not be bought by private collectors.[66] But a National Gallery had to distinguish itself from private collections on other grounds than size. Unfortunately, the 1853 report found that, 'the additions to the Collection have not been made on any definite principle; whether with a view of imparting to it completeness, of illustrating the history of art, or of raising the standard of national taste.'[67] Furthermore, if, as Aberdeen stated, the Trustees had solely been guided by the 'intrinsic merit' of the work, who had the necessary connoisseurship to judge when, as in the majority of cases, the historical pedigree could not be traced directly to the artist? There was a running controversy as to which paintings were fakes as well as which were of merit. Eastlake supported the purchase of Italian primitives for they revealed the history of Italian art and the age which produced them. He was supported by the final report of the 1853 Select Committee.[68] However, it is clear from the evidence that Peel's contrary recommendations to the effect that these

were mere 'curiosities', went far with the Trustees and with Parliament.[69] In
the meantime, many opportunities were lost, including purchases from the
Solly, Coningham and Woodburn sales. No purchase at all was made between 1847 and 1851. Time was wasted in bringing every purchase before
Parliament; judgements were rushed and mistaken. A Keeper with a good eye
but with no clear overall responsibility had no chance of expanding the
collection beyond a haphazard assortment of sometimes doubtfully authenti-
cated works.

The same story is true of cleaning and restoring policy. Already in 1835, the
large Sebastian del Piombo was being invaded by 'a colony of insects'.
Despite the fact that England was reputed to possess the best liners and
restorers in the world, the collection was in a very bad way.[70] A Commission
was appointed in 1850 to inquire into the state of the pictures in the National
Gallery, while the Select Committee of the same year included consideration
of the best mode of preserving and exhibiting them to the public. The report
urged that glass ought to be used and the backs of the pictures to be preserved. The committee forbore to express an opinion on cleaning and the
mastic varnishes being used, which were going cloudy, but it pointed out that
if such a situation continued, future bequests would be discouraged.[71] The
1853 report summarized the advantages of cleaning by mechanical and chemical means as stated in the evidence, but found it 'extremely inconclusive and
unsatisfactory', for conditions varied from picture to picture. The conflicting
evidence from Uwins and Moore was so vituperative that it led the committee
to say, 'fervent love of art seems to have kindled some personal animosity.'[72]
Moore's evidence drew attention to the removal of the alleged 'glazing' in
mistake for dirt, the rubbing out of bits of painting and a wet sponge and
duster being used for occasional cleaning. He quoted a letter to *The Times,* in
which the correspondent spoke of 'the very housemaid style of operating . . . .
The centre room also got its share of the bucket. Rembrandt, Rubens, and
Maas were considerably smartened up.'[73] General authority for cleaning
seems to have been given to the Keeper by the Trustees in 1847, the 1846
controversy ultimately having strengthened Eastlake's position. Seguier
seems to have enjoyed the same responsibility. But when Uwins was Keeper,
neither side claimed responsibility and the report concluded thus:

> Your Committee do not feel competent to decide as to such delicate points
> of difference between the Trustees and their chief officer. But the existence
> of so entire a misunderstanding, in a case where mutual confidence was so
> greatly to be desired, seems little compatible with the efficient management
> of the institution.[74]

Part of the conservation difficulties lay in the site of the collection. Even in
1836, Shee found that the National Gallery was not 'commensurate with the
greatness of this nation,' and Wilkins, the architect, testified to the alteration

of his plans.[75] The 1847-48 Select Committee drew attention to the risk of smoke, dust and impurities to the collection, for the Gallery was being used as a shelter, for appointments and refreshment. It was coping with 3,000 visitors a day, compared with 200 a day in the Berlin Gallery.[76] Thus the 1851 Report considered alternative sites. It reversed the 1847-48 decision, as did the 1853 Select Committee report, and favoured a site on the newly acquired land in South Kensington. At this point the future of the Gallery was coming increasingly into the orbit of the Royal Commission for the Exhibition of 1851 and the plan to group together all the scientific and cultural institutions of the metropolis.[77] The third report of the commissioners included the Treasury minute of 27 March 1855 which drew up the new constitution of the Gallery. Eastlake was appointed Director at a salary of £1,000 a year and his decisions as to purchase and management were final, although the Trustees could record their dissent in the minutes and submit them to Parliament. The Director was to be assisted by a salaried Keeper and Travelling Agent. Preference was to be given to fine paintings on sale abroad, especially good paintings of the Italian schools including those of the earlier masters, for little danger then existed of works already in England leaving the country. An annual purchase grant was to be voted.[78]

This was by no means the final solution. The most pressing and ever recurrent need was space to hold new purchases and bequests. Even before the Vernon collection was donated, there was no space to clean pictures. In 1850 the Vernon pictures and those in the British collection were relegated to Marlborough House, and from there with the Turner bequest to South Kensington. In 1860 the Gallery was closed for a month to enlarge one room and build a gallery. The departure of the Royal Academy in 1869 made final the decision to keep the Gallery in Trafalgar Square, but it provided only temporary relief for the accommodation problem. In the 1870s and 1880s new sets of rooms were added, but after such a delay they barely provided breathing space before the National Gallery Board had to put in new proposals to 'a dilatory and indifferent Treasury'. It took twenty years for the government to do anything about the extension proposed by the Trustees in 1887 and even then pressure for action arose from a public outcry over the proven fire risk to the pictures.[79] The flurry of action in the 1850s with Select Committees and Royal Commissions considering the purchasing, cleaning and siting of a national collection must not offer too much distraction from the fact that the government, for the most part, got away with the minimum amount of time and money which could be devoted to the institution.

IV

I beg leave to observe, that I consider the Royal Academy a much more important institution to the nation than the National Gallery; I look upon it

that a garden is of more consequence than a granary.[80]
Thus Sir Martin Arthur Shee, President of the Royal Academy, before the
Select Committee of 1836 staked the claim of the Royal Academy to live in a
building constructed with public funds on the Academy's role as a school. It
was against this role that the full weight of radical opposition was directed. Dr
Waagen in 1835 doubted the importance of academies at all, comparing them
to Dutch gardens: 'Would not any one feel a greater pleasure in the free
growth of the trees in a forest, in preference to the monotonous uniformity.'[81]
John Landseer extended the metaphor, 'They have been too much engrafted
on the vanity and glory-seeking of sovereign and despotic princes, under a
hot-house system of cultivation.'[82]

Therefore, fundamental to the controversy centred on the Royal Academy
was the increasing irrelevance and the break-down of institutionalized
academic theory. The personal squabbles – they were like an inquisition
without a pope, Haydon said – over hanging space, gloomy corners and
varnishing would never have attracted public attention had not the whole
framework been called into question during the 1830s. As Hofland stated, the
Academy had all the evils of a close corporation with additional ones, namely
that it extended its influence over the whole country.[83] It was neither producing nor encouraging the best examples of high art, nor reaching out to meet a
wider public. Its lectures and teaching were in an appalling state; its exclusive
rules banned members from exhibiting with or belonging to any other organization; it degraded the newly important role of engravers – 'whose very
essence is expansion and diffusion'[84] – to a separate category of membership.
Shee, when questioned about those who believed in a 'free trade' in art and a
greater association with design for industry, dismissed them with the words,
'the principle of commerce and the principle of art are in direct opposition the
one to the other . . .They adapt to the arts a principle which belongs only to
trade; and the moment you make art a trade you destroy it.'[85] As was
remarked thirty years later when the Academy was next brought into prominence, a close corporation had never been known to reform itself.[86] If
Quentin Bell's argument is to be followed, the Academy was so successful in
smoke-screening the opposition, the very evidence given by Shee before the
1836 hearing was tactfully expurged.[87] Shee's family condemned the whole
proceedings, detecting 'a strong bias in favour of the *Benthamite* heresy,
combined to develop the most offensive form of utilitarian dogmatism, in all
matters of political or administrative discussion.'[88] Fortunately for Shee and
the Royal Academy, there were more important reforms to occupy the
Benthamite plotters for the next couple of decades, apart from sporadic
attacks from the relentless Hume.

In 1863 a Royal Commission was appointed to inquire into the position of
the Royal Academy in relation to the Fine Arts, the circumstances of its

occupying the National Gallery building and 'to suggest such measures as may be required to render it more useful in promoting Art and improving and developing public taste.' The report was flattering, but admitted serious defects which made the institution inadequate for coping with a large increase in the number of artists. It endeavoured to give the Academy a 'clear and definite public character' instead of the anomalous and ambiguous one it had hitherto held, by suggesting a Royal Charter, thereby giving lustre to the throne as well as gratifying encouragement to artists. A number of liberalizing measures were aimed to increase the public role of the Academy. A larger membership could include architects and sculptors, with engravers being placed on a par with other members, while it considered that Associates ought to play a more important role. 'Art Workmen' whose work was of great excellence, could be given medals or certificates. The most controversial measure suggested was the introduction of lay members, some of whom 'might also render it important service elsewhere, if their presence in either House of Parliament enabled them to explain its proceedings, when required, to the Legislature.'[89] Some witnesses before the commission envisaged even greater things. Blaine thought it was very important to have a representative of the Royal Academy to advise the government on artistic patronage and commissions. Beresford Hope thought that the Academy should become an advisory body, a powerful central regulating influence, subordinate neither to the unchecked control of government nor to the vagaries of ministerial changes. For art, the Academy should act as the fountain of honour, the senate of an art university, which would be less connected to a ministerial department than was then the case.[90]

One Academician concurred with the introduction of a lay element by saying, 'I think that we are in such a sleepy state, that it would be desirable to have recourse to anything to awake us.'[91] The majority view, however, as illustrated in the Academy's 'Observations', was not deterred by the veiled threat implicit in the Commission's argument. This was that if the Royal Academy was to be given the whole of the space vacated by the National Gallery if it moved, with fixity of tenure, then the public had a right to expect the 'ready and cheerful concurrence on the part of that distinguished body' to the amendments suggested, and for old and new members of the Academy to work together for a combined object, the promotion and development of art. The Academy refused to agree to the idea of a Royal Charter. It pointed out that art workmen were already being looked after in South Kensington. Most of all, the idea of lay membership was an enlargement of the original plan and an uncalled-for innovation.[92] However, the evidence from Academicians had been fairly evenly divided between those who thought that lay members would introduce public opinion into the institution which would thereby act as a less cliquish tribunal of taste than a pack of artists, and others like

Eastlake who believed that it would require too long a study for lay members
to acquire any competencè and that, on the contrary, their judgements would
be more biased. One of the latter group rather proved the rebels' argument
when he said he thought lay members would find the proceedings so 'uncom-
monly dull' that they would give up attending.[93]

Thus the Royal Commission of 1863 gives some insight into the thought
pattern of a private institution, which was not going to enlarge upon its
original plan, despite the changing atmosphere and needs of the age. Oppé has
argued that the improvements in the position of Associates and other internal
reforms were already supported by the Academy; the cancellation of the rule
requiring artists to put their name on the list if they wanted to be candidates
for election was in fact the 'principal grievance' in 1863.[94] This is to place
foremost the Academy's own determination to 'retain its independence'.
What happened in succeeding years, despite a few reforms in management
after the occupation of the spacious premises in Burlington House, was that
as a result of its concern to remain out on a limb, it ceased to have any
relevance whatsoever, either in supporting the most progressive art and the
most advanced teaching, or improving the standards of taste in the nation at
large.[95] For Ruskin, speaking before the Commission, the reason for its
nugatory influence was more basic for the Academy was only the form
through which 'the temper of the nation' worked. So long as the country,
especially the upper classes, separated the idea of art education from other
sorts of education, there was no point in having lay members in the Academy:
the less they had to do with art, the better. He wanted the education offered
by the Academy to correspond wholly to a university education and he
outlined his scheme to the commission.[96] It is perhaps unfortunate that he
took little interest in the government art schools until after his appointment as
Slade Professor of Fine Arts at the University of Oxford.

V

In the long term, the Schools of Design represent the most serious and
elaborate foray made by the state into the fields of art and design. Anticipating the 1835-36 Select Committee report, the first national grant of £1,500 for
art education, to set up a normal school of design, was given by the government only two years after the first national grant for any sort of education. Yet
certainly until 1850 the schools exhibited the difficulties which dogged other
aspects of the diffusion process of taste throughout the country. The Schools
were in fact a failure, a confusion of teaching methods exaggerated in their
effects by administrative difficulties. The successive Directors in Somerset
House – Papworth, Dyce, Wilson and 'The Triumvirate' – all had differing
approaches, none of which seemed practically to enhance the relation
between arts and manufactures.

The head school was set under a governing body by the Board of Trade, with a membership made up of artists, manufacturers and amateurs. Public art education was controlled by this body until 1848, for it not only governed the school but administered the total government grant for art education. The artist members were all Royal Academicians determined to preserve academic teaching and life drawing for the Academy school.[97] The government school was to teach only ornamental design, which meant under the first director, Papworth, a narrow policy of drawing and modelling ornament. Thus, from the start the terms of the debate were set. There was an ideological conflict between those who sought an artist-designer education as in France, and those who conceived of the artisan's education in a much humbler sphere. The administrative conflict lay between the Board of Trade, governing council and director, between the head school's finances and those of other schools outside London. In other words, the history of the schools would epitomize all the characteristic symptoms of disorder in trying to reconcile fine and applied art with little coherent policy and few administrative instruments.

In 1837, William Dyce and Charles Wilson wrote a pamphlet on their ideas about Scottish art education. On the basis of this, Dyce was sent abroad to examine foreign systems and schools. His findings, appended to the first report, compared the French, Prussian and Bavarian methods of teaching and came out clearly in favour of the latter. Dyce preferred the elementary design classes found in all Bavarian primary schools and the scientific and technical bias of the art teaching, although in fact this did not seem to produce the best results.[98] In 1838, he became superintendent and professor of the head school. A poor start had been made for the school had proved unpopular both with manufacturers and with prospective students, who found the mechanics' institute classes cheaper and those of the Society for Promoting Practical Design more varied. Dyce was forced to reduce the fees and the limitation on life drawing was broken when in July 1841 the council appointed John Herbert to be master of figure, soon to become the most popular teacher in the school. The school was organized into seven classes, after the Bavarian model, and Dyce's Government Drawing Book, the sales of which are constantly referred to in the reports, was used as the chief means of instruction. Dyce persevered in his attempt to introduce a jacquard loom and weaving classes. The attempt was a failure, as the 1841 report concluded, for those who were already in the textile industries scarcely needed to be taught how to weave; those who were not, had no interest. Another class was set up in 1841 specifically to train art teachers in ornamental design, to replace the old-fashioned drawing master. But in general, owing to the lack of elementary education in art, the teaching had to be very basic and regimented, without the liberal education necessary to set it in context. Furthermore, the council itself was large, unwieldy and inefficient with a poor attendance record. It intervened on trifling matters but lacked real independence. Dyce explained his problems to Gladstone at the Board of Trade, but the council unfortunately could not by law be abolished. This ambiguity in the chain of command, with the director appealing straight to the Board of Trade, and the council still attempting to evade the director, continued.

Another complication was provided by the provincial schools, money having been granted for their foundation in 1840. Six were in existence by 1843, under a system dependent on government contributions being matched by those of local manufacturers. The principle was by no means sound. The schools were provided basically so that local manufacturers could make money. However, they could only be expected to flourish where there was money to spare, and that was precisely where the schools were not urgently needed. Hence, one sort of school, approximating to a drawing school, was founded in places like Norwich or York, little connected with manufactures and more bent on providing a genteel fine arts training. In Birmingham, on the other hand, there were no large magnates to provide the money. In Manchester, there seemed to be no call for original designs. Big manufacturers could obtain what they wanted by buying foreign patterns and retaining their superiority; they saw little point in benevolently aiding their lesser rivals. As for the workman, the very concept implied a slur on his present production, and the schools would only train and flood the market with rivals. Therefore, if any sort of training was favoured it was of a more academic sort – ironically, in view of the Royal Academy's preference for industrial training. In Manchester, John Zephaniah Bell provided a syllabus which tried to get rid of the distinction between high art and ornamental art. The conflict between his policy and that of the head school broke into the open when Dyce was sent north in 1843 to inspect the school, following the Education Council's decree of 1839. He found that the Manchester Management Committee backed Bell, for the Fine Art influence had improved the skill and taste of the artisans. However, classes were closed and Bell found it impossible to continue.[99] Paradoxically, Dyce resigned at the same time, having been requested by some of the Council to spend more time at the head school. He took up the less arduous task of inspector of the provincial schools.

This ambiguity of policy was accentuated by the appointment of Charles Heath Wilson to superintend the head school, whose views were diametrically opposed to those of Dyce. He was a historicist, an advocate of ancient and renaissance art, which meant in effect turning the Schools of Design into museums where students could execute exact copies of historical ornament. The third report of the council, 1843-44, emphasized this bias and inaugurated the collection of casts Wilson was making by incorporating a section on the utility of forming a collection of superior examples of ornamental work.

This would:

serve to elevate conception of the capabilities of the art, and produce a conviction that not only pecuniary gain may be derived from the study of it, but honourable distinction, and the satisfaction of benefiting the great mass of our manufacturing population by a general improvement in skill and taste in Design.

The report even went so far as to suggest that ministers abroad could easily obtain examples on the cheap. These would serve to illustrate the spirit of the age in which they were made, add to a comprehensive and liberal study of other ages and create greater refinement also.[100] This polemic could well be said to mark the beginnings of the collection which was later to become the Victoria and Albert Museum.

Less beneficial results, however, accrued from Wilson's directorship, notably the character clashes which led to the revolts of not only the students but also the teaching staff.[101] As a result, a Special Committee was set up in 1847 to investigate the complaints and to review the course of instruction and the management. The report drew a veil over the backbiting and intrigue – which is to be found in the appendix – and simply listed the grievances. Only technical skill was being taught, neither pure taste nor knowledge of the manufacturing process. It recommended preparatory schools to avoid the elementary nature of much of the teaching hitherto. Finally, it recommended that the duties of director should be redefined and a committee of instruction should receive communications from the masters. The outcome was that Wilson was quietly removed and made provincial inspector, while a committee of management consisting of Townsend, Horsley and Dyce ran the school. Naturally, this led to personality clashes; teaching deteriorated and there was trouble again in the provinces. Henry Cole, having met Lefevre, produced three reports highly critical of the way design education was going in the country, started the *Journal of Design and Manufactures* as propaganda for his views, and finally through Milner Gibson, obtained a Select Committee on the Schools of Design, which began its business in March 1849.

The Select Committee evidence summarized all the mess and grievances of the previous twelve years. The witnesses served Cole's purpose in their divided opinions in suggesting utter confusion to the public. Northcote as first witness blamed the trade depression and the jealousy and apathy of manufacturers. He suggested elementary education in drawing should be made part of national education and that more systematic instruction in the drawing of the figure was necessary, for it had a specific use in pattern, was vital for furniture design and, most important, it gave a thorough education in art, a correctness of eye and hand. For him this was the 'true catholic faith'.[102] It was, however, a view that was challenged by Cole who acknowledged that it did provide useful training but could be carried too far. If one attempted to thrust anatomy down the throats of pattern drawers, they would not attend the schools. High art did not improve other branches of art. As far as the system of drawing was concerned, it was not practical enough. Cole further castigated the whole management of the head school, stressing the failure of both the Council and the Board of Trade.[103]

Another dimension to the evidence was offered by the manufacturers themselves. In this they implicitly recognized that what they followed was the market. Witnesses spoke of the thirst for novelty and change in the public and the low standard of that taste, which preferred tawdry to good design.[104] For Herbert, the public was rarely right, for in artistic matters, it required almost as good a judgement to appreciate a beautiful thing as to execute it.[105] In fact, as neither manufacturers nor public could distinguish between good and bad design, the prime object of the Schools of Design ought to be the inculcation of improved taste first in the execution of designs and second in their application to manufacturers. As for the manufacturers' fears and jealousy, Dyce stressed that the Schools of Design dealt with principles not fashion and thus they would not affect the majority of manufacturers.[106] The obvious danger was, however, that such 'principles' would be totally unsuitable for manufactures at all.

The final report, a bowdlerized version of Cole's first draft (amended to the report),[107] made mild suggestions to improve the proportion of designers in the country who came from the Schools of Design.[108] The Board of Trade should take over entire control and there ought to be more widespread elementary teaching; at the same time, the report pointed out that it was a slow process to make a designer and quick results could not be expected. In November 1849, the Board of Trade abolished the committee of management and appointed a new committee of laymen. The Great Exhibition of 1851 enhanced Cole's reputation while it provided concrete evidence for the dissatisfaction with British designs compared with those from abroad, which had been voiced by individuals for over a quarter of a century. When it was over and the land in South Kensington purchased with the money raised, a new department of the Board of Trade was created, the Department of Practical Art. This was ruled by one permanent official, Cole, who was directly responsible to the Board of Trade. He was assisted by an artist in charge of the London school, Redgrave. It initiated a new phase in the development of art education in the country.

VI

It was Henry Cole who was responsible for setting up a national system of art education during the period 1852-73. This saw the most rapid increase of art institutions in British history, including the establishment of the first training school for art masters, the first government art examinations and teaching certificates, the first art masters' association and the first great museum of applied art, the Victoria and Albert Museum.

The first report of the Department of Practical Art laid out the guidelines of administration, its appendices the ideology which underpinned them. The proposed objectives of the department were general elementary education in art as a branch of national education, among all classes of the community, with a view to laying the foundation for correct judgement in both consumer and producer of manufactures. Secondly, it sought advanced instruction in art for specialists. Thirdly, it would encourage the application of the principles of technical art to the improvement of manufactures, and the establishment of museums. It stressed the role of the museum with an efficient circulation system and lectures, as the only effectual means whereby adults could be taught the common principles of taste, traced in works of excellence of all ages. The museums would be 'elevated from being a mere unintelligible lounge for idlers into an impressive schoolroom for every one.'[109]

The appendices include one of Cole's speeches, made at the opening of an elementary school in Westminster. He stressed instruction in the principles of design and the very elements of drawing. Armed with such training, the student, the public and the manufacturer would no longer be bound by the 'thraldom of fashionable caprice'. Art education was not a luxury but a necessity. Drawing was the power of expressing things correctly, while writing merely dealt in ideas. Cole concluded with a peculiar extension of that moral streak which flavours so much of Victorian pioneering activity in art for the masses, that 'this power will also assist them to obtain increased accuracy in all other ways, and therefore become all the more truthful and sensible of God's wisdom.'[110] Redgrave enlarged on the benefits to be accrued. It would give all a knowledge of form as a means of expressing their thoughts and an improvement among all classes in the perception of what was really excellent in design applied to the things and uses of daily life. Art acted as a universal language, a condensed shorthand. Because of the correctness of eye it encouraged, the perceptive faculties generally were improved, opening up the pleasurable perception of beauty, order and symmetry in man-made and Great Creator-made things. Furthermore:

nourishing, as it does, the love of beauty, order and perfection, it is so far the enemy of vice that he who would succeed in it must cultivate his mind, and strive to improve his general intelligence and information, making him at the same time a better workman, a better artist, a better member of society, and a better man.[111]

Redgrave insisted on utility, fitness and unity of style, using formal and symmetrical geometry as the basis of all teaching. It was a Germanic method, a training in the useful and mechanical, not the romantic and aesthetic style of teaching in the French atelier.[112] In conjunction with Cole's system, utility and pragmatism backed by a debased notion of the moral efficacy of such teaching affected every level of art teaching and made the Gladgrind image of the results not so much a caricature as has generally been supposed.[113] The system which Cole organized for training teachers of art fell into three categories: training existing school masters and mistresses, training pupil teachers and students in training colleges, and training masters for the Schools of Art. In 1852, classes for the latter were set up in Somerset House. In 1853, drawing was made compulsory in training colleges, with examinations, prizes and certificates. Technical classes were also introduced at the head school under Semper, and later workshops when the former proved to be too expensive to run.[114] The establishment of a museum from Cole's forages among the remains of the Wilson collection and his finds in the servants' quarters at Windsor proved a more lasting legacy,[115] regrettably outside the scope of these volumes. However, the main energies of the department were directed towards a battery production of art teachers for more art teachers and for more bored youths and children.[116]

In order to encourage self-support, and to remove any suggestion that local schools could expect direct grants from the department, a Science and Art minute of the Board of Trade in March 1853 laid down that from 1850, the management and costs of the Schools of Art were the responsibilities of their committees. This was the beginning of the 'payment by results' principle, fostered by Cole and successive officers in the Board of Trade, and later taken up by Lowe and applied to education generally.[117] It stemmed directly from their desire to make the local schools self-supporting and to spread the teaching of elementary drawing in the public day systems. In 1852 the department was already talking of minimum guaranteed salaries; by 1856 of 'making payments to school and master on the examination results of the poor.' The starvation of the local schools through lack of money was risked further through the allotment of the national grant undifferentiated from that given to the museum at the head school. The suspicion was that money intended for the provinces was in fact filling the coffers of South Kensington, which had so inefficient a circulation system that it was of no conceivable benefit to any museum outside London.[118] By 1863, the only fixed payments were the grants for certificates of competency held by the art masters, and a minute of 1 October of that year stopped even this. In self defence against the deprivation of the last guaranteed portion of their income, John Sparkes made contact with the art masters round his Lambeth school and founded the Association of Art Masters. They formed a deputation to see Granville, complaining first of the injustice of doing away with the masters' certificate allowances, second of the impolicy of getting rid of art pupil teachers and third, of the unfairness of spending such an overwhelming portion of the grant on South Kensington. Granville did nothing, but Northcote moved for a

Select Committee which met in 1866.

Beresford Hope in the Royal Academy Commission had condemned South Kensington as a 'Noah's art', driven from pillar to post by different directions from the administration, with the museum further complicating matters. He went on to write to the 1866 Committee, in a letter added to the appendix, that the whole teaching system was based on a fallacy. Because there existed no general recognition of the advantages of art teaching, there were not enough pupils to keep pace with the masters. The masters were creating not supplying a want. Instead of allowing the pupils to follow on their own course, the masters were dragging them along a particular course, not for their own good, but to augment the masters' incomes. In sum, as art education was the desire of the enlightened few and not popular with the still uninstructed many, results could not be made 'the foundation of the bargain', for the system only made art education more unpopular.[119]

The report of the Committee made several observations, the principle of which was that payment by results was not well adapted to the Schools of Art: 'that it has a tendency to destroy the elasticity of Art-teaching, and thus to cramp the genius of our designers, to render the schools unpopular, and to diminish the chance of local support.'[120] However, the report did point out that the certificate given to art masters was never meant to be a guarantee of annual payment. It suggested a compromise arrangement whereby a system of capital payments was regulated by the number of artisans receiving instruction from duly qualified teachers in well conducted schools. The report drew attention to the evidence on the lack of care taken with the specific needs of a locality and considered that a distinct line should be drawn between funds voted for works of art in South Kensington and those for the encouragement of provincial schools.

The Select Committee proved a failure in the eyes of Sparkes and the reformers. The certificates were not revived; a larger proportion of funds was not granted for local schools; the removal of Cole was not achieved. Paying classes, although regulation had been recommended in the report, continued to be the most remunerative form of instruction. The official history of the Schools for the rest of the century may be studied in the reports from the Department of Science and Art, while the development of the Victoria and Albert Museum is traced in those of the Commissioners for the Exhibition of 1851, the Select Committee of 1860, the correspondence, returns and building costs in the parliamentary collections of Accounts and Papers, and in the autobiography of Henry Cole. However, it is the Royal Commission on Technical Instruction of 1884 which places the running of art education in the country in its true perspective. The report attacked the existing system in two vulnerable areas. First, it pointed out that the number of children receiving any art education in England was a small proportion of the total number, compared with several western European countries, and diminishing. Furthermore, it doubted the value of the type of instruction being received. Instead of the mass of inferior drawings being sent once a year to South Kensington, it preferred an inspectorate sent from Whitehall to the schools. It stressed the necessity for sound instruction methods and competent teachers. Instead of the slow method of drawing which deprived young students of manipulative skill, it urged the rapidity and boldness of freehand drawing.[121]

One sentence sums up the second and more basic failure of the Schools to fulfil the aims of the 1836 report:

Large grants of public money for teaching art to artisans in such classes can scarcely be justified on any other ground than its industrial activity.

Yet the teaching of industrial design in the art schools had been all but ignored since Cole took over. Indeed, from the closing of the Museum workshops by Poynter in 1877 there had been no practical craft work at the schools. Grants were given for designs on paper not for applied work. Furthermore, since both the government and employers refused to provide scholarships, artisans had to pay their own way. The report compared the crowded classes organized gratuitously for artisans abroad with the situation in this country. It recommended that intelligent youths of the artisan class should have access both to secondary and technical education via numerous scholarships; that tradesmen teachers should be employed; that employers should take a greater interest and that the localities should bear a proportion of the cost.[122]

The 1889 Technical Instruction Act which permitted the levy of a penny rate for science and art teaching initiated the municipal takeover of responsibility for the Schools of Art. At the same time, the influence of the Arts and Craft Movement was permeating the system. Since the foundation of the Art Union, Felix Summerly's Art Manufactures and the firm of Morris, Marshall and Faulkner had successfully combined art with manufactures on a small scale. Morris's firm, although without educational aims, influenced many of the founders of the Art Workers' Guild, who discussed art and architecture and formed a society to organize exhibitions. The society's first chairman was Walter Crane and it set new standards of taste, encouraging many artisans to enroll in craft classes which were organized in London in the 1890s. Crane lectured in the National Art Training Schools, became Director of Design at the Manchester Municipal School of Art and in 1898, Principal of the South Kensington School, now named the Royal College of Art. He said he found the College 'a sort of mill in which to prepare art teachers'.[123] When the Science and Art Department merged with the new Board of Education in 1899, a Council of Advice was formed to direct the nation's art education policies. The reorganization of the College in 1901 to incorporate a Design department with craft classes, together with Lethaby's work at the Central School ensured that the influence of the Art Workers' Guild helped to stop the rot in the South Kensington system until the 1930s. However, the most radical innovations to connect art and design with mass-manufactured, mass-consumed factory products in the Bauhaus did not reach England until after the second world war. Similarly, the advances made by Marion Richardson, Cizek and Viola did not influence art teaching in schools generally until the 1940s. It was a century since the question had been first posed: how to improve the nation's taste and its products. These parliamentary papers reveal the varying approaches attempted and the purpose which underlay them. They underline the fact that art for the Victorians was not an aesthetic emotion reserved for the privileged few. Art had a social purpose, a moral and educational role to play, which was essential for the country's prosperity and well-being.

Footnotes

1 'London Art Union Minutes of Committee', 4 vols. MS British Museum II, 62. Quoted in Anthony King, 'George Godwin and the Art Union of London 1837-1911', *Victorian Studies,* VIII (1964) p.107.

2 See Nikolaus Pevsner, *Academies of Art* (Cambridge, 1940), pp.148-52.

3 'L'effet du commerce sont les richesses; la suite des richesses, le luxe, celle de luxe, la perfection des arts.' Montesquieu, *L'Esprit des Lois,* liv.21. ch.6. Quoted in D. Robertson Blaine, *On the Laws of Artistic Copyright and their Defects* (London, 1853), pp.1-2. For examples of academies founded in the late eighteenth century with commercial as well as artistic considerations in mind see N. Pevsner, *Academies of Art,* pp.152-75.

4 *Report of the Select Committee on Arts and Manufactures,* HC 1836 (568) IX, p.iii. IUP series Design 1.

5 *Minutes of Evidence,* HC 1835 (598) V, qus.670, 1598, 1721. HC 1836 (568) IX, qus.245, 270. IUP series Design 1.

6 *Minutes of Evidence,* HC 1835 (598) V, qus.1724-27. HC 1836 (568) IX, qu.330. IUP series Design 1.

7 *Minutes of Evidence,* HC 1835 (598) V, qu.1460. HC 1836 (568) IX, qus.1973-74. IUP series Design 1. Shee first stressed the incompatibility of the principles of art and trade in the preface to his *Rhymes on Art* (London ed.1805), obviously deriving his argument from Sir Joshua Reynolds's first *Discourse on Art* (London, 1769).

8 *Minutes of Evidence,* HC 1835 (598) V, qu.1566. IUP series Design 1.

9 *Minutes of Evidence from the Select Committee on the National Gallery,* HC 1852-53 (867) XXXV, qus.5943-72, 5991-93. IUP series Fine Arts 4.

10 *Hansard,* 3rd ser., XLIX, cols.717-20 (24 July, 1839), cols.1007-38 (30 July, 1839); LXXVI, cols.1246-49 (22 July, 1844).

11 *Minutes of Evidence from the Select Committee on Arts and Manufactures,* HC 1836 (568) IX, qus.1835-40. IUP series Design 1.

12 (James Dennistoun), 'The National Gallery Report', *Edinburgh Review,* XCIX (1854) 549.

13 *Observations of the Members of the Royal Academy of Art upon the Report of the Royal Academy Commission,* HC 1864 (3332) XIX Pt.1, pp.1-3, 12-13. IUP series

Fine Arts 5, pp.757-59, 768-69. See also *Hansard*, 3rd ser., CLXXVI, cols.236-53 (24 June 1864).

14   ('An Artist'), 'Amateur Government of British Art', *Athenaeum*, No.923 (1845) pp.664-65.

15   For Peel's artistic activities see Norman Gash, *Sir Robert Peel* (London, 1972), pp.290, 687-89.

16   For the Sheepshanks bequest see *Appendix D to the Fourth Report of the Commissioners for the Exhibition of 1851*, HC 1861 (2819) XXXII, pp.102-05.

17   See James Johnston Auchmuty, *Sir Thomas Wyse, 1791-1862* (London, 1939). W.A. Munford, *William Ewart, M.P. 1798-1869* (London, 1960). Also, the speech made by Wyse at a meeting of artists and engravers in 1842, quoted in John Pye, *Patronage of British Art* (London, 1845), pp.176-85.

18   See Archibald Prentice, *History of the League* (London, 1853), II, pp.315-41.

19   Quoted in Sir Henry Cole, *Fifty Years of Public Work* (London, 1884), II, pp.208-20.

20   *Report from the Select Committee on the South Kensington Museum*, HC 1860 (527) XVI, pp.iv-vi.

21   There is scarce a common trade, which does not afford some opportunities of applying to it the principles of geometry and mechanics, and which would not therefore gradually exercise and improve the common people in those principles, the necessary introduction to the most sublime as well as the most useful sciences. Adam Smith, *Wealth of Nations*, quoted in 'Elementary Drawing', *The Times*, 7 October 1876 and repeated in H. Cole, *Fifty Years of Public Life*, I. pp.280-81.

22   For the memorials presented, unsuccessfully, to the Council of the School of Design, by the wood engravers to petition against the class of instruction in wood engraving for ladies at the School, see the *Art-Union*, V (1843) p.271. VI (1844) p.123. When Cole took over, the class was reorganized under Cole's friend, John Thompson. *First Report of the Department of Practical Art*, 1852-53 (1615) LIV, pp.20-21. IUP series Design 4, pp.270-71.

For the complaints against the cheap, monopoly service offered by the South Kensington photographic department (headed, incidentally, by Thurston Thompson, John Thompson's son) by professional photographers, led by Roger Fenton, see *Report from the Select Committee on the South Kensington Museum*, 1860 (527) XVI, pp.vi-vii. Also, *Minutes of Evidence*, qus.350-60, 1564-1620.

23   See H. Cole, *Fifty Years of Public Work*, I.

24   Quoted in H. Cole, *Fifty Years of Public Work*, II, pp.305-08.

25   See Benjamin Robert Haydon, *Autobiography* (1926 ed.). Also, *The Diary of Benjamin Robert Haydon*, ed. Willard Bissell Pope (Cambridge, Mass., 1960-63).

26   See, for example, *The Abuses of the National Gallery* (London, 1847), *Revival of Vandalism at the National Gallery* (London, 1853), written by Moore under the pseudonym of 'Verax'.

27   It claimed to have a subscription list of 15,000 in 1849 when it changed its name to the *Art Journal*. For a not unbiased account of its role, see Samuel Carter Hall, *Retrospect of a Long Life* (London, 1863), I, pp.338-63.

28   See H. Cole, *Fifty Years of Public Work*, I, pp.390-92.

I

29   For the history of academic theory and practice see N. Pevsner, *Academies of Art*. Also Quentin Bell, *The Schools of Design* (London, 1963), pp.1-37. Stuart Macdonald, *The History and Philosophy of Art Education* (London, 1970), pp.23-59.

30   *Minutes of Evidence from the Select Committee on the Promotion of Fine Arts*, HC 1841 (423), VI, qu.861; IUP series Fine Arts 2, pp.84-85.

31   For a summary of the contemporary arguments put forward in favour of history painting see Edward Edwards, *The Fine Arts in England* (London, 1840), pp.185-87.

32   See (Elizabeth Eastlake), 'The Late Prince Consort', *Quarterly Review,* CXI (1862) pp.176-200. Also Winslow Ames, *Prince Albert and Victorian Taste* (London, 1967), who quotes Ford Madox Brown on the subject, p.51. The theory was discounted in the memoir compiled by Lady Eastlake in Sir Charles Lock Eastlake, *Contributions to the Literature of the Fine Arts* (London, 1870 ed.), p.172. See also, Keith Andrews, *The Nazarenes* (Oxford, 1964), pp.84-85.

33   *Minutes of Evidence,* HC 1841 (423) VI, qus.259, 743-62. IUP series Fine Arts 2, pp.38, 74-76.

34   For the full exchange see *Appendices 8,10 and 11 to the Third Annual Report of the Commissioners on the Fine Arts,* HC 1844 (585) XXXI, pp. 21-24, 26-30. IUP series Fine Arts 2, pp.455-58, 460-64.

For the relationship between high art and British historical painting see Edgar Wind, 'The Revolution of History Painting', *Journal of the Warburg Institute,* II (1938) pp.116-27. Charles Mitchell, 'Zoffany's "Death of Captain Cook",' *Burlington Magazine,* LXXXIV (1944) pp.56-62. 'Benjamin West's "Death of General Wolfe" and the Popular History Piece', *Journal of the Warburg and Courtauld Institutes,* VII (1944), pp.20-33. 'Benjamin West's "Death of Nelson",' *Essays in the History of Art presented to Rudolf Wittkower,* ed. Douglas Fraser, Howard Hibbard, Milton J. Lewine (London, 1967), pp.265-73.

35   *Minutes of Evidence,* HC 1841 (423) VI, qus.356-60, 367, 401-07, 713-16. IUP series Fine Arts 2, pp.45-46, 48, 72.

36   *Report from the Select Committee on Art Unions,* HC 1845 (612) VII, pp.xviii-xx. *Minutes of Evidence,* qu. 2185. IUP series Fine Arts 1.

For the exclusion of art from church and state see (William Carey), *Observations on the Probable Decline or Extinction of British Historical Painting* (London, 1825). Also, 'Historical Painting in England', *Art-Union,* II (1840) pp.64-65.

37   *Report from the Select Committee on Art Unions,* HC 1845 (612) VII, pp.xxiv-xxv. *Minutes of Evidence,* qus.2140, 2217, 3330. IUP series Fine Arts 1.

For the use of lotteries in the eighteenth century by Hogarth, Copley and Boydell, the print dealer, see Gerald Reitlinger, *The Economics of Taste* (London, 1961), pp.66-68, 77. Also, Henry Cole, 'Public Galleries and Irresponsible Boards', *Edinburgh Review,* CXXIII (1866) pp.54-57 which refers to the 1753 plan to raise funds for the British Museum by public lottery, supported by the highest dignatories of church and state; he adds that 'public feeling' would not allow such a plan to take place now.

38   *Minutes of Evidence from the Select Committee on Arts and Manufactures,* HC 1835 (598) V, qus.653-61, HC 1836 (568) IX, qus.248, 1798-99, 1905-07. IUP series Design 1.

39   *Report from the Select Committee on National Monuments,* HC 1841 (416) pp.vi-viii, 91. *Minutes of Evidence,* qu.1849. IUP series Fine Arts 2, pp.120-22, 217.

40   *Hansard,* 3rd ser., CXII, cols. 814-15 (1 July 1850).

41   *Minutes of Evidence from the Select Committee on the National Gallery,* HC 1852-53 (867) XXXV, qus.7011, 7136-53, 7390-92. IUP series Fine Arts 4. Also, *Minutes of Evidence of the National Gallery Site Commission,* HC 1857 (2261) XXIV, qus.2653, 3294. *Appendix II, No.2 to the Report,* pp.157-59. IUP series Fine Arts 3, pp.295, 333-34, 347-49.

For similar sentiments, voiced in connection with the liberal opening hours at South Kensington, see *Report from the Select Committee on the South Kensington Museum,* HC 1860 (527) XVI, p.vii. Also, *Correspondence &c., relative to the Establishment of the Bethnal Green or East London Museum,* HC 1872 (759) xlvi.

42   (J.W. Croker), 'Life of Haydon', *Quarterly Review,* XCIII (1853) pp.582-83.

II

43 *Minutes of Evidence from the Select Committee on Fine Arts*, HC 1841 (423) VI, qus.446-52, 863, 911, 926. IUP series Fine Arts 2, pp.51, 85, 90.

44 *Report from the Select Committee on Fine Arts*, HC 1841 (423) VI, p.x. IUP series Fine Arts 2, p.18.

45 *Thirteenth Report of the Commissioners on the Fine Arts*, HC 1863 (3141) XVI, pp.8-9. IUP series Fine Arts 3, pp.426-27.

46 *Report from the Select Committee on Arts and Manufactures*, HC 1836 (568) IX, p.vii. *Minutes of Evidence*, qus.46-65. IUP series Design 1.

47 *Minutes of Evidence from the Select Committee on Copyright of Designs*, HC 1840 (442) VI, qu.684. IUP series Design 2.

48 *Minutes of Evidence from the Select Committee on Copyright of Designs*, HC 1840 (442) VI, qus. 3656, 3672, 3681-89. IUP series Design 2.

49 *Minutes of Evidence from the Select Committee on Copyright of Designs*, HC 1840 (442) VI, qus.4965, 4984, 5019, 5079. IUP series Design 2.

50 *Minutes of Evidence from the Select Committee on Copyright of Designs*, HC 1840 (442) VI, qu.372. IUP series Design 2.

51 *Minutes of Evidence from the Select Committee on Copyright of Designs*, HC 1840 (442) VI, qus.2214-24. IUP series Design 2.

52 *Minutes of Evidence from the Select Committee on Copyright of Designs*, HC 1840 (442) VI, qu.8421. IUP series Design 2.

53 *Report from the Select Committee on Art Unions*, HC 1845 (612) VII, pp.xiv-xvi, xxii-xxiii. IUP series Fine Arts 1.

54 Anthony King, 'George Godwin and the Art Union of London 1837-1911', *Victorian Studies*, VIII (1964) pp.101-30.

55 *Minutes of Evidence from the Select Committee on Art Unions*, HC 1845 (612) VII, qus.862-98. IUP series Fine Arts 1.

III

56 *Minutes of Evidence from the Select Committee on the Fine Arts*, HC 1841 (423) VI, qus.763-64, 784-86. IUP series Fine Arts 2, pp.76, 78.

57 *Appendix 2 to the Sixth Report of the Commissioners on the Fine Arts*, HC 1846 (749) XXIV, p.10. IUP series Fine Arts 2, p.548. *Twelfth Report of the Commissioners on the Fine Arts*, HC 1861 (2806) XXXII, pp.7-8. IUP series Fine Arts 3, pp.399-400.

58 'Styles and Methods of Painting suited to the Decoration of Public Buildings', *Appendix 6 to the Second Report of the Commissioners on tne Fine Arts*, HC 1843 (499) XXIX, pp.56-65. IUP series Fine Arts 2, pp.418-27. *Appendix 2 to the Fifth Report of the Commissioners on the Fine Arts* HC 1846 (685) XXIV, pp.11-25. IUP series Fine Arts 2, pp.521-35. Reprinted in Sir Charles Eastlake, *Contributions to the Literature of the Fine Arts*, (London 1848), pp.125-79.

59 *Report from the Select Committee on Art Union Laws*, HC 1866 (332) VII, p.iii. IUP series Fine Arts 6, p.577.

60 See A. King, 'George Godwin and the Art Union of London', pp.119-21.

61 *Minutes of Evidence from the Select Committee on Art Union Laws*, HC 1866 (332) VII, qu.537. IUP series Fine Arts 6, p.614.

62 (James Dennistoun), 'The National Gallery Report', *Edinburgh Review*, XCIX (1854) p.528. See also *Hansard*, 3rd ser., CXXIV, col.1313 (8 March 1853).

63 *Report from the Select Committee on the National Gallery*, HC 1852-53 (867) XXXV, pp.iii-v. IUP series Fine Arts 4.

64 *Minutes of Evidence from the Select Committee on Arts and Manufactures*, HC

1836 (568) IX, qu.1443. IUP series Design 1.

65 *Minutes of Evidence from the Select Committee on the National Gallery,* HC 1852-53 (867) XXXV, qus.5283, 5286, 7225-26, 6809. IUP series Fine Arts 4.

66 *Report from the Select Committee on Arts and Manufactures,* HC 1836 (568) IX, p. x. IUP series Design 1.

67 *Report from the Select Committee on the National Gallery,* HC 1852-53 (867) XXXV, p.vi. *Minutes of Evidence,* qu.5307. IUP series Fine Arts 4.

68 *Report from the Select Committee on the National Gallery,* HC 1852-53 (867) XXXV, p.xvi. IUP series Fine Arts 4.

69 *Minutes of Evidence from the Select Committee on the National Gallery,* HC 1852-53 (867) XXXV, qus.6023-30. IUP series Fine Arts 4.

70 *Minutes of Evidence from the Select Committee on Arts and Manufactures,* HC 1836 (568) IX, qus.1543-57, 1803-23. IUP series Design 1.

71 *Report from the Select Committee on the National Gallery,* HC 1850 (612) XV, pp.iv-v. IUP series Fine Arts 3, pp.26-27.

72 *Report from the Select Committee on the National Gallery,* HC 1852-53 (867) XXXV, pp.vi-xi. IUP series Fine Arts 4.

73 *Minutes of Evidence from the Select Committee on the National Gallery,* HC 1852-53 (867) XXXV, qu.2379. IUP series Fine Arts 4.

74 *Report from the Select Committee on the National Gallery,* HC 1852-53 (867) XXXV, p.ix. IUP series Fine Arts 4.

75 *Minutes of Evidence from the Select Committee on Arts and Manufactures,* HC 1836 (568) IX, qus.2034, 1207-08, 1402-03. IUP series Design 1.

76 *Report from the Select Committee on the National Gallery,* HC 1850 (612) XV, p.iv. IUP series Fine Arts 3, p.26.

77 See the *Second Report of the Commissioners for the Exhibition of 1851,* HC 1852-53 (1566) LIV.

78 *Appendix K to the Third Report of the Commissioners for the Exhibition of 1851,* HC 1856 (2065) XXIV. pp.174-84.

79 See Sir Charles Holmes and C.H. Collins Baker, *The Making of the National Gallery 1824-1924* (London 1924) pp.49-64.

IV

80 *Minutes of Evidence from the Select Committee on Arts and Manufactures,* HC 1836 (568) IX, qu.2041. IUP series Design 1.

81 *Minutes of Evidence from the Select Committee on Arts and Manufactures,* HC 1835 (598) V, qu.95. IUP series Design 1.

82 *Minutes of Evidence from the Select Committee on Arts and Manufactures,* HC 1836 (568) IX, qu.2045. IUP series Design 1.

83 *Minutes of Evidence from the Select Committee on Arts and Manufactures,* HC 1836 (568) IX, qus.1264-66. IUP series Design 1.

84 J. Pye, *Patronage of British Art* p.296. Pye gives a useful account of the grievances felt in artistic circles during the 1840s. pp.289-301.

85 *Minutes of Evidence from the Select Committee on Arts and Manufactures,* HC 1836 (568) IX, qus. 1973-74. IUP series Design 1.

86 *Minutes of Evidence of the Royal Academy Commission,* HC 1863 (3205) XXVII, qus. 2904-08. IUP series Fine Arts 5, p.346.

87 Quentin Bell, 'Haydon versus Shee', *Journal of the Warburg and Courtauld Institutes,* XXII (1959) pp.347-58.

88   M.A. Shee, *Life of Sir Martin Arthur Shee* (London, 1860) II, p.47.

89   *Report of the Royal Academy Commission*, HC 1863 (3205) XXVII, pp.v-ix. IUP series Fine Arts 5, pp.18-21.

90   *Minutes of Evidence of the Royal Academy Commission*, HC 1863 (3205) XXVII, qus.2865, 3015-18, 4208-09, 4228-29, 4238. IUP series Fine Arts 5, pp.342, 356-57, 490, 492-94.

91   *Minutes of Evidence of the Royal Academy Commission*, HC 1863 (3205) XXVII, qu.1191. IUP series Fine Arts 5, p.169.

92   *Observations of the Members of the Royal Academy of Arts upon the Report of the Royal Academy Commission*, HC 1864 (3332) XIX Pt.1 pp.1-3. IUP series Fine Arts 5, pp.757-59.

93   *Minutes of Evidence of the Royal Academy Commission*, HC 1863 (3205) XXVII, qu.1785. IUP series Fine Arts 5, p.235.

94   A. Paul Oppé, 'Art', in *Early Victorian England*, ed. G.M. Young, (Oxford, 1934) II, p. 139.

95   See H.C. Morgan, 'The Lost Opportunity of the Royal Academy: an assessment of its position in the nineteenth century', *Journal of the Warburg and Courtauld Institutes*, XXXII (1969) pp. 410-20. An official history is given in Sidney C. Hutchison, *The History of the Royal Academy 1768-1968* (London, 1968).

96   *Minutes of Evidence of the Royal Academy Commission*, HC 1863 (3205) XXVII, qus.5082, 5087, 5093, 5095-99. IUP series Fine Arts 5, pp.585-88.

V

97   Etty, the only Academician in favour of life drawing classes for the artisan, became interested mainly in the School of Design, established in his native York, where the curriculum was in sympathy with his ideas. S. Macdonald, *The History and Philosophy of Art Education*, p.70.

98   *Report from Mr. Dyce to the President of the Board of Trade on Foreign Schools of Design*. HC 1840 (98) XXIX, pp.1-56. IUP series Design 3, pp.9-64. For Dyce and his philosophy see S. Macdonald, *The History and Philosophy of Art Education*, pp.78-80. 118-26.

99   For an account of the chequered history of the Manchester School of Design see the evidence of Potter, a local textile manufacturer. *Minutes of Evidence from the Select Committee on Schools of Art*, HC 1864 (466) XII, qus.2206-33. IUP series Fine Arts 6, pp.172-76. For the branch schools in general see Q. Bell, *The Schools of Design*, pp.99-141. S. Macdonald, *The History and Philosophy of Art Education*, pp.84-88, 102-10.

100   *Third Report of the Council of the School of Design*, HC 1844 (566) XXXI, pp.18-21. IUP series Design 3, pp.112-15.

101   *Report of a Special Committee of the Council of the Government of the School of Design*, HC 1847 (835) LXII, pp.5-144. IUP series Design 3, pp.247-388. For an account of the revolt of the masters and the Special Committee see Q. Bell, *The Schools of Design*, pp.154-210.

102   *Minutes of Evidence from the Select Committee on the Schools of Design*, HC 1849 (576) XVIII, qus.111, 114-17, 259, 412, 414, 445. IUP series Design 3, pp.462-64, 475, 491-92, 494. For a summary of his view see (Stafford H. Northcote), 'Schools of Design', *Edinburgh Review*, XC (1849) pp.473-96.

103   *Minutes of Evidence from the Select Committee on the Schools of Design*, HC 1849 (576) XVIII, qus.1886, 1953, 2000-04. IUP series Design 3, pp.611-12, 623, 627-28.

104   *Minutes of Evidence from the Select Committee on the Schools of Design*, HC

1849 (576) XVIII, qus.1064, 1319, 2164-66, 3775. IUP series Design 3, pp.546, 565, 653, 775.

105 *Minutes of Evidence from the Select Committee on the Schools of Design*, HC 1849 (576) XVIII, qus.1776-77. IUP series Design 3, p.602.

106 *Minutes of Evidence from the Select Committee on the Schools of Design*. HC 1849 (576) XVIII, qus.759-62. IUP series Design 3, pp.516-17.

107 *Report from the Select Committee on the Schools of Design*, HC 1849 (576) XVIII, pp.i-vi. *Amended Draft Reports*, pp.xi-xli. IUP series Design 3, pp.401-06, 411-51.

108 *Report from the Select Committee on the Schools of Design*, HC 1849 (576) XVIII, pp.iii-iv. IUP series Design 3, pp.403-04.

VI

109 *First Report of the Department of Practical Art*, HC 1852-53 (1615) LIV, p.30. IUP series Design 4, p.280.

110 *Appendix II (A) to the First Report of the Department of Practical Art*, HC 1852-53 (1615) LIV, pp.54-59. IUP series Design 4, pp.304-09.

111 *Appendix II (B) to the First Report of the Department of Practical Art*, HC 1852-53 (1615) LIV, pp.59-63. IUP series Design 4, pp.309-13.

112 See S. Macdonald, *The History and Philosophy of Art Education*, pp.233-41, 284-90 on Redgrave's teaching philosophy and methods, and those of the French ateliers.

113 See K.J. Fielding, 'Charles Dickens and the Department of Practical Art', *Modern Language Review*, XLVIII (1953) pp.270-77. Also, S. Macdonald, *The History and Philosophy of Art Education*, pp.228-33.

114 For Semper's methods see N. Pevsner, *Academies of Art*, pp.251-58. The workshops established by Cole to help in the building of the museum were disbanded on his resignation. See S. Macdonald, *The History and Philosophy of Art Education*, pp.171-72, 233, 293.

115 See S. Macdonald, *The History and Philosophy of Art Education*, pp.177-81 for the development of the South Kensington Museum, the loan collections and the Travelling Museum. Also, the *Report from the Select Committee on the South Kensington Museum*, HC 1860 (527) XVI. *Correspondence between the Treasury and the Science and Art Department relative to New Buildings for the Museum*, HC 1866 (441) XL. &c.

116 For the stultifying methods of art teaching see George Moore, *Modern Painting* (London, 1893), pp.63-67.

117 See S. Macdonald, *The History and Philosophy of Art Education*, pp.207-24.

118 *Report from the Select Committee on Schools of Art*, HC 1864 (466) XII, pp.xvii-xviii. *Minutes of Evidence*, qus.1690-94. IUP series Fine Arts 6, pp.25-26, 148-49. To be compared with the more favourable impression gained in the *Report from the Select Committee on the South Kensington Museum*, HC 1860 (527) XVI, pp.iv-v.

119 *Minutes of Evidence of the Royal Academy Commission*, HC 1863 (3025) XXVII, qus. 4240-42. IUP series Fine Arts 5, p.494. *Appendix 20 to the Report from the Select Committee on Schools of Art*, HC 1864 (466) XII, pp.457-58. IUP series Fine Arts 6, pp.487-88.

120 *Report from the Select Committee on Schools of Art*, HC 1864 (466) XII, p.xvii. IUP series Fine Arts 6, p.25.

121 *Report of the Royal Commission on Technical Instruction*, HC 1884 (c.3981) XXIX, pp.518-20. IUP series Scientific and Technical 5, pp.590-92.

122   *Report of the Royal Commission on Technical Instruction,* HC 1884 (c.3981) XXIX, pp.536-40. IUP series Scientific and Technical 5, pp.608-12.

123   Quoted in S. Macdonald, *The History and Philosophy of Art Education,* p.296, which also gives the best summary of the trends in art education in England during the present century.

Bibliography

General
Winslow Ames, *Prince Albert and Victorian Taste.* (London, 1967).
T.S.R. Boase, *English Art 1800-1870* (Oxford, 1959).
Stuart Macdonald, *The History and Philosophy of Art Education.* (London, 1970).
A. Paul Oppé, 'Art' in *Early Victorian England 1830-1865,* ed. G.M. Young (Oxford, 1934).
Nikolaus Pevsner, *Academies of Art, past and present.* (Cambridge 1940).
John Steegman, *Victorian Taste* (London, 1970 ed.).
Palace of Westminster
T.S.R. Boase, 'The Decoration of the New Palace of Westminster 1841-1863', *Journal of the Warburg and Courtauld Institutes,* XXVII (1954) pp.319-58.
Copyright of Designs
Reginald Winslow, *The Law of Artistic Copyright* (London, 1889).
Art Unions
Anthony King. 'George Godwin and the Art Union of London 1837-1911', *Victorian Studies,* VIII (1964), pp. 101-30.
National Gallery
Sir Philip Hendy, *The National Gallery* (London, 1955).
Sir Charles Holmes and C.H. Collins Baker, *The Making of the National Gallery 1824-1924* (London, 1924).
Royal Academy
Sidney C. Hutchison, *A History of the Royal Academy 1768-1968* (London, 1968).
George Dunlop Leslie, *The Inner Life of the Royal Academy* (London, 1914).
H.C. Morgan, 'The Lost Opportunity of the Royal Academy: an assessment of its position in the nineteenth century', *Journal of the Warburg and Courtauld Institutes,* XXXII (1969) pp.410-20.
William Sandby, *The History of the Royal Academy of Arts* (London, 1862).
Schools of Design
Quentin Bell, *The Schools of Design* (London, 1963).
Quentin Bell, 'Haydon versus Shee', *Journal of the Warburg and Courtauld Institutes,* XXII (1959) pp.347-58.
Frank P. Brown, *South Kensington and its Art Training* (London, 1912).
K.J. Fielding, 'Charles Dickens and the Department of Practical Art', *Modern Language Review,* XLVIII (1953) pp.270-77.
John C.L. Sparkes, *Schools of Art* (London, 1884).

Contemporary writings on art
Sir Charles Lock Eastlake, *Contributions to the Literature of the Fine Arts* (London, 1848).
Edward Edwards, *The Fine Arts in England* (London, 1840).
Benjamin Robert Haydon, *Lectures on Painting and Design* (London, 1844).
George Moore, *Modern Painting* (London, 1893).
John Pye, *Patronage of British Art* (London, 1845).
Martin Arthur Shee, *Elements of Art* (London, 1809).

Biography
Sir Henry Cole, *Fifty Years of Public Work* (London, 1884).
Lady Eastlake, Memoir of Sir Charles Lock Eastlake in *Contributions to the Literature of the Fine Arts* (London, 1870).
Samuel Carter Hall, *Retrospect of a Long Life: from 1815 to 1883* (London, 1883).
Benjamin Robert Haydon, *Autobiography* (London, 1926 ed.)
The Diary of Benjamin Robert Haydon, ed. Pope, Willard Bissell. (Cambridge, Massachusetts 1960-1963).
F.M. Redgrave, *Richard Redgrave, a Memoir* (London, 1891).
Martin Arthur Shee, *The Life of Sir Martin Arthur Shee* (London, 1860).

Periodicals, especially the *Art-Union Journal* and the *Journal of Design and Manufactures,* the *Edinburgh Review* and the *Quarterly Review* provide extensive coverage of many of the main topics of interest in Victorian fine art and design.

THE DOCUMENTS

FINE ARTS

Fine Arts Volume 1

REPORTS FROM THE SELECT COMMITTEE ON ART UNIONS WITH MINUTES OF EVIDENCE, APPENDIX AND INDEX, 1845

576 pp

The Art Union movement was introduced into England from Germany about 1834. The union consisted of artists, businessmen and industrialists who endeavoured to encourage the arts by providing financial support. About 1840 their method of distributing art prizes by lottery brought the activities of the art unions under suspicion of the Treasury. This inquiry sought to assess the constitutions, functioning and achievements of the art unions, their position in relation to the law, and whether they deserved approval.

Artists themselves generally supported the policies of the unions. The committee was of the opinion that the unions were contributing much to the encouragement and development of art, and were bringing the enlightening influence of art to the masses in a way that was not possible under a system of private patronage. The volume gives an insight into the thinking in artistic circles at the time and contains accounts of a number of unions in European countries.

Original reference

1845　　(612)　　VII　　　Art Unions, Sel. Cttee. Rep., mins. of ev., etc.

Fine Arts Volume 2

REPORTS FROM SELECT COMMITTEES ON THE PROMOTION OF FINE ARTS AND ON NATIONAL MONUMENTS AND WORKS OF ART WITH MINUTES OF EVIDENCE, APPENDICES, INDEX AND REPORTS FROM THE COMMISSIONERS ON FINE ARTS, 1841-1847

586 pp

Two Select Committee reports were presented to parliament in 1841 on the influence of public buildings and national monuments in promoting the arts and developing public taste and appreciation. The first of these dealt with the importance of public patronage of the Fine Arts in connection with the rebuilding of the Houses of Parliament. The application of British art to the rebuilding of Parliament was considered a major opportunity "of encouraging the arts and of associating them with our Public Architecture, our Legislation, our Commerce and our History". Witnesses who gave evidence included Charles Barry, the architect involved, Sir Martin Archer Shee, President of the Royal Academy and William Dyce, Professor of the Theory of Arts at King's College. The matters considered ranged over the use of paintings, sculpture, frescoes and the ability of British artists to achieve the necessary standards in content and techniques. Directly related to this are the reports of the Fine Arts Commissioners which include sections on the English School of Painting and extensive information on the process of fresco painting and the methods of the Italian masters.

The Select Committee on National Monuments and Works of Art examined the facilities available to the public at the British Museum, the National Gallery, the Tower, Hampton Court Palace, Greenwich Hospital, Westminster Abbey and St. Paul's Cathedral.

Original references

1841	(423)	VI	Promotion of the Fine Arts of this country in connection with the rebuilding of the Houses of Parliament, Sel. Cttee. Rep., mins. of ev., appendix, index.
	(416)		State of National Monuments and Works of Art, Sel. Cttee. Rep., mins. of ev., appendix.
1842	[412]	XXV	Fine Arts, Com. 1st Annual Rep., appendix.
1843	[499]	XXIX	Fine Arts, Com. 2nd Annual Rep., appendix.
1844	[585]	XXXI	Fine Arts, Com. 3rd Annual Rep., appendix.
1845	[671]	XXVII	Fine Arts, Com. 4th Annual Rep., appendix.
1846	[685]	XXIV	Fine Arts, Com. 5th Annual Rep., appendix.
	[749]		Fine Arts, Com. 6th Annual Rep., appendix.
1847	[862]	XXXIII	Fine Arts, Com. 7th Annual Rep., appendix.

Fine Arts Volume 3

REPORTS FROM SELECT COMMITTEES AND COMMISSIONS ON WORKS OF ART AND ON THE NATIONAL GALLERY WITH MINUTES OF EVIDENCE, APPENDICES, INDICES AND REPORTS FROM THE FINE ARTS COMMISSIONERS, 1847-1863

434 pp   4 plans

The presentation of Robert Vernon's collection of 157 pictures to the nation in 1847, housed temporarily in the National Gallery, made the problem of accommodation for future bequests acute. The 1847-48 Select Committee recommended the use of Parliamentary grants to provide the necessary space by constructing an enlarged National Gallery on the existing site. This subject was again examined in 1850 by a Select Committee and in 1857 by a Royal Commission. The commission examined the Select Committee reports and received evidence from many noted artists and architects on the best means of preserving and displaying pictures, on the effect of atmospheric impurities and on various proposed sites. The effects of the London atmosphere on pictures, including Turner's works the *Cave of Queen Mab* and the *Deluge*, are described and there is more evidence on the injuries to the works of such artists as Holbein, Poussin, Bellucci and others. The final conclusion of the commission on a suitable site was that the existing site enlarged and with modern means of protecting and preserving works of art would be the most suitable for a National Gallery.

This volume also includes a report on the lighting of picture galleries by gas and the eighth to the thirteenth (and final) reports from the Commissioners on Fine Arts (see IUP volume Fine Arts 2).

Original references

1847-48	(720)	XVI	Works of Art (Providing additional room), Sel. Cttee. Rep.
1849	[1009]	XXII	Fine Arts Commissioners, 8th Annual Rep.
1850	(612)	XV	National Gallery, Sel. Cttee. Rep., mins. of ev., etc.
1850	[1180]	XXIII	Fine Arts Commissioners, 9th Annual Rep.
1851	(642)	XXII	Site for a New National Gallery, Com. Rep.
1854	[1829]	XIX	Fine Arts Commissioners, 10th Annual Rep.
1857 Sess 2	[2261]	XXIV	National Gallery Site, R. Com. Rep., mins. of ev., etc.
1857-58	[2425]	XXIV	Fine Arts Commissioners, 11th Annual Rep.
1859 Sess 2	(106)	XV	Lighting of picture galleries by gas, Com. Rep.
1861	[2806]	XXXII	Fine Arts Commissioners, 12th Annual Rep.
1863	[3141]	XVI	Fine Arts Commissioners, 13th Annual Rep.

Fine Arts Volume 4

REPORT FROM THE SELECT COMMITTEE ON THE MANAGEMENT OF THE NATIONAL GALLERY AND ON NATIONAL MONUMENTS OF ANTIQUITY AND FINE ART WITH THE PROCEEDINGS, MINUTES OF EVIDENCE, APPENDICES AND INDEX, 1852-53

1024 pp   9 folding plans

The Select Committee of 1852-53 was "appointed to Inquire into the Management of the National Gallery; also, to consider in what mode the collective Monuments of Antiquity and Fine Art possessed by the Nation may be most securely preserved, judiciously augmented and advantageously exhibited to the Public."

The investigations of the committee into the management and administration of the Gallery covered the duties and responsibilities of the Board of Trustees, of the Keeper of the Gallery and of the Gallery staff. Among the proposals examined were the creation of a Combined Department of art in the National Gallery, the need for definite regulations and identification of staff duties, the abolition of the office of Keeper and the appointment of a Director. Sir Charles Eastlake, President of the Royal Academy, who submitted extensive evidence to the committee was appointed to this newly created post of Director in 1855. The admission of the public and of students was debated and a great deal of attention was paid to the cleaning and restoration of pictures, proper arrangement for display and conditions in continental galleries and museums. Of special value in this connection is the evidence on picture cleaning; according to Mr Morris Moore, artist and picture dealer, every picture cleaned under the superintendence of Sir Charles Eastlake and Mr Seguier was injured by removal of the glazings. Evidence of such damage during cleaning and restoration was given in relation to specific paintings — *The Judgement of Paris* by Rubens, the *Embarkation of the Queen of Sheba* by Claude, and many others. The appendices to the report contain valuable proposals on the management of the gallery and on the arrangement and completion of the collection of paintings. Lists of masters of several German, Italian, French, Spanish and English schools of painting are given.

Original reference
1852-53 (867)   XXXV   National Gallery, Sel. Cttee. Rep., mins. of ev.,
                              appendices, index.

Fine Arts Volume 5

REPORT OF THE COMMISSIONERS ON THE PRESENT POSITION OF THE ROYAL ACADEMY IN RELATION TO THE FINE ARTS WITH MINUTES OF EVIDENCE, APPENDIX, INDEX AND OBSERVATIONS OF THE MEMBERS OF THE ROYAL ACADEMY ON THE REPORT, 1863-1864

776 pp

In this outstanding report the commissioners examined the constitution of the Academy, its functions, funds, exhibitions, teaching system and buildings. The evidence is an invaluable source of contemporary expert opinion on the whole subject of art and art teaching, particularly with regard to painting, sculpture and architecture. Most of the witnesses were men with established reputation as writers, artists and public servants, e.g. Charles Landseer, John Ruskin, W Dyce, etc. The appendices to the report provide details of the rules and regulations of the Academy since its founding in 1768, lists of members from that date, and extracts from the regulations of foreign academies. The qualifications for membership and associate membership were fully debated and the advantages of incorporating other artist societies (e.g. the Watercolour societies) in the Royal Academy were considered. The observations on the report by Royal Academy members relate to the provision of a Charter for the Academy, the introduction of "lay" members, the mode of election to the academy and to other points raised in the report.

Original references

1863	[3205]	XXVII	Present position of the Royal Academy in relation to the Fine Arts, Royal Com., Rep., mins. of ev.
	[3205-I]		Present position of the Royal Academy in relation to the Fine Arts, Royal Com. appendix and index.
1864	[3332]	XIX Pt. I	Present position of the Royal Academy in relation to the Fine Arts, observations on the Commissioners' Rep.

Fine Arts Volume 6

REPORTS FROM SELECT COMMITTEES ON SCHOOLS OF ART, ART UNION LAWS, PURCHASES FROM THE PARIS EXHIBITION AND THE ANCIENT MONUMENTS BILL WITH PROCEEDINGS, MINUTES OF EVIDENCE, APPENDICES, INDICES, AND ADDITIONAL REPORTS ON WORKS OF ART, 1864-1897

846 pp   15 charts and plans

The principal report in this volume deals with government supported schools of art. The committee paid particular attention to the Science and Art Department's relationship with the several schools of art throughout the country. Valuable details are given on the location and housing of the schools, the numbers of students, prizes won, etc. The committee's recommendations mention a central training school for teachers, state scholarships and the more efficient use of the South Kensington Collections. The Select Committee on Art Union Laws heard much damaging evidence against the unions. Since their introduction from Germany in 1834 the Art Unions were accused in high quarters of debasing public taste by fostering bad art and strongly criticised for the lottery system of distribution of art objects (see IUP volume Fine Arts 1). Among the other shorter papers published here are reports on the circulation of art objects on loan for exhibition and the housing of the Lady Wallace Collection.

Original references

1864	(466)	XII	Schools of Art (Sums granted by Parliament for the promotion of National Education in Art), Sel. Cttee. Rep., mins. of ev., etc.
1866	(332)	VII	Art Union Laws. Sel. Cttee. Rep., mins. of ev., etc.
1867	(433)	X	Purchases from the Paris Exhibition for the Benefit of Schools of Science and Art, Sel. Cttee. Rep., mins. of ev., etc.
1877	(317)	VIII	Ancient Monuments Bill, Sel. Cttee. Rep., mins. of ev., etc.
1881	[C.2836]	LXXIII	Circulation of Art Objects on Loan for Exhibition, Rep.
1897	[C.8445]	LXXII	Housing of the collection of works of art bequeathed to the nation by the late Lady Wallace, Treasury Dept, Cttee. Rep., mins. of ev., etc.

THE DOCUMENTS

DESIGN

Design Volume 1

REPORTS FROM SELECT COMMITTEES ON ARTS AND MANUFACTURES
WITH MINUTES OF EVIDENCE, APPENDICES AND INDEX, 1835-1836

560 pp   4 plans

These reports deal principally with extending art and design principles throughout the United Kingdom, particularly among the manufacturing classes. In its examination of the state of art in Britain and in other countries as manifest in their different manufactures, it discovered that by comparison British products were dull and lacking in original design. The evidence indicated, however, a public demand for education in artistic matters and the committee criticise the lack of facilities for this. Among the means considered for promoting art were public galleries, museums of art, government publications and the provision of public money for galleries and for decoration of public places with frescoes and sculptures. Investigated also were the problems of piracy of designs caused by inadequate copyright protection and the academic attitudes of institutions such as the Royal Academy. Those interviewed as witnesses included many notable artists and art critics of the time, e.g., John Martin the landscape painter, Benjamin Robert Haydon and others. John Landseer, father of the painter and then president of the Royal Academy, T Jones Howell, a factory inspector, the keeper of the National Gallery in Pall Mall and experts on continental art institutions also gave evidence.

Original references

1835	(598)	V	Arts and manufactures (extending a knowledge of the arts and of the principles of design among the manufacturing population), Sel. Cttee. Rep., mins. of ev.
1836	(568)	IX	Arts and manufacturers (extending a knowledge of the arts and of the principles of design among the manufacturing population), Sel. Cttee. Rep., mins. of ev.

Design Volume 2

REPORT FROM THE SELECT COMMITTEE ON COPYRIGHT OF DESIGNS
WITH MINUTES OF EVIDENCE, APPENDIX AND INDEX, 1840

628 pp

Copyright of design should, in the opinion of the committee, be extended. This brief resolution prefaces the extensive evidence presented on the subject. The aim of the committee was to collect and analyse the evidence for and against the proposed extension of protection for designers and manufacturers provided by the copyright laws. The industry selected for investigation was the clothing industry. The effects of piracy on British design, the comparison between the quality of British and continental European designs and the registration of and current developments in design were investigated. Witnesses claimed that the best artists were not employed because lack of protection led manufacturers to spend little on design. With extended copyright protection, a twelve month period, or in some cases two years (for furniture chintzes) or three years (for paper-staining) trade would improve, according to some opinions; other witnesses, however, believed that copyright protection even as it existed was damaging to the home trade. The chairman of the committee, Sir J E Tennent subsequently sponsored the Copyright of Design Bill which became law. William Ewart, MP, a member of the committee was involved in the establishment of the schools of design at Somerset House, London (see IUP volumes Design 3 and 4), a direct result of the report contained in volume 1 of this set.

Original reference

1840   (442)   VI   Copyright of designs, Sel. Cttee. Rep., mins. of ev., appendix, index.

Design Volume 3

REPORTS FROM THE SELECT COMMITTEE AND FROM SPECIAL COMMITTEES AND COUNCIL REPORTS ON SCHOOLS OF DESIGN WITH REPORTS ON SCHOOLS OF DESIGN IN FOREIGN COUNTRIES, 1840-1849

978 pp 1 diagram

The reports on foreign schools of design dealt with German and French institutes. The syllabus of instruction used in Prussian schools for artizans was given and the Ban Academie was described. Classes in the Ban Academie differed from those of the Royal Academy because architecture was treated as a science rather than as an art. Qualifications required by masters who taught in Bavarian schools and details of Bavarian agricultural and industrial schools were given. Also included in these reports was an address (in French) given in December 1837 to prizewinning students of the Ecole des Beaux Arts, the only wholly state directed school of art in France.

Progress in both the central school of design at Somerset House and schools in the provinces was recorded in a series of five reports from the Design School Council. The way in which the government grant of £10,000 was distributed to the provincial schools was detailed. Each report followed similar pattern and the two special committee reports, which brought the series to an end, dealt with complaints made about the system of instruction and the lack of knowledge of the manufacturing process. Twenty-four resolutions were adopted dealing with subjects such as the director's and secretary's duties, courses and prize medals. The Select Committee report of 1849 is devoted to details of the management and policies of the School of Design.

Original references

1840	(98)	XXIX	Schools of Design in Prussia, Bavaria, France, Mr Dyce, Rep.
1841	(65)	XIII	School of Design, Provisional Council Rep.
1843	[454]	XXIX	School of Design, Council, Rep.
1844	[566]	XXXI	School of Design, Council, 3rd Rep.
1845	[654]	XXVII	School of Design, Council, 4th Rep.
1846	[730]	XXIV	School of Design, Council, 5th Rep.
1847	[835]	LXII	School of Design, Special Cttee. Rep.
	[850]		School of Design, measures for carrying out the recommendations of the special committee, 2nd Special Cttee. Rep.
1849	(576)	XVIII	Schools of Design, Sel. Cttee. Rep., mins. of ev., appendix, index.

Design Volume 4

REPORT FROM THE SELECT COMMITTEE ON THE SCHOOL OF DESIGN, REPORTS ON THE HEAD AND BRANCH SCHOOLS OF DESIGN AND FIRST REPORT FROM THE DEPARTMENT OF PRACTICAL ART, 1850-1853

646 pp

Three reports on the state and progress of the schools of design give detailed accounts of each of the provincial design schools. These accounts include information on works sent in by the students for inspection and the number accepted; students whose works were accepted by manufacturers; prizes and the rules and regulations of the schools. The prospectus for a fourteen-lecture course on ornamental art in government schools is included as well as correspondence on the purpose of schools of design. The first (and only) annual report from the department of practical art is contained here. The department was based at Marlborough House. The report summary shows that the system of elementary instruction in art was available to all classes of the community, that the system was nearly self-supporting, that schools of design in the country had been improved and nominations to scholarships had been extended from the London area to the provinces. In addition a museum of manufactures was established and there were special classes for technical instruction. Appendices include details which cover the management of local schools of practical art, previously the schools of design, at Somerset House and Gower Street and information on the technical instruction given by the department, on the Queen's private collection of arms at Windsor Castle on print work and lace making and on casts taken of the Temple of the Sun at Balbec.

Original references

1850	(730)	XLII	State of the Head and Provincial Schools of Design, Reps.
	(731)		State of the•Head and Provincial Schools of Design, Reps.
1851	[1423]	XLIII	Schools of Design, Reps.
1852-53	[1615]	LIV	Department of Practical Art, 1st Rep., appendices.

EDUCATION:
THE BRITISH MUSEUM

Edward Miller

Commentary

Introduction

In the opening decades of the nineteenth century the British Museum had become to many an object of ridicule. Founded in 1753, it had slept away the eighteenth century and was only now slowly adjusting itself to contemporary conditions. Its exclusive air, the difficulties which the ordinary man experienced in gaining admission to its reading room or even to the exhibition galleries – though these had been greatly eased under the enlightened administration of Joseph Planta, Principal Librarian from 1799 to 1827 – infuriated a growing number.

The Museum seemed a creature of aristocratic privilege, its Trustees for many years drawn almost exclusively from the ranks of the nobility. Despite the large sums of public money spent upon its upkeep or in enabling it to secure valuable additions to its collections, it was widely regarded as both incompetent and useless.

Cobbett voiced the general distrust; the Museum was no more than 'a place intended only for the curious and the rich', a comfortable refuge for 'clergymen who employed poor curates to perform their duty . . . whilst they were living in indolence and affluence here in London.'[1]

Growing criticism

As the century progressed there was more serious criticism from another quarter. The eighteenth century had considered the Museum primarily as a scientific institution. Though much had been added since – books, manuscripts, coins, prints and antiquities of many periods – to scientific men at least it was still above all a museum of natural history and that it was that 'for which the British Museum was mainly founded'.[2] Scientists were now an increasingly powerful force and their opinions counted for much. Yet scarcely any had ever been appointed trustees and the suspicion grew that the noble amateurs who largely composed the Board were not only undistinguished but not even interested in science. It was asserted that from inadequate care the natural history collections were deteriorating badly and that the Trustees' indifference was wreaking havoc among the nation's scientific treasures. Some of these suspicions were justified. The Trustees were probably less interested in their natural history collections than in rare manuscripts or Greek vases. A former Keeper of Natural History[3] got rid of what he described as 'zoological rubbish' by burying or burning it, until 'some persons in the neighbourhood complained and threatened with legal action, because they thought the moths were introduced into their houses by the cremations in the Museum garden'.[4] Not one insect was said to remain out of the 5,394 collected by Sir Hans Sloane, and which formed part of the founding collections. Though this was probably due to the original faulty methods of preservation, yet it did seem to indicate a lack of care for collections on which a great deal of public money had been spent. As Sir Humphrey Davy, himself one of the very few scientific Trustees, had said, 'Our national establishment is unworthy of a great people . . . the present is the best moment for attempting a . . . fundamental change in . . . this ancient, mis-applied and . . . useless, Institution'.[5]

What with the criticisms of disgruntled radicals and the fears and frustrations of the scientists, it would indeed seem that the Museum had 'become too prominent a mark for nuisance-haters and notoriety hunters to be passed over'.[6]

The Select Committee of 1835

Their chance came in 1835. A John Millard, having briefly held a post in the Department of Manuscripts and then dismissed for inefficiency, now gained the sympathy of Benjamin Hawes, the radical M.P. for Lambeth, who succeeded in getting a Select Committee appointed to enquire into every aspect of the Museum.

Though much seemed to be wrong, in particular the high-handed attitude which many officers, especially the Principal Librarian, Sir Henry Ellis, took towards the general public, the Committee discovered no trace of sinecurism or corruption whilst Millard had undoubtedly been rightly dismissed. No witnesses, however, had as yet been heard from the Department of Printed Books, a department which was itself coming under increasing criticism. It was therefore recommended that a further Select Committee should be appointed to complete the enquiry.

The progress of the investigation had been followed with interest by many. Amongst them was a young man destined to play a part not only in the affairs of the Museum but even more so in the movement for the establishment of a national municipal public library system.

This was Edward Edwards, the self-educated son of a London bricklayer. He was already interested in the problems of libraries and, as a radical, resented the pretensions of the Museum which he considered often unjustified, its air of snobbish exclusiveness disguising an inefficient administration and a defective library. In February 1836 Edwards published a pamphlet[7] criticising the evidence presented by the Museum and in particular, a point glossed over by the Committee, the fact that 'several valuable collections had been lost to the British Museum, and in a great measure to the public, by the fault or neglect of the Museum itself'.[8]

Such cogent criticism by one so young and of such humble birth aroused considerable interest (also considerable opposition, at least within the Museum) and Edwards was invited to give evidence before the new Committee.

The Select Committee of 1836

This was a smaller and more able body than its predecessor, and it seemed probable that it would spend less time smelling out imaginary abuses and more in carrying out a thorough investigation into what was really wrong. Despite the improvements which had taken place during the previous thirty years, in particular since the appointment of its present Keeper, the Reverend Henry Baber, the Department of Printed Books was constantly criticised. It was, after all, the only library in London readily available to the public and yet many undoubtedly regarded it as extremely poor. 'Bad editions, bad catalogues, a bad reading room and tedious and frequent delays'.[9] It was still considerably smaller than many comparable foreign institutions and was rightly held to be quite unworthy of the richest and most powerful nation in the world.

The man who was to change entirely this state of affairs was already a member of the staff. This was Antonio Panizzi, a political refugee, who had joined the department in 1831. He had since greatly distinguished himself and was clearly destined for high office. In 1835 he had been sent by Baber on a 'bibliographical tour' of the principal libraries of Western Europe, so that an accurate and up to date comparison might be made between these institutions and the Museum. Panizzi's evidence before the 1836 Committee was outstanding. Edwards, also an admirable witness, ungrudgingly admitted this.

One of the best results of that Committee . . .was the opportunity it gave to Mr. Baber and to Mr. Panizzi of advocating the claims of the National Library to largely increased liberality on the part of Parliament. The latter in particular did it with an earnestness and with a vivacity of argument and of illustration which I believe won for him the respect of every person who enjoyed (as I did) the pleasure of listening to his examination.[10]

The Mid-Century Museum

From July 1837 Panizzi was himself Keeper of Printed Books and, in so far as he was able, proceeded to put his ideas into practice. But the next ten years at the Museum were to be filled with violent controversies and bitter personal antagonisms, news of which was soon common property.

In particular, the feud between Panizzi and Sir Frederic Madden, Keeper of Manuscripts which on the latter side at least was of a pathological intensity, was widely commented on. The intense jealousy and hatred felt by Madden for his far more successful rival was almost equalled by the dislike shown both by Josiah Forshall, Secretary to the Trustees, and by John Gray, Keeper of Zoology. Gray had inspired and may have even written Sir Nicholas Harris Nicolas' pamphlets which precipitated the setting up of the Royal Commission in 1847, and had written several other pamphlets under his own name fiercely attacking his colleague. The rivalry between Gray and his former superior König, Keeper of Geology, was equally bitter and there was scarcely an individual among the staff not drawn into these disputes. Outside the Museum Panizzi was supported by many of the Whig notables, Palmerston, Russell and Clarendon and the young Gladstone amongst them. Ellis and Madden on the other hand were favoured by Aberdeen, Monckton Milnes, and a number of lesser figures. None of this did anything to enhance the opinion in which the Museum was generally held. More and more it seemed out of the main stream of progress. It never seemed open when it could be visited by the majority and the extensive rebuilding which was taking place throughout this period added to the confusion and annoyance. A cartoon of 1846, 'The British Museum on a British Holiday',[11] sums up the position. Enormous crowds are standing before the old narrow gateway, whilst the new buildings, surrounded by scaffolding, are glimpsed above the half demolished outer wall. Though it is Boxing Day the Museum is shut! A disconsolate family, obviously up for the day, look on in bewildered despair. They just do not understand why they cannot see the Museum. Their two small children, being obviously under eight, would not have been admitted anyway. Other families wait patiently for something to happen or are about to go home in disgust. A smart carriage bowls contemptuously by. Special arrangements would be made for its occupants' visit on a private day, when the Boxing Day crowds would be safely at work, and when even the smallest children, it would seem, might freely accompany their parents round the Museum galleries.

In 1841 a Select Committee had reported that notwithstanding the fears of some of the officers, the experiment of admitting the general public to the Museum on annual holidays had been a resounding success.[12] But further attempts to extend the hours or even to permit Sunday opening met with repeated failure.[13] The strong feelings of resentment to which this gave rise, the feeling that a large proportion of the general public were being barred from viewing their own treasures, provoked a growing exasperation with the Museum authorities. The eighteenth century had accepted the fact that a public institution might be virtually closed to all but a few privileged visitors. The nineteenth century, to an increasing extent, would not.

Among the professional classes annoyance with the alleged deficiencies of both library and reading room continually increased, whilst the scientific world was once more troubled by the state of the natural history collections. The genuine difficulties of the Museum staff were largely ignored, and every mistake, real or imagined, was put down to the gross inefficiency inseparable from an institution dominated by noble amateurs and run, for the most part, by venal foreigners.

The Royal Commission

Early in March 1847 it was rumoured that under pressure from various radicals a Committee might be set up to look into the affairs of the Museum. It was, however, the scientists who precipitated the inquiry. On 10 March 1847 a memorial was addressed to the Prime Minister, Russell, from the British Association and other organizations expressing their profound dissatisfaction at the undue number of non-scientists on the Board of Trustees and with the Museum's general attitude towards scientific studies.[14]

Three months later, on 17 June, a Royal Commission was appointed to 'inquire into the Constitution and Government of the Museum'.[15] It is not impossible that Panizzi himself had had a hand in its origin. He had frequently called for a public inquiry into the many attacks which had been made both on him and on his administration of the library. He was on friendly terms with many of the Whig leaders and with these now in power here was his opportunity. There is little doubt, however, that had Panizzi really been the incompetent charlatan that his enemies declared him to be, he would have received no mercy. All that he demanded, and this he was to receive, was the chance to plead his case before an impartial tribunal.[16] The Commission was of course to look into other matters, in particular the general administration of the Museum undermined by the bumbling incompetence of Ellis, the Principal Librarian, but to most people, at least in literary circles, the prime task of the Commission was to investigate the alleged shortcomings of the national library and of its foreign-born head.

When in March 1850 the Commission issued its report Panizzi was completely exonerated. What was fundamentally wrong with the Museum was the usurpation by its Secretary, Josiah Forshall, of powers that more properly belonged to the Principal Librarian or to the individual keepers[17] and that this had exacerbated, even if it had not caused, the bitter antagonisms and frustrations among the staff over the last fifteen years. Radical changes were proposed in the Museum's administration in order, it was hoped, to make it more efficient – changes that with one partial exception – the appointment of Professor Richard Owen to be Superintendent of the Natural History Departments – were never carried out.

The report was on the whole well received. *The Athenaeum* considered that Panizzi 'commanded our admiration by the manly spirit in which he faced all difficulties, and grappled with all opponents'[18] whilst most other papers were equally friendly. Edwards, on the other hand, considered the report to be 'a mass of rubbish,[19] whilst in the view of Sir Frederic Madden, Keeper of Manuscripts and Panizzi's bitter enemy, 'a more partial enquiry never yet was made and it is disgraceful to the character of English gentlemen to lend themselves to the plans of an Italian vagabond whose only merit lies in his powers of misrepresentation'.[20] Nevertheless, as a result of the Commission's activities, many misapprehensions concerning the Museum were swept away, whilst under Panizzi's wise rule, the Museum itself became a far happier and more efficient institution.

But new troubles arose, for the most part from the gross overcrowding of the Museum. Already Sir Robert Smirke's vast neo-classical edifice was felt to be inadequate as well as unsuitable. The Royal Commission had been scathing: 'a warning, rather than a model, to the architect of any additional structure'.[21] The Committee of 1838 had been misled by Smirke and Forshall as to the amount of space needed, and none could have foreseen the enormous increase in the number of books, and in antiquities of every description. In 1846 Panizzi had secured an annual grant of £10,000 for the purchase of books and had also vigorously enforced the copyright regulations. The excavations of Layard and others in Mesopotamia had also resulted in many more antiquities arriving at the Museum. A solution to the problems of the library had been achieved by the construction of the present Reading Room and its surrounding bookstacks in 1857. To relieve the growing pressure on the other departments, it would seem essential, however, that a large part of the remaining collections should be transferred elsewhere. Panizzi, now Principal Librarian, favoured the instant removal of the Natural History departments, as well as the ethnographical, prehistoric and medieval collections.

Men of his generation tended to despise such objects. To them 'antiquities' meant those of Greece and Rome. Even Egyptian and Assyrian remains were of doubtful respectability and not really needed. The new scientific spirit and the growing realisation that man had been on earth for an immensely longer period than had hitherto been thought, provoked a new interest in pre-history and in the artefacts of surviving primitive races, whilst medieval relics were of far greater appeal to a romantic generation than they had been to their fathers.

Pressure was put on the Museum to increase its almost negligible holdings. Under the direction of Augustus Franks, from 1851 in charge of medieval antiquities, the expansion was remarkable. More space must be found and something must go. The scientists took alarm and protested vigorously once more at the Museum's apparent discrimination against its scientific collections.

The Select Committee of 1860 and after

In April 1860 a Select Committee was appointed to go into the question. They considered it quite wrong that the popular natural history collections should leave for distant Kensington or such other possible sites as Victoria or the Thames Embankment. 'Sufficient reason had not been assigned for the removal of any part of the ... collections ... except that of Ethnography, and the portraits and drawings'.[22] Conditions at the Museum nevertheless grew worse. By 1878 the natural history collections were preparing to move and by 1883 the last of them had left for their fine new home at South Kensington.

Problems could still arise. A dispute between the Royal Irish Academy and the Museum had to be investigated by a Departmental Committee in 1899[23] and the rule laid down, which is still adhered to, that in general Irish, Scottish and now of course Welsh antiquities or other rare objects, should go to the national museums of those countries. Sir Edward Maunde Thomson, the Museum's Director, nevertheless strongly emphasized the true role of that institution:

> It is not a London Museum, it is not an English Museum, it is a 'British Museum', and as such we naturally have to look after its interests, and make our collections as perfect as possible, to represent every portion of the British Empire[24]

and indeed as far as it is now practicable the whole world. This dispute did not, fortunately, mar the excellent relations which existed and which continue to exist between the Museum and other comparable institutions both in Great Britain and abroad.

During the preceeding fifty years the Museum had undergone four major investigations. Though few of their recommendations, in particular of the Royal Commission, had been adopted, the light thus thrown upon the workings of a great national institution had been of benefit both to the general public and to the Museum itself. Governments rarely take the advice of those bodies set up to investigate such questions and, moreover, it was now felt that Panizzi and his successors had brought about such striking improvements that the wholesale reform of the Museum was no longer necessary. From the evidence placed before these, on the whole sympathetic, enquiries, the educated public had been led to appreciate how a great museum and library functioned, the problems and difficulties with which it was faced and the steps necessary to overcome them. Born of genuine grievances as well as of much malignant and ill-informed criticism, these investigations revealed to an ever more sympathetic audience how a great national institution should be run. The very different position that the British Museum held in popular esteem by the end of the nineteenth century was due in no small measure to this masterly series of reports.

Bibliography

A comprehensive general history of the British Museum appeared early in 1974, Edward John Miller, *That Noble Cabinet. A History of the British Museum, 1753-1972.* (London: Deutsch, 1974). One of the best general histories is still Edward Edwards, *Lives of the Founders of the British Museum* (London: Trübner & Co., 1870). Despite his own unhappy experiences, Edwards is always extremely fair when dealing with the nineteenth-century Museum. It contains much information, especially on the earlier collections not readily available elsewhere. A summary account will be found in Edward John Miller, *A Brief History of the British Museum* (London: Pitkin Press, 1970). A.J.K. Esdaile, *The British Museum Library. A short history and survey* (London: Allen & Unwin, 1946) is the standard history of the library departments. It is somewhat sketchy, particularly in dealing with the early years, but is an invaluable work of reference. There are of course numerous works on the contents of the Museum. An excellent compilation is *The Treasures of the Museum* (London: Thames & Hudson, 1971), which contains, in addition, short accounts of the history of the various collections by members of the staff. Another recent work is J. Mordaunt Crook, *The British Museum* (London: Allen Lane, the Penguin Press, 1972), which, however, deals primarily with the architectural history of that institution.

The nineteenth-century Museum — the background to the various Parliamentary enquiries — is dealt with by a number of mostly contemporary works. Of these the most valuable is Robert Cowtan *Memories of the British Museum* (London: R. Bentley & Son, 1872). Cowtan, for many years an attendant and then an assistant at the Museum, gives a vivid picture of that institution from the point of view of the junior staff. His fervent admiration for Panizzi should be set against the far more critical view taken by Francis Espinasse, *Literary Recollections and Sketches* (London: Hodder & Stoughton, 1893). Much information on the nineteenth-century Museum as well as of an earlier period will be found in G. F. Barwick, *The Reading Room of the British Museum* (London: Benn, 1929) and in the relevant chapters of William A. Munford, *Edward Edwards, 1812-1886* (London: Library Association, 1963).

There are several biographies of Sir Anthony Panizzi covering the years 1831 to 1866 at the Museum. Of these two had the advantage of an intimate personal knowledge of their subject, Robert Cowtan, *A Biographical Sketch of Sir Anthony Panizzi* (London: Asher, 1873) and Louis Fagan, *The Life of Sir Anthony Panizzi.* 2 vol. (London, Remington, 1880). More modern studies are Constance Brooks, *Antonio Panizzi, Scholar and patriot* (Manchester: University Press, 1931), which deals, however, more with his activities as an Italian patriot than as an English librarian, and Edward J. Miller *Prince of Librarians. The Life and Times of Antonio Panizzi of the British Museum* (London: Deutsch, 1967). The latter deals fully with Panizzi's connection with the various Parliamentary investigations and contains a comprehensive bibliography. Cecil B. Oldman's *Sir Anthony Panizzi and the British Museum Library* (London: H.K. Lewis, 1958) deals very thoroughly with the events of Panizzi's keepership of Printed Books from 1837 to 1856, but not with his subsequent activities.

Two manuscript sources are of importance as a background to the various Parliamentary enquiries, in particular the Royal Commission of 1848-50: Edward Edwards' *Diaries,* 1844-84 (Department of Printed Books, British Museum) and Sir Frederic Madden's *Journals* (1819-73), of which the original is in the Bodleian Library and a photographic copy in the Department of Manuscripts, British Museum.

Other manuscript collections which supplement the printed sources are the official papers of Panizzi, 1837-56, in the Archives of the Department of Printed Books; Panizzi's correspondence and papers, 1797-1877 (BM. Add.MSS 36,714-36,729) and the papers of Sir Henry Ellis, also in the Department of Manuscripts.

Footnotes

1 *Hansard,* 3.s. 14 August 1833.

2 Evidence of Charles Konig, Keeper of Natural History, 1813-51. *Report of the Commissioners appointed to inquire into the constitution and government of the British Museum,* p.163. HC 1850 [1170] XXIV, 211. IUP series Education: British Museum 3.

3 George Shaw, Keeper of Natural History, 1807-13.

4 *Report from the Select Committee on the condition, management and affairs of the British Museum,* p.197. HC 1835 (479) VII, 201. IUP series Education: British Museum 1, p.197.

5 John Davy, *Memoirs of the Life of Sir Humphry Davy, Bart.* 2 vol. (London: Longman 1836), II, 342, 3.

6 'The British Museum', *Quarterly Review,* no.175 (1850), p.145.

7 Edward Edwards, *A Letter to Benjamin Hawes . . . being strictures on the "Minutes of Evidence" taken before the Select Committee on the British Museum* (London: Effingham Wilson, 1836).

8 E. Edwards. *A Letter to Benjamin Hawes,* p.45.

9 *Times,* 18 November 1825.

10 Edward Edwards, *Lives of the Founders of the British Museum,* 2 vol. (London: Trübner, 1870), II, 542.

11 William Johnson Fox, 'The British Museum closed', *Howitt's Journal,* 16 January 1847.

12 *Report from Select Committee on National Monuments and Works of Art,* p.151. HC 1841 (416) VI, 599.

13 Charles Cavendish Fulke Greville, *The Greville Diary,* edited by Philip W. Wilson. 2 vol. (London: Heinemann, 1927), II. 293, 4.

14 *A Copy of a Memorial to the First Lord of the Treasury, presented on the 10th day of March, by members of the British Association for the Advancement of Science . . . respecting the Management of the British Museum.* HC 1847 (268) XXXIV, 253.

15 *Report of the Commissioners,* p.iii.

16 Some, such as Edwards and Sir Frederick Madden, Keeper of Manuscripts at the Museum, considered it far from impartial and that it had been packed with Panizzi's supporters, so as to bring in a favourable verdict on his administration. This does not seem to be true. Though many of the Commissioners were his friends, others were his

implacable enemies. The general opinion was that Commission conducted its work honestly and fairly, despite the machinations of its Secretary John Payne Collier, who was a determined antagonist of Panizzi.

17 *Report of the Commissioners,* p.6.

18 *Athenaeum,* 11 May 1850.

19 Edward Edwards, *Diary,* 28 March 1850. [Manuscript now in the Department of Printed Books, British Museum].

20 Madden, *Journal,* 26 May 1849. [Manuscript now in the Bodleian Library, Oxford.]

21 *Report of the Commissioners,* p.36.

22 *Report from the Select Committee on the British Museum,* p.xiii, HC 1860 (540) XVI, 185. IUP series Education: British Museum 4, p.53.

23 *Celtic Ornaments found in Ireland . . . Report of Committee, etc.* HC 1899 (179) LXXVII, 685. IUP series Education: British Museum 4, p.377.

24 *Celtic Ornaments Report,* p.4.

THE DOCUMENTS

BRITISH MUSEUM

British Museum Volume 1

REPORT FROM THE SELECT COMMITTEE ON THE CONDITION, MANAGEMENT AND AFFAIRS OF THE BRITISH MUSEUM WITH MINUTES OF EVIDENCE, APPENDIX AND INDEX, 1835

640 pp   4 plans

This report presents extensive information on every aspect of the management and affairs of the museum up to 1835. This information is contained in the oral evidence of the museum staff and in a three-hundred page appendix of statistics, extracts from documents relating to the museum, etc. Each collection is described and discussed, references are made to new accessions, particularly a collection of pictures including works by Titian, Rubens and Rembrandt donated to the museum by Sir George Beaumont. The income and expenditure of the museum is described. Sections of the appendix deal with bequests, parliamentary grants and other sources of income.

The suspension of work on the index to the museum collections is the subject of a good deal of oral evidence. The work on the index was terminated because of the expense involved but most witnesses felt that the value of such an index would outweigh the expense. Luke G Hansard, a member of the famous printing family gave evidence in this connection on the work of John Milliard in compiling indexes to the parliamentary papers. The importance of museums, libraries, etc. as public educational institutions was stressed by witnesses and it was suggested that the government should be willing to spend more money on them. Information on similar institutions in many foreign countries is provided in the index. As in other respects there was an anxiety lest France should be better provided than England with museums and libraries.

Original reference

1835   (479)   VII   The British Museum, Sel. Cttee. Rep., mins. of ev., appendices, index.

British Museum Volume 2

REPORT FROM THE SELECT COMMITTEE ON THE CONDITION AND

MANAGEMENT OF THE BRITISH MUSEUM WITH MINUTES OF EVIDENCE,
APPENDIX AND INDEX, 1836

944 pp   2 plans   1 diagram

This committee continued and completed the work of the 1835
committee. Among the witnesses were members of the museum staff,
authorities in the natural sciences, the Archbishop of Canterbury and
Sir Robert Smirke one of the architects responsible for the rebuilding
of the museum (1828-57). A good deal of further evidence deals with
the management and affairs of the museum. The problem of providing
indexes and catalogues for the collections was again discussed, the
systems used for this purpose in other institutions are examined. In the
evidence and in the resolutions there was an awareness of the
importance of the museum both to scholars and to the general public.
Consequently it was urged that a policy of management calculated to
achieve the best results be pursued. The resolutions recommended an
expansion of the museum to include new departments, longer opening
hours to facilitate the public and overall reform of the organisation and
management of the museum. Evidence also contains information on the
collections in the museum, on museums in foreign countries and on the
collections of various organisations at home. The appendix contains a
copy of the will of Sir Hans Sloane (1739). His bequests formed the
basis for the establishment of the British Museum.

Original reference
1836   (440)   X   The British Museum, Sel. Cttee. Rep., mins. of ev.,
                                appendices, index.

British Museum Volume 3

REPORT OF THE ROYAL COMMISSION APPOINTED TO INQUIRE INTO
THE CONSTITUTION AND GOVERNMENT OF THE BRITISH MUSEUM,
1850

1056 pp

Additional to the stated terms of this report the commission directed
their inquiry "towards the ground of various complaints by the public
and by officers of the Museum". The administration of the museum by
its trustees was directed by the principal librarian and the secretary.
The committee were forced to conclude that the trustees did not
manage the museum in the best way. The committee were agreed that

the offices of principal librarian and secretary should be abolished and that an executive council should be appointed. The report gives a valuable contemporary picture of the museum, its various departments, accounts and building requirements.

Original reference

1850   [1170]   XXIV   The constitution and government of the British Museum, R. Com. Rep., mins. of ev., etc.

British Museum Volume 4

REPORTS FROM SELECT COMMITTEES AND OTHER REPORTS ON THE BRITISH MUSEUM, 1837-1899

354 pp   10 maps

This final volume in the British Museum set includes the important paper of 1857-58 requesting increased accommodation for the department of antiquities. This was the focal point of a group of reports from several departments at the time which lead to subsequent improvements and extensions to the museum. There is also a paper of 1899 on the subject of Celtic ornaments offered for sale to the British Museum. This deals with how competition between Irish and Scottish Museums and the British Museum could be reduced. The relaxation of the regulations of the museum for parting with any of its acquisitions was also a subject of the inquiry.

The Select Committee inquiry of 1860 dealt with future extensions to the museum buildings and with the question of whether part of the collections should be removed to separate sites. The volume also includes a report of the plans and estimates for the completion of the museum building presented in 1837-38.

Original references

1837-38	(545)	XXIII	British Museum, plans and estimates for the completion of the building, Sel. Cttee. Rep.
1857-58	(434)	XXXIII	British Museum, accommodation, Keeper of the dept. of antiquities, Rep.
1860	(540)	XVI	British Museum, Sel. Cttee. Rep., mins. of ev., appendix.
	(540-I)		British Museum, Sel. Cttee. index.
1899	(179)	LXXVII	Celtic ornaments found in Ireland offered for sale to the British Museum, Dept. Rep., mins. of ev.

EDUCATION:
PUBLIC LIBRARIES

Edward Miller

Commentary

Introduction

The campaign for the establishment of free municipal public libraries, which was brought to a successful conclusion by William Ewart's Act of 1850,[1] forms an integral part of that spread of elementary education which was so prominent a feature of Victorian England. It too had its enemies who feared lest libraries, like classrooms, might become mere schools of agitation and sedition,[2] while its friends considered it to be a part — and an important part — of that 'gigantic struggle for intellectual elevation now going on.'[3]

It is of course a truism that politics and education were indissolubly linked. Chartists and others of a like persuasion were fully alive to the importance of educating the masses, of relieving them from that apathetic misery in which all too many of them were sunk. Durham Political Union had, in 1840, urged that its members should study 'the works of history and especially the history of our own country . . . their bearing on our present state, and tracing the entire chain of development by which the constitution of society has been unfolded.'[4]

It was more than half a century since Joseph Lancaster had opened his first school and had thereby taken a timid step towards the general education of the poor. Now with increasing government assistance, the two rival but flourishing bodies, the Anglican National Society and the undenominational British and Foreign School Society, founded by Lancaster's supporters, had done much to enable the lower classes at least to learn to read. There was much still to be done. No more, it was said, than one in eight and probably no more than one in thirteen of the nation's children attended school.[5] Nonetheless, in Brougham's words, the schoolmaster was abroad[6] and, in co-operatives, in mechanics institutes, and in trade unions, men were banding together to obtain knowledge.[7]

But, as a witness before the Select Committee on Public Libraries of 1849 testified: 'Yet the fact is that we give the people in this country an appetite to read, and supply them with nothing. For the last many years in England, everybody has been educating the people, but they have forgotten to find them any books'.[8]

And it was not merely the lack of books. Leisure was still scanty, domestic conditions too often appalling and only the most ambitious would have the resolution and the courage to persevere in the face of almost overwhelming difficulties. It was to make the lot of such men a little easier, to provide both the books and, if needs be, a place wherein they might be studied, that the public library movement was born.

The Public Library Movement

As with many other nineteenth century reform movements it was essentially a movement from above, enlightened members of the middle classes deciding what was good for their inferiors. Books were to be 'a means of elevating the character of the labouring classes, and improving the social condition'.[9] They must, of course, be the right books; on no account either immoral or subversive — and the interpretation of both these terms was, to say the least, generous. If left to themselves the majority of the working classes would read nothing other than newspapers, for the most part of a highly undesirable nature, or the trashiest of popular fiction. The numerous religious works so generously distributed among the deserving poor by the pious, had not had the effect which was expected of them. Books — books of the right sort— easily and freely available, would at least keep the working classes off the streets and out of the clutches of Chartists and of similar unwholesome influences.

It was felt that on the whole things were done better abroad or even in Scotland. The evidence of Edward Edwards of the British Museum before the Public Libraries Select Committee of 1849 is full of assertions as to how much easier it was to obtain books from foreign libraries than it was in this country, assertions which his enemies claimed to be largely false.[10]

It was certainly true that conditions in England left much to be desired. Nothing, it was said, struck an American more forcibly on coming to England than to see 'how little reading there is among the labouring or business classes.'[11] Facilities for borrowing books, particularly to read at home, were extremely limited. Cathedral and parochial libraries were for the most part moribund, whilst their contents were scarcely of the sort to appeal to the majority of working class readers. The professional libraries were virtually restricted to their own members, whilst the circulating libraries, such as Mudie's, founded eight years previously, were largely a middle-class preserve, their subscriptions alone putting them far beyond the reach of the poor.

The itinerant libraries founded in East Lothian by Samuel Brown in 1817, with the object of providing 'a library within a mile-and-a-half of every inhabitant of the country',[12] had attracted a considerable number of working class readers, whilst during the previous two decades several small libraries had been set up by philanthropic employers in factories or in collieries. Most mechanics' institutes possessed libraries, but even here all too often the small subscription was beyond the means of the poorer students, whilst many of the books themselves — politics being almost always excluded — were unattractive to working class readers.

The British Museum Library, although free and in theory open to anyone pursuing a serious course of study, was widely felt to be unduly restrictive[13] and its catalogues and service to readers were far from perfect. Moreover its books might not be borrowed nor was it ever open in the evenings.

These were the two essential conditions in the radical demand for municipal public libraries. The report of the 1849 Committee emphasized 'that they should be freely accessible to all the public; that they should be open during the evening; and that they should be, as far as possible, lending libraries'.[14] To be of any real benefit, the working classes must have books that they could read either at home or of an evening in warm, well-lighted reading rooms.

Lighting was always a problem in early Victorian England. There was an inherent danger of fire in almost every form of artificial lighting then used. Ten years later the Trustees of the Museum went into the matter and on expert advice decisively rejected any idea of lighting by gas either their galleries or the reading rooms.[15] Those who gave evidence before the two Select Committees were largely unaware of the full extent of the problem and of the great risk to priceless collections which almost any form of artificial lighting then involved. There were other difficulties. Merely to have a reading room opened, at least in a great library like the British Museum, without access to the bookshelves, was largely a waste of the reader's time, as Panizzi pointed out to the Select Committee of 1850.[16] Not until the introduction of electric light later in the century was a satisfactory solution to be arrived at.

In March 1849 a Select Committee of the House of Commons was set up under the chairmanship of William Ewart to go into the whole question of the lack of adequate public library facilities and to suggest a solution.[17] Although such well-known politicians as Disraeli and Monckton Milnes were on the Committee, they seem to have shown little interest in the proceedings. Much of the work seems to have been done by Joseph Brotherton, member for Salford. Brotherton, a retired cotton manufacturer was famous for his views on temperance, vegetarianism and good works generally. Other active members were James Wyld, MP for Bodmin and naturally, the Chairman, William Ewart.

On 23 July 1849 it issued its report, 'The establishment of Public Libraries, freely accessible to all the people' would, they felt, have only beneficial results and trusted, somewhat optimistically, that Great Britain 'will not long linger behind the people of other countries in the acquisition of such valuable institutions.'[18]

The Report was well received. *The Athenaeum* considered that it was 'one of the best blue-books connected with literature that Parliament has given to the public for a very long time' and that it abounds in 'sensible recommendations', in particular by suggesting that Parliament should pass an Act enabling Town Councils to levy a small rate 'for the erection and support of Town Libraries',[19] the solution that was ultimately adopted. The evidence given, however, by Edward Edwards, adversely comparing, it would seem, the British Museum with foreign libraries, had greatly offended his superior Antonio Panizzi, Keeper of Printed Books at the Museum, an offence which was compounded by an article he wrote on the Report of the Committee in the *Quarterly Review*.[20] Edwards' evidence had likewise been strongly criticised by his colleague, Thomas Watts, under the pseudonym *Verificator* in a series of articles in *The Athenaeum*,[21] which did much to cast doubts on its value. Edwards was hated by Panizzi who considered that "he was not . . . to be trusted" and was heartily disliked by many of his other colleagues. He was a difficult man, despite his enthusiasm and love of learning and never seems to have fitted in either at the Museum or elsewhere. Edwards had fallen foul of Panizzi in 1848 for allegedly using official stationery in Museum time on an unofficial project. "A person like Mr. Edwards who had had repeatedly to be warned & reprimanded for neglecting his duty, who had twice been convicted for making false entries in his diary . . . ought no longer to be allowed to remain in the Museum.", thundered his irate superior.

Ewart and his family had formerly been friendly with Panizzi, but in recent years had increasingly come to mistrust him and William Ewart in particular, by this time regarded the Italian-born librarian with considerable distaste. On 14 February 1850 Ewart introduced a bill to enable town councils to establish public libraries and museums by levying a halfpenny rate.[22] Pressure, much of it from the Museum authorities, who felt that the views of the national library had hitherto not been properly represented, led to the appointment of a further Select Committee on the very day that the bill was introduced.[23] Panizzi was now convinced that Edwards presented a threat to his beloved Museum and that, therefore, he must be utterly discredited. With the cunning and perseverance of a prosecuting council — he was, of course, a distinguished lawyer — he set about providing the Committee, in particular his friend Lord Seymour, helped by various agents and friends, with the evidence to complete Edwards' discomforture.[24]

The principal witness before this new Committee was Panizzi himself, who continued to do his best to throw doubt on Edwards' evidence. However the statistics so generously provided by Edwards might not always be accurate, but essentially he was right. As Thomas Greenwood, Edwards' first biographer, wrote 'The nation was practically bookless so far as accessibility to the public was concerned, and the weight of this fact is overlooked, and he is told that he has put a place in Spain which he should have placed in Portugal'.[25] Facilities in Great Britain were just not adequate enough for the increasing numbers wishing to take advantage of their new found literacy. Edwards, the self-educated son of a London bricklayer, was indeed a difficult man and the evidence he gave too often coloured by prejudice, but from his own experience he was able to appreciate the needs and desires of those, who to the vast majority of the Victorian upper and middle classes, were a race apart.

Panizzi, for instance, was by no means opposed in principle to public libraries,[26] but his attitude was one that would have had the sympathy of his Whig friends: that public libraries were desirable but was this bill the best way, was even the assumption correct that there was a large number of unsatisfied working class readers crying out for the facilities which the bill sought to provide? Surely, it would be better to wait and see until the demand manifested itself more plainly.[27] It was this reluctance to do anything unless the demand was overwhelming which continually plagued the protagonists of a widespread municipal library system, as it did almost all other nineteenth century reformers.

The Act of 1850 and its results

To all too many, any change was for the worse and there was also the fear, even in radical circles, of a possible infringement of a man's inalienable rights to do what he would with his own. Such very different members as the eccentric Tory Colonel Sibthorp and the radical John Bright were both critical of Ewart's bill. Sibthorp's old-fashioned paternalism was revolted by attempts by reformers, however well-meaning, to impose their tastes and habits on the working classes. He declared: 'He did not like reading at all and he hated it when at Oxford'[28] and was clearly of the impression that the majority of the population shared his aversion.[29] Bright's view, like that of otherwise sympathetic members, was that while warmly approving of the bill in principle, he deplored any regulation which entailed ratepayers being taxed for something of which they had not specifically approved, that it gave 'the town council powers of taxation without consent'.[30]

Such objections and the more hostile atmosphere engendered by Panizzi's evidence and *Verificator's* articles forced Ewart to accept modifications to his original proposals, but the bill eventually passed by a small majority.[31]

So in this modest way, with inadequate funds and hedged by restrictions, the municipal library began. For many years few councils availed themselves of the Act's powers, even after these were increased and the permitted rate raised to one penny five years later.[32] Nevertheless, to an ever increasing extent the public library became an integral part of the Victorian desire for self-improvement. Edwards himself laid the foundations well in Manchester, at the Free Library from 1851 onwards, and up and down the country other devoted men followed his example.

The evidence laid before the two Select Committees made very plain the almost complete lack of adequate facilities for people of modest means desirous of studying or indeed of merely reading for pleasure, whether at home or in a public reading room, at a time convenient to themselves. The Acts of 1850 and 1855 were the first hesitant steps to remedy this solution.

Progress was slow. All too often the new libraries were hampered by local prejudice and municipal parsimony. Charles Dickens might regard the public library as a 'great free school, inviting the humblest workman to come in and to be a student',[33] but for many years the local public library was regarded primarily as a service, grudgingly bestowed, to provide newspapers and light literature for the working classes, and therefore to be run as economically as possible. The middle classes still preferred to use, as they were to do for at least another century, the circulating libraries.

The Public Library Acts and the Select Committees which gave rise to them form an essential part of that great movement for municipal reform which, during the latter half of the nineteenth century, transformed to an increasing extent the foetid slums thrown up by the Industrial Revolution into clean and pleasant cities. In these, the municipal library, like parks and sports grounds, formed an important feature, a state of affairs undreamed of by the early reformers, and due almost entirely to the efforts of such men as Ewart and Edwards, who, in the face of hostility, ridicule and apathy, succeeded in opening men's eyes to a great and abiding need.

Bibliography

Two books which throw considerable light on the spread of education and the creation of that demand which led to the two Select Committees on Public libraries and the subsequent Legislation are Mary Sturt, *The Education of the People. A history of primary education in England and Wales in the nineteenth century* (London: Routledge & Kegan Paul, 1967) and Robert K. Webb, *The British Working Class Reader, 1790-1848* (London: Allen & Unwin, 1955). The extensive quotations from primary sources make the first of these an invaluable work of reference, as well as a most useful general history, whilst the second is particularly illuminating in its examination of the close relationship between education and politics in the early nineteenth century, and of the reaction by the upper classes to the supposed threat offered by an increasingly literate working class. The popular and unstamped presses are fully explored by Patricia Hollis, *The Pauper Press* (Oxford: OUP, 1970) and Joel H. Wiener, *The War of the Unstamped* (New York: Cornell U.P. 1969).

For the general background to the period George Kitson Clark *The Making of Victorian England* (London: Methuen, 1962) is invaluable, especially chapters Two and Five, 'Progress and Survival in Victorian England' and 'The People'. Other useful general works are J. F. C. Harrison, *Early Victorian Britain* (London: Weidenfeld & Nicholson, 1971) and Geoffrey Best, *Mid-Victorian Britain* (London: Weidenfeld & Nicholson, 1971).

The history of the Public Library movement itself is covered by several books. Of these easily the best is William A. Munford, *Penny Rate. Aspects of British public library history* (London: Library Association, 1951). It is extremely well documented and full of most useful information. The author is particularly successful in relating the development of the public library system to the general historical background. It is to be regretted that there is no bibliography. Other useful histories are John L. Thornton, *A Mirror for Librarians. Selected readings in the history of Librarianship* (London: Grafton & Co., 1948), covering both English and American sources; John Minto, *A History of the Public Library Movement in Great Britain and Ireland* (London: Allen & Unwin, 1932), a somewhat pedestrian book; and Raymond Irwin's *The English Library. Sources and history* (London: Allen & Unwin, 1960). This deals for the most part with the library in antiquity and in the Middle Ages, but Part Two, *The English Domestic Library,* is well worth reading.

The background to the two Select Committees on Public Libraries is extensively covered by William A. Munford's two biographies, *William Ewart, M.P., 1798-1869. Portrait of a radical* (London: Grafton & Co., 1960) and *Edward Edwards, 1812-1886* (London: Library Association, 1963). The first is probably the best study available for the early public library movement and for other popular causes which enjoyed Ewart's support. The second makes extensive use of Edwards' diaries and other primary sources and is particularly interesting when dealing with Edwards' years at the British Museum and his activities in connection with the two Select Committees on Public Libraries.

Edward Miller's *Prince of Librarians. The life and times of Antonio Panizzi of the British Museum* (London: André Deutsch, 1967) deals in detail with Panizzi's evidence before the Select Committee of 1850 and gives the story of his feud with Edwards. Other background material may be found in *That Noble Cabinet. A history of the British Museum.* (London: André Deutsch, 1974) by the same author.

An older but still valuable biography of Edwards is that by Thomas Greenwood, *Edward Edwards. The chief pioneer of municipal public libraries* (London: Smith, Greenwood & Co., 1902). It has the advantage that the author knew Edwards personally and was himself an outstanding worker in the same field.

Edwards's own works on librarianship give a clear picture of his beliefs and aspirations and are essential for any understanding of the vital part he played in the struggle for a free municipal public library system. His *Memoirs of Libraries.* 2 vol. (London: Trübner, 1859), a solid painstaking work, presents with a wealth of detail a complete conspectus of the contemporary library world, as seen by a dedicated librarian.

Of more immediate concern are Edwards's two pamphlets. *A Letter to the . . . Earl of Ellesmere . . . on the desirability of a better provision of public libraries* (London, 1848) and *Remarks on the Paucity of Libraries freely open to the public . . . together with a succinct statistical view of the existing provision of Public Libraries in the several states of Europe* (London, 1849). These consist essentially of his evidence before the Royal Commission on the British Museum of 1849-50 and the Select Committees on Public Libraries of 1849 and 1850, in which he stresses the better provision with regard to libraries enjoyed by many European cities as compared with those of Great Britain. The second pamphlet deals also with the alleged deficiencies of British libraries, especially the British Museum, as compared with their foreign rivals. Though both pamphlets suffer from Edwards's excessive earnestness and lack of humour, they give much valuable information not readily found elsewhere.

Edwards also kept a diary from 1844 to 1884, which is now in the Department of Printed Books, British Museum. This throws considerable light on his efforts to assist Ewart with the two Select Committees and to pass the Public Libraries Act, and his quarrel with Panizzi as well as on his later life in Manchester and elsewhere.

Much relevant material will be found in the *Library History Journal,* published by the Library History Group of the Library Association and in H. J. de Vleeschauwer's 'Survey of Library History', *Mousaion* 63-66, (Pretoria, 1963).

Footnotes

1 13 & 14 Vict. c.65 (An Act for enabling Town Councils to establish Public Libraries and Museums).

2 Sir Robert Inglis, M.P. for Oxford University, considered that the halfpenny rate envisaged by Ewart's bill 'was clearly adapted not merely for the purpose of procuring books, but also of creating lecture rooms which might give rise to an unhealthy agitation' *Hansard,* 3 s., 13 March 1850.

3 *Eliza Cook's Journal,* 5 May 1849.

4 *Northern Liberator,* 19 September 1840. Quoted in Robert F. Wearmouth, *Some Working-Class Movements of the Nineteenth Century.* (London: Epworth Press, 1948), p.142.

5 Speech of W. J. Fox, M.P. for Oldham. *Hansard,* 3 s., 26 February 1850. However, a large number of children did receive some sort of education, if only a very brief one. See Robert Kiefer Webb, *The British Working Class Reader, 1790-1848.* (London: Allen & Unwin, 1955), chap. 1.

6 *Hansard,* n.s., 29 January 1828.

7 For a more extended treatment of this subject see the essay on the education of the poorer classes by J. R. B. Johnson, above.

8 *Report from the Select Committee on Public Libraries,* p.85. HC 1849 (548) XVII, 129. IUP series Education: Public Libraries 1.

9 *Report from the Select Committee, 1849,* p.85.

10 *Report from the Select Committee, 1849,* pp.2-11. See also the maps in the *Report.*

11 *Report from the Select Committee,* 1849, p.105.

12 *Report from the Select Committee,* 1849, p.111.

13 It was open from nine till four from September to April, nine till seven for the rest of the year. For conditions of admission, see *Statutes and Rules for the British Museum*. (London, 1833), p.25. The Chartist, William Lovett, said that he had experienced no difficulty in obtaining admission, but confirmed that few working men ever used the library. *Report from the Select Committee, 1849*, p.181.

14 *Report from the Select Committee, 1849*, p.xii.

15 British Museum (Lighting by Gas). HC 1861 (348) XXXIV, 225.

16 *Report from the Select Committee on Public Libraries*, p.65. HC 1850 (655) XVIII, 71. IUP series Education: Public Libraries 2.

17 *Commons Journal, CIV*, p.142.

18 *Report from the Select Committee, 1849*, pp.iii, xiv.

19 *Athenaeum*, 1 September 1849.

20 Edward Edwards, 'Libraries and the People', *British Quarterly Review*, XI (1850), p.61.

21 *Athenaeum*, 17 November; 24 November; 8 December 1849; 5 January 1850. A number of Edwards's other colleagues seem to have contributed to the articles. Though some of the criticism is trifling, the general effect was to throw considerable doubt on the reliability of Edwards's evidence and on the means by which it had been secured.

22 *Hansard*, 3 s., 14 February 1850.

23 *Commons Journal*, CV, p.69.

24 Panizzi employed Henry Stevens, the Museum's American agent and Adolphus Asher, the principal European agent, to gather evidence on Edwards's activities and those of his ally, C. R. Wyld, Librarian of the Royal Society. Although sometimes wrong in detail, and Wyld had in fact never visited some of the libraries he claimed to have inspected, the general accuracy of Edwards's figures was subsequently vindicated by the statistical returns received through the Foreign Office and published as Appendix 2 to the 1850 Report.

25 Thomas Greenwood, *Edward Edwards, the chief pioneer of public libraries* (London: Scott, Greenwood & Co., 1902), p.103.

26 In 1836 Panizzi had declared 'The fact is, that the library of the British Museum being the only library for a million and a half of inhabitants will never be satisfactory to everybody . . . so long as it is the only one in London. There ought to be at least two public libraries for education, and they ought to be formed on very different principles from those of the library of the British Museum'. *Report from the Select Committee on the condition, management and affairs of the British Museum*, p.391, HC 1836 (440), 399. IUP series Education: British Museum 2. Panizzi obviously had in mind the supply of cheap textbooks for the use of students. See also *Report from the Select Committee, 1850*, p.61.

27 *Report from the Select Committee, 1850*, p.65.

28 *Hansard*, 3 s., 13 March 1850.

29 'However excellent food for the mind might be, food for the body was what was now most wanted for the people'. *Hansard*, 3 s., 13 March 1850. 'He had no hesitation in saying that the city which he represented [Lincoln] did not desire any such measures as this; at least he had never heard of it'. *Hansard*, 3 s., 10 April 1850.

30 W. R. Miles, *Hansard*, 3 s., 13 March 1850.

31 *Hansard*, 3 s., 30 July 1850. An amendment, prohibiting the provisions of the bill being extended to Ireland, was carried by forty-three votes. *Hansard*, 3 s.p 30 July 1850.

32 18 & 19 Vict. c.70. *(An Act for further promoting the Establishment of Free Public Libraries in Municipal Towns.)*

33 Speech at the opening of the Free Library, Manchester, 2 September 1852. Manchester Free Library, *Report of the Proceedings at the Public Meetings, etc.* (Manchester, 1852), p.19.

THE DOCUMENTS

PUBLIC LIBRARIES

Public Libraries Volume 1

REPORT FROM THE SELECT COMMITTEE ON PUBLIC LIBRARIES WITH
THE PROCEEDINGS OF THE COMMITTEE, MINUTES OF EVIDENCE,
APPENDIX AND INDEX, 1849

452 pp   12 maps

The Select Committee on Public Libraries examined the state of
existing libraries and the means by which the number of public libraries
could be increased. Librarians gave evidence on the state of libraries,
numbers of books in them, their geographical distribution and the
extent to which the general public were allowed access to them. The
committee classified libraries into four types, university, cathedral,
parochial and village. Evidence from university representatives led the
committee to recommend that university libraries, especially the
copyright deposit libraries were especially deserving of public support
as they were major research centres. The committee noted that the
increasing level of education in both rural and urban areas would
inevitably lead to an increase in public demand for library facilities.
Evidence on the advanced state of public libraries in the United States
and on the Continent led the committee to recommend that Britain's
existing village libraries should be improved and greatly increased in
numbers. They also urged that the duty on imported books should be
abolished as they considered it a tax on knowledge.

Original reference

1849   (548)   XVII   Public libraries, Sel. Cttee. Rep., mins. of ev.,
appendix, index.

Public Libraries Volume 2

REPORTS FROM SELECT COMMITTEES ON PUBLIC LIBRARIES WITH
MINUTES OF EVIDENCE, APPENDICES AND INDEX, 1850-1852
508 pp

The reports contain a comprehensive survey of Library facilities in
Britain, Europe, the Americas and Russia. Particular attention was paid

by the committee to investigating the operation and requirements of large libraries especially university libraries. Evidence was heard on the physical condition, accommodation, lighting and ventilation of many famous libraries, including the British Museum, Vatican and Munich libraries. British librarians explained to the committee the criteria on which they based their book purchasing. The need to promote the international dissemination of knowledge, especially the results of original research, led the committee to examine the possibility of international exchange of books between libraries and the speed with which libraries were able to obtain scientific journals. A large section of the volume is devoted to returns relating to overseas libraries and their organisation and stocks were detailed. These returns were compiled by foreign librarians in response to a British request for information on library facilities abroad.

Original references

1850	(655)	XVIII	Public libraries, Sel. Cttee. Rep., mins. of ev., appendix, index.
1851	(630)	X	Public libraries, Sel. Cttee. Rep., mins. of ev., appendix.
1852	(532)	V	Public libraries, Sel. Cttee. Rep., mins. of ev., appendix.

SECONDARY EDUCATION: THE EDUCATION OF THE MIDDLE CLASSES

Gillian Sutherland

Commentary

Introduction

The Reports and evidence of the three Royal Commissions which inquired into secondary education in England during the nineteenth century, the Clarendon Commission of 1861-4, the Taunton Commission of 1864-7 and the Bryce Commission of 1894-5[1] are no less public and self-conscious documents than any other nineteenth-century blue books. The peculiar importance of these three inquiries as sources for study lies in their isolation. Systematic national provision for secondary education was inaugurated only by the Education Act of 1902. Thus, unlike the Report of the Newcastle Commission, and even more, that of the Cross Commission, they cannot be made points of focus in an ever-increasing flow of information, both from government and outside it, about educational provision in the country at large. They are the only national surveys of secondary school provision: as it were, two cross-sections of the society, separated by an interval of thirty years. Whatever our reservations about the bias of their inquiries, we have to use their data and up to a point, their systems of classification, since we have not enough to construct alternatives. At the same time, if we pursue the comparison with the elementary education sources further, a countervailing factor can be perceived. Just as elementary education was defined in terms of a social group — the labouring poor — rather than in terms of an age group, so was secondary education defined in terms of its clientèle, the middle and upper classes. This does not make the Clarendon, Taunton and Bryce discussions the less biased but it does mean that they are less remote from the actual experience of pupils, teachers and parents. They have their manipulative aspects; but they also offer glimpses of the élite discussing the training and recruitment of its own members and its own children.

1. The Circumstances surrounding the creation of the three Commissions

i

All three Reports were, in classical fashion, a response to the pressures of 'public opinion'; although on each occasion public opinion expressed itself in significantly different ways, reflecting in some degree the rise and increasing sophistication of pressure group politics and tactics. The state of the older public schools had been an intermittent target for attack since the beginning of the century; and the great series of inquiries into charitable trusts in general, inaugurated by Brougham in 1818, had resembled a continuing sniper's fire.[2] A new phase of attack was launched at the end of the 1850s. The indefatigable Brougham presented a petition to parliament with 40,000 signatures praying for the improvement of middle-class education;[3] and the first of a series of letters signed 'Paterfamilias' in the *Cornhill* in May 1860 inaugurated a vigorous debate in the periodicals.[4] A more effective parliamentary lobbyist than the ageing Brougham presented himself in the person of Mountstuart Elphinstone Grant Duff, Liberal MP for Elgin Burghs. He recorded in his diary for 1861:

> All through this spring I was much occupied in urging the expediency of a Royal Commission to inquire into the Public Schools, circulating a paper of reasons in favour of it to all members of the House of Commons and communicating with Northcote, the two Russells, the Head Masters of Harrow and Rugby etc., besides Gladstone and Sir George Lewis who were the members of the government who took most interest in the matter. After much negotiation all ended happily and the commission was issued.[5]

For one of the most garrulous of nineteenth-century diarists (he eventually published fourteen volumes of extracts from his journals) Grant Duff was curiously uninformative about his motives. His readiness to act as spokesman for the critics of public schools may have had something to do with his own secondary education — at Edinburgh Academy; but like many another distinguished nineteenth-century Scot he had then gone up to Balliol and had many contacts within that extraordinarily influential Balliol connexion in nineteenth-century education.[6] He had taken a keen interest in the activities of the Royal and Executive Commissions for the reform of the University of Oxford and it may be that he saw a Royal Commission as providing a similar catalyst in the case of the public schools, assisting them to put their own houses in order before a real confrontation developed.[7]

Grant Duff had initially asked the Home Secretary, Sir George Cornewall Lewis, for a Commission to inquire into all 'the higher school Education of England and Wales'; and for a time it looked as if the terms of reference of the Clarendon Commission would include all endowed schools.[8] But in the end they were confined to the nine foundations of Eton, Winchester, Harrow, Rugby, the Charterhouse, Westminster, St. Paul's, Merchant Taylors and Shrewsbury. Public discussion of the general issue did not, therefore, subside. In his *A French Eton, or Middle Class Education and the State,* first published between 1863 and 1864 as a series of articles in *Macmillan's Magazine,* Matthew Arnold argued that the schools which most needed reform were not Eton and its 'eight co-respondents' but the decaying grammar schools and the great mass of private and proprietary schools, claiming to offer a cheap but sound education for the children of 'the great mass of middling people, with middling incomes'. With heavy irony he quoted from advertisements in *The Times* offering an ' "Educational Home" where "discipline is based upon moral influence and emulation and every effort is made to combine home-comforts with school-training. Terms inclusive and moderate." ' [9]

Some sections of the government, which employed Matthew Arnold as an Inspector of elementary schools, were not unsympathetic. In 1860 Ralph Lingen, the Permanent Secretary to the Education Department, had commented to his political chief, Lord Granville, the Lord President of the Council:

> The education of the (thrifty) middle class, that is to say, of the class below the richer professional class and the richer commercial class is worse provided for than that of the classes over and under them. It is very undesirable to extend *Government* action to this class; but their schools want what inspection does for the schools of the poor. [10]

When in the summer of 1864 a deputation from the National Association for the Promotion of the Social Sciences waited on the Prime Minister, Lord Palmerston, to urge an investigation into *all* endowed schools, Lord Granville responded with alacrity and the Taunton Commission was set up that autumn.

ii

The Bryce Commission also represented a response to debate, but in a situation where the vested interests had become a great deal more complex. By 1890 demand for the direct involvement of the state in the provision of secondary education had built up considerably; and it was beginning to be powerfully reinforced by increasing anxiety about Britain's competitive position internationally. [11] An initial gesture of sorts was made towards this by the Technical Instruction Act of 1889, which established county and county borough councils as local authorities responsible for technical education and empowered them to spend the proceeds of a penny rate in promoting it. From 1890 these were augmented by a share of the purchase tax on liquor, the celebrated 'whisky money'. [12] In 1889 also the Welsh Intermediate Education

Act empowered Welsh county councils to begin to make provision for some kind of post-elementary education.[13]

But national action on secondary education as a whole was not a simple matter of expanding the powers of county and county borough councils. Some account had to be taken of the fact that local government agencies for elementary education already existed.[14] The earliest elementary schools had been the product of voluntary enterprise and were usually denominational in character. Debate about the propriety of government subsidy to denominational — usually Anglican — teaching — the 'religious problem' — had inhibited government action since the 1830s; and the Elementary Education Act of 1870 attempted to circumvent the problem by creating a dual system. It compelled the creation of a new, directly-elected local authority, the school board, with powers to build and run non-denominational schools only in areas where there were no schools, or not enough schools. In areas where existing denominational voluntary schools provided enough places, a majority of the ratepayers could choose whether or not to establish a board. Where a board was established, it was responsible for enforcing attendance provisions in the district as a whole, but otherwise had no part in the conduct of the voluntary schools. This produced a kind of double patch-work, with parishes with and without school boards side by side, and in parishes with school boards sometimes board and voluntary schools side by side. The complications were compounded by the different financial arrangements obtaining for board and voluntary schools. Board schools drew income not only from government grants and children's fees but also from the rates. Voluntary schools had only grants, fees, subscriptions and the occasional endowment. These last were neither as secure nor as capable of growth as rates. Thus voluntary schools' committees of management found it more and more difficult to respond to increased expectations in elementary education, let alone contemplate any responsibility for secondary school provision.

At the same time, some school boards had begun to stake out a kind of claim to such provision. The Code of regulations governing grants to elementary schools allowed older children to tackle some quite advanced work; and elementary schools were also able to apply for grants from the Science and Art Department for scientific and technical work. Only a handful of the larger urban school boards had either the resources or the demand to engage systematically in work at this level; but at the end of the 1870s several took the logical step of concentrating such work in a central school, known as a Higher Grade school, which siphoned off the older children from all the surrounding board schools. To call such schools 'elementary', however, was stretching the term and their dubious legality was the subject of continuing debate and dispute.[15]

With the dual system the legislation of 1870 had given administrative and institutional dimensions to the traditional religious problem. The equally traditional alignment of Tories with Anglicans and Whigs with Dissent was transmuted into the commitment of most Liberals to school boards and their extension, and the commitment of most Conservatives to their abolition or reconstruction. Thus, neither politically nor administratively was it possible simply to graft responsibility for secondary education on to the existing framework for elementary education.

The Bryce Commission was specifically intended to begin to hack a way through this tangle of conflicting interests — incidentally also offering an extreme case of the interdependence of politician and pressure group, of decision-maker and client. A. H. D. Acland, Vice-President of the Committee of Council 1892-5 and thus the political head of the Education Department, was that rare animal, a serious politician who was also a committed educational reformer.[16] In 1892, with Hubert Llewellyn Smith, he had published *Studies in Secondary Education,* a survey of existing provisions, with a final chapter arguing strongly for immediate action. But Gladstone's last ministry was in no position to undertake major education legislation. Gladstone himself was preoccupied with Home Rule, the rest of the Cabinet were squabbling over the succession, and for their parliamentary majority they depended upon the Irish. In September 1892 Acland wrote to his old friend Michael Sadler, who had succeeded him as Steward of Christ Church, Oxford and Secretary of the University Extension Committee:

I have in view — this is quite *between ourselves* — some informal conference between Headmasters' Conference, Teachers Guild, College of Preceptors etc. County Council Ass. Univ. Ext. Auths., one or two from each — at the Education Office on Secondary Education Orgn. Registration & Training of Teachers etc. — But it may turn out very difficult to bring this about.

Please help me from the point of view of a wide survey of what we need nationally and can *do,* if with a small majority behind us. We must make hay while the sun shines.[17]

The 'informal conference' at the Education Office did not materialise. But early in 1893 Michael Sadler was to be found organizing a petition from the resident members of the University of Oxford to the Hebdomadal Council to arrange a national conference on secondary education. The conference duly took place and in turn prompted a memorial to the Prime Minister from the Convocation of Oxford in November 1893, calling for a Royal Commission on secondary education. The Bryce Commission was created early in 1894, with Sadler and Llewellyn Smith among its members.[18]

2. The personnel of the Commissions

i

As the circumstances of its creation indicate, the membership of the Bryce Commission reflected both careful packing and a wide range of actual or potential vested interests. Bryce deferred to Acland in their selection; and one of his Cambridge friends commented: 'the prevailing idea is that Acland has packed it so as to get a scheme passed which he has ready made.'[19] But apart from Sadler and Llewellyn Smith, and possibly Henry Hobhouse the Liberal-Unionist politician, who had introduced a private member's bill in 1893, empowering county councils to aid general secondary education, which was remarkably similar to one promoted by Acland himself as a private member the previous year,[20] few of the others could be as obviously identified with the Vice-President. Bryce himself had impeccable credentials for a chairman's job. He was not only a solid Liberal elder statesman, he had been Regius Professor of Civil Law at Oxford and an Assistant Commissioner to the Taunton Commission.[21] Sir Henry Roscoe and Dr Richard Wormell were the representatives of science. The affiliations of J. H. Yoxall, as ex-president of the National Union of Elementary School Teachers, were fairly clear.[22] The women's interest was represented by Sophie Bryant, who was to become the headmistress of the North London Collegiate School in 1895, and Eleanor Sidgwick, Principal of Newnham College, Cambridge, wife of the philosopher and educational reformer Henry Sidgwick, and last but by no means least, sister of Arthur Balfour.[23] These two were professionals; the third woman, Lady Frederick Cavendish, widow of the ill-fated Chief Secretary to Ireland, was not. But she was well-known for her voluntary work and again part of an influential family network, as sister of yet another Commissioner, the Hon. Edward Lyttelton, headmaster of Haileybury, later to be headmaster of Eton; and daughter of the fourth Lord Lyttelton, who had sat on both the Clarendon and Taunton Commissions.[24] In addition her presence represented some guarantee to the Established Church that its interests would not be wholly neglected. The Dean of Manchester, Dr Maclure, was clearly there to give support; while Sir Richard Jebb, Regius Professor of Greek at Cambridge, but also one of the two MPs for the University, was to play the dual role of distinguished academic and spokesman for Anglican interests.[25]

ii

Labels of vested interest were less easy to affix to the members of the Commissions of the 1860s, although some equally careful packing went on. The obvious radicals on the Clarendon Commission were Henry Halford Vaughan, former Regius Professor of Modern History at Oxford,[26] and his erstwhile friend Edward Twistleton, who had been a member of the Executive Commission to reform Oxford under the 1854 Act. In the event, Vaughan functioned alone, displaying a considerable talent for bewildering witnesses with the complexity of his questions. Twistleton was totally ineffective, disabled perhaps by a shattering quarrel with Vaughan in 1861, and certainly by his wife's death in 1862.[27] The other man with something of a reputation in university reform, William Hepworth Thompson, Regius Professor of Greek at Cambridge, was almost equally ineffective, but largely, according to his fellow-Commissioner Lord Lyttelton, through indolence.[28] Lyttelton and the remaining members, Northcote, Devon and Clarendon came from that category of men on which any Royal Commission draws heavily, men who are generally acceptable, both politically and intellectually, who may be described as 'sound'. The fourth Lord Lyttelton had been at Eton and Trinity, was bracketed equal first classic with C. J. Vaughan, and had won the Chancellor's Medal. He shared his classical interests with his brother-in-law, W. E. Gladstone.[29] Northcote had been at Eton and Balliol, and with Charles Trevelyan had reported on the reform of the Civil Service in 1853. He was the nearest to a Gladstonian Chancellor of the Exchequer that the Tory party was able to produce.[30] The eleventh Earl of Devon had been at Westminster and Christ Church, and served as Secretary of the Poor Law Board from 1850 to 1859. The fourth Earl of Clarendon had been at Christ's Hospital, although with his own private tutor, and at St. John's College, Cambridge. He was to become Foreign Secretary in Gladstone's first ministry in 1868 and was the brother-in-law of George Cornewall Lewis, the Home Secretary who had appointed the Commission.[31]

In putting together what became the Taunton Commission, Lord Granville and H. A. Bruce, Cornewall Lewis's successor as Home Secretary, attempted initially to see whether members of the Clarendon Commission would serve again. Clarendon replied immediately:

At this moment it would be impossible for me to fix the sum that would induce me to get upon a Middle Schools drag. I will only say generally that it must be something that I could settle upon Hyde [his son] and thereby raise him from the pauper to the millionaire class . . . Lyttelton would make a very good chairman — the only one of the late lot who would. Devon is weak, Northcote pedantic, Thompson idle, Twistleton quirky, Vaughan mad; yet they all had merits and worked usefully together except Vaughan, who, though a man of real genius, is unmanageable.[32]

On this last point Lyttelton was in entire agreement — 'there really ought to be a record in the Home Office that he must never be employed in such a way' — and stipulated that he would serve again, although not as chairman, only if Vaughan were excluded. He, too, but at much greater length, favoured Granville with a pen-portrait of the late Commission; rating both Devon and

Northcote higher than Clarendon had done.[33] Lyttelton and Northcote were the only two who served on both.

To these Granville and Bruce added Lord Taunton, Secretary of State for the Colonies 1855-8, thought likely to make a sound chairman; Lord Stanley, Eton — from which he was expelled for stealing — Rugby and Trinity and heir to the Earldom of Derby; W. F. Hook, the Dean of Chichester, whose work as Vicar of Leeds had been the classic demonstration of what might be done in an urban industrial parish by a devoted clergyman;[34] Dr John Storrar, prominent in organizing London University; A. W. Thorold, another clergyman active in parochial and educational work, and in 1874 to become Bishop of Rochester; Sir Thomas Dyke Acland, the eleventh baronet, active in the Devon-based county school movement and a founder of the Oxford and Cambridge middle class examinations;[35] W. E. Forster and Edward Baines, respectively representing the moderate and extreme voluntarist wings of Dissent;[36] Peter Erle, one of the Charity Commissioners, as their legal expert; and finally, after much persuasion, the Rev. Frederick Temple, currently headmaster of Rugby and perhaps the epitome of the Balliol connexion already referred to. Educated at Blundell's and Balliol, supported by scholarships, he had been brought from his Balliol Fellowship at Lingen's suggestion, to be made Principal of the Kneller Hall training school for Poor Law schoolmasters. When this had failed, through no fault of his, he had been transferred to the elementary education Inspectorate, whence he had been appointed to Rugby. After Rugby he was to become successively Bishop of Exeter, Bishop of London and Archbishop of Canterbury.[37] In the 1860 Memorandum for the Lord President already mentioned, Lingen had concluded by referring Granville to Temple as an authority on middle class education whom they both acknowledged.[38] Temple advised on the composition of the Commission well before he himself finally consented to join; and he also brought in H. J. Roby, formerly Secretary to the Cambridge Local Examinations Syndicate and now a master at Dulwich, who was appointed the Commission's Secretary.[39]

3. The Reports: structure, contents and significance

i

The brief given the Clarendon Commission was obviously far more straightforward than those given the other two, and this was reflected in the way they organised their work. The Clarendon Commissioners prepared a questionnaire on finance and invited written submissions from interested parties; but for the most part they relied on the standard technique of oral examination of witnesses, some volunteers, some invited.

The Taunton Commission had a far more intractable problem — and the actual terms of their brief gave Granville a lot of trouble. Grant Duff had talked initially about 'all Higher School Education', while the subject of 'middle-class education' figures largely in the public debates. But, as Bruce pointed out to Granville in August 1864:

What is a middle class school? Are all between public schools and elementary to be so considered? Is the inquiry to be made not only into Endowed Grammar Schools, and Proprietary Schools, but into Private Schools?

If, on the other hand, for middle class schools are understood schools for sons of Tradesmen, Farmers etc. in which the classics are *not* taught, the result will be that vast numbers of endowed and other schools, much and in some cases chiefly frequented by the middle classes, will be excluded from the inquiry — and probably no schools need investigation more than these.

If the object be to inquire into all schools whether endowed or not, classical or not, in which the middle classes are instructed, how can the line be drawn with any approach to accuracy? Most of the poorer gentry and clergymen send their sons to grammar schools at which they meet no inconsiderable number of the classes socially inferior to them and usually designated as 'middle'.[40]

Temple was firmly of the opinion that 'to inquire into the education of the middle classes generally would be too vague an undertaking' and might be taken as evidence of the state's intention to intervene in their organization in a systematic way; and he advised an investigation of endowed schools only, as did Lingen.[41] But Granville and Bruce continued to incline towards vagueness;[42] until, towards the end of the year, Temple wrote that he found:

in so many important quarters so strong a feeling against the phrase "middle class" that I think it better even at this eleventh hour to suggest the expediency of avoiding it. Some of the best grammar schools dislike it so much that they may possibly refuse to answer our questions if it is used.

He proposed instead the utter neutrality of an inquiry into the education of children not covered by either the Clarendon or the Newcastle Commissions, and a consideration of 'how far and in what way the Grammar Schools and other Educational Endowments may be made available for its improvement';[43] and this was the formula that was ultimately adopted.

Neutral it might be, vague it certainly was; and the Commissioners were thus left to define the precise extent of their inquiry themselves. It left them free to include proprietary and private schools. It also left them free to include girls' schools — a request first made by Emily Davis, the future foundress of Girton College, to Lyttelton in October 1864, passed on to Granville and presumably endorsed by him.[44] But the net effect was to give them a total number of schools to investigate, so they calculated, of the order of 4,000. Thus they had to make extensive use of written questionnaires and depend heavily on the work in depth of Assistant Commissioners in sample areas.

Their team of Assistant Commissioners was an impressive one, including as it did T. H. Green, the neo-Hegelian philosopher and yet another Balliol man,[45] James Bryce, and two of the ablest Inspectors of elementary schools in J. G. Fitch and D. R. Fearon.[46] Matthew Arnold, inevitably, was packed off to the Continent; while the Reverend James Fraser, the future Bishop of Manchester, who had already distinguished himself as an Assistant Commissioner to the Newcastle Commission, was sent off to report on North America. Their reports comprise the bulk of the volumes of evidence; and it is perhaps worth noting that, unlike the Newcastle Commission, neither their statistics nor their judgements on standards of work in the schools were seriously challenged by contemporaries.

The Bryce Commissioners took the Taunton investigations as one of their principal reference points and thus organized their inquiries and set out their findings in similar fashion. Together, the evidence presented by the two Commissions is an unique source for the actual extent and nature of secondary school provision for both boys and girls, in the second half of the nineteenth century, which has yet to be fully exploited. The Commissioners themselves attempted to present a national picture, insofar as there was such a thing; but both Reports rightly stressed the extraordinary local diversity. The Commissions' material could provide the backbone for a series of local studies; and the range of material available in most localities makes it relatively straightforward to pierce the discreet anonymity of Assistant Commissioners' references to individual schools, while adding information about some of the more ephemeral institutions.[47]

ii

But as important as such maps of school provision is any information to be gleaned from the inquiries as to the exact nature and social location of the provision, and the roles of the Reports in shaping its development. We want to know not only what secondary schools there were, but also who went and who was expected to go to them; what he learned and was expected to learn; and whether these things changed over time. We need therefore to consider the representative status as well as the unique qualities of the sources; to establish the context in which they are to be located, and the other evidence against which they must be juxtaposed before they can be weighed and weighted.

An important first clue to the context is provided by the difficulty Granville and the Taunton Commissioners had in defining the Commission's terms of reference in any positive fashion. For the demand for secondary education in the nineteenth century was not a unified one. Its diversity is one of its most important characteristics, yet one which has so far been relatively neglected in the secondary literature. A major distinction needs to be drawn between those parents who had crossed or wished their children at least to cross what Professor Coleman has described as 'the great social divide' between Players and Gentlemen,[48] and those who were content with the lesser achievement of 'respectability'. The former group are those who have received the lion's share of attention in the secondary literature. Their sons monopolized the boarding schools, staying at least till sixteen, or often till eighteen, or even twenty; perhaps they went to the University; and if they aimed at specific occupations at all, aimed at the ancient professions or the services. Not all such parents were noticeably affluent; but many made up in status and aspirations what they lacked in wealth. Such a one was Mrs Phoebe Catherine Prior, widow of a Chancery barrister who had been killed by a fall from his horse, leaving her with ten children to bring up in the 1850s. She used what money she had to buy a house in Harrow, in order to get her sons taken into the school as foundation scholars, educating her daughters herself and taking in boarders to make end meet.[49] She might be described as a heroic example of the 'sojourners' to be found at both Harrow and Rugby in the first half of the nineteenth century.[50]

This type of demand was well established by the 1840s. The first wave of proprietary boarding schools, such as Cheltenham and Marlborough, was as much a response to demand already felt as a factor in creating it. Arnold's reforms at Rugby can hardly be seen as a catalyst; rather the deification of Arnold through A. P. Stanley's *Life,* first published in 1845, reflected the already established trend.[51] By 1800 six of the nine schools investigated by the Clarendon Commission in 1861-4, Eton, Winchester, Rugby, Harrow, Westminster and Charterhouse, were already national schools, that is, attracted pupils from all over the country.[52] Of the remaining three, Shrewsbury under Butler would soon become so, while St. Paul's and Merchant Taylors were special cases as metropolitan day schools. As early as 1810 the trustees of the Harpur Trust at Bedford set out to reorganize the grammar school there as a boarding school, explicitly following the example of Rugby.

The activities of the Harpur Trustees are of double interest. For in 1764 they had secured a private act of Parliament allowing them to establish a modern school, teaching English and elementary subjects, besides the grammar school; and this grew and flourished in the later eighteenth century while the grammar school, teaching classics, languished.[53] This juxtaposition underlines the existence of a distinct demand for education from parents who were not prepared or could not afford to make 'gentlemen' of their boys, while nevertheless being unprepared to allow them to associate in schools with the children of the labouring poor. These children were far less likely to board; would leave schools at fourteen or at the latest sixteen, aiming at commercial or white-collar clerical, sub-professional occupations, or occasionally, skilled craft work. This group is numerically far more significant that the former, equally as important and far less well-known.

Professor Perkin has pointed out that 'the rise of the first great industrial civilization called forth ever-expanding numbers of more specialized non-manual workers' in discussing changes in the occupational structure during the nineteenth century.[54] But there are some striking indications that this second type of demand also had made itself felt before 1800. Analysis of a sample of grammar schools functioning in the eighteenth century, drawn from fourteen counties and London has shown that almost ninety per cent of those actually founded in the eighteenth century provided for the teaching not only of Latin and Greek but also of English and elementary subjects. Where there is evidence of curriculum change during the eighteenth century again, the overwhelming bulk of the changes, nearly eighty per cent, entailed the introduction of English, writing and arithmetic.

It is conceivable, of course, that some of this demand could more properly be described as working-class, particularly if the grammar school were free— although, of course, it was quite common for schools which provided free teaching in Latin and Greek to charge for other subjects. Of the sample already referred to, 152 schools provided everything free to foundation scholars, 115 charged for other subjects besides Latin and Greek, and 46 charged for everything. The question could only really be resolved by systematic admissions data, which simply does not exist in most cases. But it is worth noting that at Christ's Hospital during the eighteenth century the children of clerical workers were a steadily increasing group, while the children of unskilled workers disappeared.[55] In addition, recent work on Lancashire at the end of the eighteenth and the beginning of the nineteenth century suggests that although the provision of schools of all types was expanding it was not keeping pace with population growth, and the social group which lost out most heavily was the unskilled labouring poor.[56] There is a major field for investigation here.

The Trustees of Leeds Grammar School were quite clear what clientèle they wished to attract when they initiated proceedings in Chancery, in their celebrated attempt to change the terms of their trust, between 1779 and 1805.

The Parish of Leeds [they declared] contains upwards of sixty thousand inhabitants is wholly mercantile and nine tenths of the boys are brought up to trade and commerce. In consequence they are taken from school about the age of fourteen years and put out apprentices or are placed in the counting houses of the merchants — To such boys arithmetic and low algebra may and will be of use; and the Committee found so much difficulty in limiting the number of boys to be taught writing that they are of opinion writing should be wholly excluded — They conceive that a master appointed merely for algebra and mathematics will not be so useful to the inhabitants of the town of Leeds as a master to teach low algebra and arithmetic, as they conceive the boys in general are taken from school at too early an age to avail themselves of algebra and mathematics.[57] While they are very clear they want nothing fancy like 'high' algebra, let alone Latin and Greek, they are equally clear that they do not want a writing school either: they are not an elementary school doing the most basic work.

Although with his celebrated judgement elaborating the doctrine of *cy-près* Lord Eldon would not allow the Leeds Grammar School Trustees to abandon classical teaching, they were not debarred from opening a commercial department beside the classical school. This they promptly did; and were imitated by grammar school trustees in Wolverhampton, Norwich, Nottingham and Bury St. Edmunds. As the clergyman who devised the Wolverhampton scheme commented: 'it is evident that . . . a large class unprovided with public education will remain between the Grammar School and the parochial and similar schools.'[58]

An alternative course of action for the Leeds and Wolverhampton trustees would have been to try to build up their classical schools by taking boarders — as Rugby and Harrow had done before them and as Bedford began to do in 1810. The Harpur Trustees were fortunate under the terms of the 1764 Act in being able to conduct both a classical and a commercial school; and general legislation of 1840 made this a possibility for some other schools. But in a number of cases, however, local circumstances and the particular terms of the trust made a response to demand of this range and flexibility impossible. The first half of the nineteenth century saw a series of sharp conflicts over the use and remodelling of particular trusts. In 1860, for example, Sir John Romilly, Master of the Rolls, finally refused the trustees of Bristol Grammar School permission to take boarders, on the ground that the school was to fulfil primarily a local demand. He commented:

Either the school becomes a school for the rich, that is, for what may be termed the high branch of the middle classes, or it becomes a school from which they are practically withdrawn. It is in the nature of things that it should be so. The regard paid to wealth in this country gives an unusual degree of importance to boys whose parents are supposed to possess it, over those whose parents are supposed to be wanting in that respect . . . I think that the eventual harmonious admixture of classes is much better attained by keeping distinct the schools in which boarders are admitted and those in which free scholars are admitted.[59]

In a significant number of cases the charitable trusts concerned were mixed ones and the conflict was considerably intensified by the fact that educational expansion and/or change would have to use funds formerly devoted to eleemosynary purposes. Even in Bedford a substantial group of local tradesmen tried to reduce the proportion of the endowment devoted to the grammar school in order more effectively to sustain the almsgiving. They lost only after a ten-year battle and yet another protracted and expensive Chancery suit. Similar protests were made, unsuccessfully, at Norwich and Nottingham.[60] Another major battle, in which the local freemen were more successful, was fought at Coventry. Efforts to make the monies in Sir Thomas White's Charity more accessible resulted in a series of schemes being laid before Chancery between 1853 and 1855. These generated proposals from the recently-created Charity Commission. The local grammar school had a moribund classical side but a reasonably healthy commercial side. They proposed that money from the charity should be used to build up its endowment, thereby enabling the headmaster to be paid a proper salary; fees should be put up all round, although freemen's sons would continue to get preferential treatment; and the staff should be empowered to run boarding houses. This provoked a massive series of protests about alienation of the charity from the deserving poor in Coventry; and, as W. H. Gardner put it at one of a series of public meetings:

> they had no idea of giving and it was not intended to give, what was called a classical education to the children of weavers and watchmakers. What they required was an education which would qualify their sons to become good mechanics and men of business and their daughters good wives and mothers.

The Coventry and Warwickshire MPs were mobilised and the scheme was eventually dropped. In 1860 Chancery finally accepted a much more limited freemen's scheme, for the creation of an industrial school for the orphan daughters of freemen.[61]

iii

These Chancery battles and the activities of the early Charity Commission, which need to be far more fully investigated, allowed the articulation of demand for secondary education in two distinct forms, sometimes competing for the same resources, but apparently considered unable to coexist in the same school. The leading publicists of 'middle-class' education in mid-century perceived alternative patterns of development for secondary schools in much the same terms. Both the Reverend J. L. Brereton and the Reverend Nathaniel Woodard argued, from the 1840s onwards, for a segregation and a stratification according to parents' incomes and aspirations and both founded schools accordingly.[62]

By the 1860s, therefore, the notions of distinct types of demand, to be separately provided for, had become familiar ones. It would have been surprising if the Clarendon and Taunton Commissioners had either failed to take account of them or developed a radically different interpretation. Instead, they crystallized and elaborated them. The burden of their recommen-

dations was the formalization and systematic extension of segregated secondary schools and the ordering of these schools in a hierarchy.
Superficially, this may appear a curious description of the Clarendon Commission's work. For the sheer *domesticity* of their proceedings is striking. Discussions are conducted between equals, almost between intimates. Witness and Commissioner quote Latin at each other, neither requiring a translation. Commissioners inquire minutely after diet, sleeping arrangements, timetable, for all the world like anxious parents choosing a school for their son. But this is the point. They had attended these schools themselves: they would send their sons to them. This is the élite discussing its own education and the education of its successors. It is an elaboration and, at times, a celebration of the ideal-type of a public school education, and as such it will become the standard by which to judge and to which to relate all other types of secondary education.

Their utter certainty about the virtue and pre-eminence of the system so far evolved is plainly shown in the last paragraphs of the general section of their Report:

It remains for us to discharge the pleasantest part of our task, by recapitulating in a few words the advances which these schools have made during the last quarter of a century, and in the second place by noticing briefly the obligations which England owes to them — obligations which, were their defects far greater than they are, would entitle them to be treated with the utmost tenderness and respect. . .

Among the services which they have rendered is undoubtedly to be reckoned the maintenance of classical literature as the staple of English education, a service which far outweighs the error of having clung to these studies too exclusively. A second, and a greater still, is the creation of a system of government and discipline for boys, the excellence of which has been universally recognised, and which is admitted to have been most important in its effects on national character and social life. It is not easy to estimate the degree in which the English people are indebted to these schools for the qualities on which they pique themselves most — for their capacity to govern others and control themselves, their aptitude for combining freedom with order, their public spirit, their vigour and manliness of character, their strong but not slavish respect for public opinion, their love of healthy sports and exercise. These schools have been the chief nurseries of our statesmen; in them and in schools modelled after them, men of all the various classes that make up English society, destined for every profession and career, have been brought up on a footing of social equality, and have contracted the most enduring friendships, and some of the ruling habits, of their lives; and they have had perhaps the largest share in moulding the character of an English gentleman. The system, like other systems, has had

its blots and imperfections; there have been times when it was at once too
lax and too severe — severe in its punishments, but lax in superintendence
and prevention; it has permitted, if not encouraged, some roughness,
tyranny and licence; but these defects have not seriously marred its whole-
some operation, and it appears to have gradually purged itself from them in
a remarkable degree. Its growth, no doubt, is largely due to those very
qualities in our national character which it has itself contributed to form;
but justice bids us add that it is due likewise to the wise munificence which
founded the institutions under whose shelter it has been enabled to take
root, and to the good sense, temper and ability of the men by whom during
successive generations they have been governed.[63]

This comes perilously near arrogance; and makes the relaxed and gentle-
manly tone of the proceedings appear less engaging than ominous, in the
sense that they are conversations between equals blinkered by self-
satisfaction. The sense of the Commissioners' closed-mindedness is reinforced by their discussion of the curriculum and the place of science. Edward
Twistleton's one contribution had been to prepare a list of eminent scientists
— as Clarendon put it, 'all the biggest swells in science'[64] — to be invited to
give evidence on the place science should occupy in the public school.[65] The
most profound and telling criticism of the limitations of the present curriculum dominated by classics came, perhaps inevitably, from Michael Faraday, the man with virtually no formal education. He pinpointed the practical
weakness of the argument that classics provided a *training* for the mind:

Up to this very day there come to me persons of good education, men and
women quite fit for all that you expect from education; they come to me and
they talk to me about things that belong to natural science; about mes-
merism, table-turning, flying through the air, about the laws of gravity;
they come to me to ask me questions, and they insist against me, who think
I know a little of these laws, that I am wrong and they are right, in a manner
which shows how little the ordinary course of education has taught such
minds. Let them study natural things and they will get a very different idea
to that which they have obtained by that education. It happens up to this
day. I do not wonder at those who have not been educated at all, but such as
I refer to say to me, ''I have felt it and done it, and seen it, and though I have
not flown through the air, I believe it.'' Persons who have been fully
educated according to the present system, come with the same proposi-
tions as the untaught, and stronger ones, because they have a stronger
conviction that they are right. They are ignorant of their ignorance at the
end of all that education.[66]

Unfortunately for Faraday, the only member of the Commission who really
took the point — who, indeed, had elicited that answer — was Vaughan. It
forms the core of his dissenting Appendix to the final Report.[67] But here it is

wrapped up in such complexities and subtleties as almost wholly to lose its force. The contrast between these convolutions and the simplicity and vivid clarity of Faraday's statement helps explain why Vaughan drove both Clarendon and Lyttelton to distraction; and perhaps goes some way to explaining why the unanimity of the 'eminent swells' on the deficiencies of public school education left so little mark on the Report. The Commissioners *hoped* the public schools would give more time to science;[68] but this carries far less force than their ringing assertion of the essentially classical nature of a public school education.

Given such arrogant self-satisfaction, it is understandable that the Clarendon Commissioners proposed no root-and-branch reconstruction. The specific changes recommended really amounted to tinkering; and the draft bill which resulted from their Report concerned itself chiefly with the clarification of the position of the headmaster vis-à-vis both staff and governors, the management of certain endowments, and the removal of the last vestiges of local connection and foundation rights from Harrow and Rugby.[69] Harrow already had a commercial school, intended for the sons of local tradesmen. It was proposed to create another like this at Rugby and in both places turn foundation privileges for local boys into scholarships open to general competition.

It is through these last proposals that the system which the Commissioners had glorified can be seen to have its manipulative and exploitative dimensions. For as the inhabitants of Rugby and Harrow hastened to point out, the charities of Lawrence Sheriff and John Lyon were being transformed into national institutions at the expense of the localities in which and for which they had been founded. They rehearsed their grievances before a Select Committee of the House of Lords in 1865, which was considering the draft bill. The proceedings of this Committee are of great importance and need to be read in conjunction with both Clarendon and Taunton Reports. They show precisely what was entailed in making an endowed school a national institution, reminding us that even apparently archetypal public schools had originated as endowed grammar schools. They underline the point that the conflict over the use of endowments for secondary education was a national phenomenon in the first half of the nineteenth century, an obvious consequence of, and important evidence for, the differentiation of demand already mentioned.

The proceedings of the Committee also help to complete the point about the intimate and intricate connection of the Clarendon and Taunton Reports. For the witness their Lordships took most seriously and whose views their conclusions largely reflected, was none other than the Reverend Frederick Temple, headmaster of Rugby. Temple decisively rejected all local claims to special privileges in charities of this kind:

the founding of these schools very much partook of the character of a national movement, every man doing his best to educate his own bit of the country and . . . although his primary object was this general education, yet nobody thought of any way of giving it than by providing a good education just round his own spot.

In the reconstruction of the endowment, 'it appeared to me that the persons I was bound to consider were these:— First, the poorer foundationers and secondly the general public of England.' For those of the foundationers who were truly local, he saw the solution to be 'a first-rate middle school (in which)·. . . the children of the tradesmen might receive an exceedingly good education, first-rate of its kind . . . there might be also not a few of the poorer gentry who would be glad to get such teaching.' For the rest:

Those sojourners who are on the average two thirds of the foundationers I consider to represent the people of England generally . . . In dealing with this matter you have to consider that there is so much money to spend on free education which you cannot increase; and that the question is how best you shall select those who shall be the recipients of it . . . How are we to choose? As it is at present, we are making a sort of blind choice; that is, we give a free education to those who, for one reason or another are able to come and live in Rugby. There may be hundreds of others a great deal more deserving both on account of character and on account of talent, all of whom are not taken into consideration at all.

For this the only solution was entrance scholarships open to national competition. This would be fairer for all children and in particular give proper opportunities to those,

to whom the want of high cultivation is the greatest loss. It is a comparatively slight loss to boys of a low scale of intellect if they do not get a very high kind of education. In fact I can see every now and then that there are boys who get very little benefit except the mere benefit of association with their fellows, from the teaching at the school. Their intellects will not take in any more, and though it is good for them, no doubt, to live among their fellows, I cannot say that the education as far as the books are concerned does really very much for them. But to a boy who has real ability it is the greatest possible loss to be unable to cultivate it; it is to him a real deprivation. Those are the boys, therefore, who have, it seems to me, the first claim — I may say that just as to them it is the greatest loss if they do not get it, so also to them is it the greatest boon if they do get it. They are the boys who afterwards are able to use it to advantage, and as they rise in the world, they find that every step only brings them more and more into the position that is natural to them.[70]

Temple thus combined the stratification of secondary schools by parental occupation and aspirations with a stratification by merit in which the best was represented by the public school; and he offered the possibility of a limited, highly structured mobility through scholarships. This view of the proper pattern of development for secondary education and the guiding principles for the remodelling of endowments formed the core of the Taunton Report, large parts of which, of course he drafted.[71]

As Temple had done in 1865, the Commission considered what interpretation might be offered of founders' intentions; and went on to offer an interesting summary of the process of diversification of demand for secondary education:

> One great service, which till a very late period was rendered to this country by the grammar schools, was that so many boys of more than ordinary capacity found in them, what they could hardly have found elsewhere, the means of rising to eminence in all professions and especially in literature. Our history is full of names of men who have risen by their learning and not a few from comparative obscurity. And in a great majority of cases these men obtained their early education in the first instance from the nearest county grammar school, and sometimes not only their early education but exhibitions to enable them to complete that education at the Universities . . .
>
> This service was, perhaps more certainly than anything else which the grammar school can now do, a main object of the founders. To say that they intended to teach Latin and Greek to no more than the few who now desire to learn it, or to say that they intended to teach something useful to the mass of the population who are now within reach of their schools, is rather to distort than to represent their original purpose. But that they intended boys of more than average ability to find in these schools the means of a first-rate education, which would qualify them afterwards for useful service to the Church and State, can hardly admit of any doubt at all.
>
> The value of the service and the certainty that it was within the meaning of the founders, would be very strong arguments for leaving the grammar schools alone, if they still continued to do what they did even till the beginning of the present century. But this excellent work, which they have done so long, they have at last ceased to do.
>
> The fact is that they could do this work only so long as education was comparatively simple and uniform, and all classes could be educated together. While the upper classes were content with such classical teaching as the nearest grammar school followed by the University could give, and the middle classes, if they did not want so much classics, still were content with the same teaching continued for a shorter period, the schools could be sustained with vigour, and any genius that appeared found a fit soil and a congenial atmosphere for his growth. But education has become varied and complex. The different classes of society, the different occupations of life,

require different teaching. Many who once would have been content with next to no education at all, now, not only require education, but require an education suited to their special needs and will not accept that which was before provided for everybody. The upper classes have found the advantages of large schools and free intercourse between many boys, and will not allow their children to grow up with no school companions but their immediate neighbours, but send them off where they will see a wider range of character and enter at once on a larger world. Many in the middle classes are not content with Latin and Greek when Latin and Greek no longer means association with the sons of the gentry . . .

It is useless to endeavour to restore what is plainly past. It must be confessed — in confessing it we are but recording a plain fact — that it is no longer possible to keep all education in one groove, and by giving precisely the same education to all classes to make it easy for talent in every class to rise to its natural level . . . Everywhere it is acknowledged that the problem of education is no longer simple, but that different solutions will be required in different circumstances. It will be seen that we also propose to accept the distinction that we already find and to classify schools side by side, so that a parent, according to the destination for which he intends his son, may place him from the first in a school of the third grade, or of the second, or of the first. The three grades do not lead one into the other, but stand side by side, starting it may be said from the same point but leading to different ends.

First grade schools, 'generally classical schools' were for those leaving at eighteen. In populous urban areas they might be day schools; elsewhere they would be boarding schools. Second-grade schools were for those leaving at sixteen and third-grade schools for those leaving at fourteen. Considerations of expense would almost certainly ensure that both of these were day schools.

The Commissioners were at some pains to stress that schools of the various grades would perform different but equally valuable functions. But they could not avoid the question of the relationship between the grades; and, indeed, with their paean of praise for the ancient functions of the grammar schools they had raised the question of mobility themselves. As they put it:

We cannot think it well that the old glory of the grammar schools should be entirely lost, and that it should be henceforth impossible for ability to find aids to enable it to achieve distinction. Nor do we think it a necessary consequence of what we have proposed.

The schools of the third grade are not, and are not intended to be, preparatory to schools of the second; nor schools of the second to schools of the first. But provided only there be still maintained some one leading study as a link between the three, we still think it quite possible and even easy to arrange that real ability shall find its proper opening.

They recommended that Latin should be a common study in all three grades; and that endowments should be used to provide exhibitions, so that 'talent, wherever it was would be discovered and cherished and enabled to obtain whatever cultivation it required'.[72] Ultimately they did see their three grades as an hierarchy, with the classical school at the apex.

iv

In considering finally the question of their influence on subsequent policy the Clarendon and Taunton Reports cannot be separated. The tinkerings with endowments recommended by the Clarendon Commission finally reached the statute book in 1868,[73] delayed chiefly by the activities of vested interests and the preoccupations of successive governments with parliamentary reform. The real importance of the Report lay in its elaboration of the 'best' type of secondary education, the topmost rung of the hierarchy of schools, the model for the Taunton first grade schools.

The bulk of the Taunton recommendations were very quickly embodied in a draft bill, no doubt owing something to the fact that W. E. Forster was appointed Vice-President of the Committee of Council on Education in Gladstone's first ministry. But the more ambitious section of the bill, creating a national administrative structure to link all grades of school and provide for their inspection, excited considerable controversy. Forster was eventually driven to sacrifice it as the price for getting through straightaway the first part of the Bill, which provided for the appointment, for three years in the first instance, of special Commissioners with powers to remodel educational endowments.

The first three Endowed Schools Commissioners were Lord Lyttelton, Canon H. G. Robinson, formerly Principal of York Training College, and Arthur Hobhouse, Q.C., who was already a Charity Commissioner. H. J. Roby was appointed their secretary. As might be expected, they took the guidelines of the Taunton Report very seriously, provoking thereby a series of collisions with vested interests, most notably in Gloucester and in London. This led to another Select Committee in 1873, which, in some ways, stands in the same relation to the Taunton Report as the Lords Select Committee of 1865 to the Clarendon Report. Again aggrieved local residents made their voices heard; again we begin to perceive something of the actual costs and effects in individual localities of the remodelling of ancient endowments.

These rows ensured that the Endowed Schools Commission's life would not be prolonged; and by legislation of 1874 rather weaker powers to remodel educational endowments were given to the Charity Commission. A detailed study of their educational work in individual localities has yet to be done and is long over-due. It is the only way to establish with certainty how powerful the Taunton guide-lines remained. It seems likely that while developing demand for secondary education in the later nineteenth century did not altogether fit the Taunton categories, they largely shaped the ways in which the demand was met.

This hypothesis finds some support in the proceedings of yet another Select Committee investigating disputed schemes for schools, this time in 1886. The account the Charity Commissioners gave of their policy is not very different from that given by the Endowed School Commissioners in 1873.[74]

v

Much more important is the evidence represented by the Bryce Report. As has been mentioned, the Bryce Commissioners deliberately chose to conduct their inquiries in the same terms as Taunton; and they found it not incongruous to adopt the same principles of classification of schools.

First grade schools [they declared] are those whose special function is the formation of a learned or a literary, and a professional or cultured class. This class comprehends the so-called learned professions, the ministry, law, medicine, teaching of all kinds and at all stages, literature and the higher sciences, public life, the home and foreign civil service, and such like. This is the class whose school life continues till 18 or 19 and would naturally end in the universities . . .

The Second Grade Schools are those whose special function, although it does not at all exclude an ideal of culture, is the education of men with a view to some form of commercial or industrial life.

The Third Grade Schools are those whose special function is the training of boys and girls for the higher handicrafts or the commerce of the shop and the town.[75]

They noted the apparent weakness of demand in certain areas for second grade schools; and concluded that Taunton had underestimated the drawing power, both social and intellectual, of schools of the first grade. The classical public school appeared to be an influential model for many great urban day schools besides those in London. They also devoted much time and energy to a consideration of the demand for third-grade education which they saw as expressing itself through the progressive extension of the elementary school curriculum and the creation of 'Higher Grade' schools. But at no point did they seriously consider that this could be interpreted as a challenge to the basic horizontal stratification.[76] They continued to think of mobility as something to be provided for by a scholarship system. In discussing the recruitment of their 'cultured class' they commented:

the more highly organised our civilisation becomes, the more imperative grows the need for men so educated and formed, the more generous ought their education to become and the greater the necessity for recruiting their ranks with the best blood and brains from all classes of society. And we conceive one of our functions to save this higher education from becoming the prerogative or preserve of any special order, and to make the way into it, and into all it leads to, more open and accessible to capable and promising minds from every social class.[77] While Temple and the Taunton Commissioners had cast their plea for elitism in terms of the gain to the individual's development, the Bryce Commissioners thus presented theirs in terms of the interests of the state. But apart from this altered emphasis they have no major new programmatic statement to make about secondary education: more of the same kind of thing, with local authority support, is the substance of their Report.

In part this seems to have been because they were so heavily preoccupied with the administrative tangles which had developed over the responsibility for and legality of local authority spending on education other than elementary; and they were under pressure from Acland to report quickly.[78] But in part it is surely also testimony to the continuing power of the ideas elaborated and crystallised in the Clarendon and Taunton Reports. The congruence between these and the pattern of development after 1902 is, yet again, an area for further, more detailed investigation. Although the Bryce Commissioners had worked so hard to construct an administrative compromise, the interaction between the administrative and political dimensions of the situation was such that it took the Conservatives from 1896 to 1902 to carry through legislation to provide systematic central and local government aid for secondary education in general.[79] But the continuing preeminence of the classical curriculum and the stratification of schools with the restricted, structured mobility of a scholarship system are there for all to see in the local authority secondary schools created after 1902.[80]

Bibliography

Secondary education

The best general introduction to the subject remains R.L. Archer, *Secondary Education in the Nineteenth Century* (Cambridge, 1921). A.S. Bishop, *The Rise of a Central Authority for English Education* (Cambridge, 1971), provides a clear and thorough account of changing central administrative and governmental structures; while John Roach, *Public Examinations in England 1850-1900* (Cambridge, 1971), provides a useful account of certain increasingly important structural factors. But there is a marked imbalance in the distribution of more detailed and specific studies. There is a wealth of material on the public schools, a dearth of material on endowed grammar schools, private schools and local authority activity in secondary and technical education.

Many public schools have full admissions registers for all or part of the period. A general framework of information is provided by T.W. Bamford,

The Rise of the Public Schools (London, 1967), and there are a host of studies of individual schools, of which Brian Heeney, *Mission to the Middle Classes: The Woodard Schools 1848-1891* (London, 1969) and David Newsome, *A History of Wellington College 1859-1959* (London, 1959), are the most distinguished examples. David Newsome has also provided a model study of four public-school headmasters, Arnold, Prince Lee, Christopher Wordsworth and E.W. Benson, in *Godliness and Good Learning* (London, 1961). T.W. Bamford, *Thomas Arnold* (London, 1960) attempts a modern critical reassessment. G.R. Parkin, *The Life and Letters of Edward Thring* (London, 1910), although written soon after Thring's death in a glow of devotion, includes major extracts from the diaries and correspondence of one of the few headmasters who challenged prevailing élitist notions. Alicia Percival, *Very Superior Men: some early public school headmasters and their achievements* (London, 1973), is rather heavily anecdotal. Dr Bamford and Miss Percival have also contributed essays on these themes to a recent collection, *The Victorian Public School,* ed. Brian Simon and Ian Bradley (Dublin, 1975).

The image and status of the public school are at least as important as the actual details of its organization. The pioneer studies of this are E.C. Mack, *Public Schools and British Opinion 1780-1860* (London, 1938) and *Public Schools and British Opinion since 1860* (New York, 1941). More recently, there is an article by Patrick Scott, 'School Novels as a Source Material: with a selective bibliography' in *Bulletin of the History of Education Society* v (Spring 1970), pp. 46-56 and an essay by the same author, 'The School and the Novel: *Tom Brown's School Days'* in *The Victorian Public School* ed. Simon and Bradley, pp. 34-57. V.A. McClelland, *English Roman Catholics and Higher Education 1830-1903* (Oxford, 1973), provides some evidence about the power of the image even within the relatively closed world of English Roman Catholicism; while W.A.C. Stewart, *The Educational Innovators Vol. II: Progressive Schools 1881-1967* (London, 1968), offers some evidence for the reaction against public schools at the end of the century.

Of course, as has been pointed out, a large number of public schools had originated as endowed grammar schools. The criteria for the achievement of public school status by an endowed grammar school – or a proprietary or private boarding school – are discussed by J.R. de S. Honey, *The Victorian Public School 1828-1902: the School as a Community* (unpublished Oxford D. Phil. thesis, 1969). Some of Professor Honey's material is now more generally accessible in his essay, 'Tom Brown's Universe' in *The Victorian Public School* ed. Simon and Bradley, pp. 19-33; and it is to be hoped that the book based on his thesis will soon appear. But the material on the endowed grammar schools which remained as such, and the proprietary and private schools of modest aspirations, is thin on the ground. Richard S. Tompson, *Classics or Charity? The Dilemma of the Eighteenth-Century Grammar School* (Manchester, 1971), has important implications for the study of such schools in the early nineteenth century. Some of the grammar schools have admissions registers and anniversary histories. Margaret Bryant has indicated what might be done, even for some of the more ephemeral institutions, in her excellent article, 'Topographical resources: private and secondary education in Middlesex from the sixteenth to the twentieth century' in *Local Studies in the History of Education* ed. T.G. Cook (London: History of Education Society, 1972), pp. 99-135; and there are two complementary local studies, Zena Crook and Brian Simon, 'Private Schools in Leicester and the County 1789-1840' and Brian Simon, 'Local Grammar Schools 1780-1880' in *Education in Leicestershire 1540-1940* ed. Brian Simon (Leicester, 1968), pp. 103-155.

David Wardle has a brief, inadequately documented, survey of provision in Nottingham in *Education and Society in Nineteenth-Century Nottingham* (Cambridge, 1971); and Joyce Godber includes a short account of its educational activities in her account of *The Harpur Trust 1552-1973* (Bedford, 1973). Otherwise, one is left hoping that some of the rich material in F.E. Balls, *The Origins of the Endowed Schools Act 1869 and its operation in England 1869-1895* (unpublished Cambridge Ph.D. thesis, 1964), will find its way into print.

Material on the early local authority activity, that is, higher grade schools and county council subsidization of technical education, is almost equally patchy. E.J. Eaglesham discusses the administrative complication caused by higher grade schools within a rather narrow frame of reference in *From School Board to Local Authority* (London, 1956). But Patrick Keane's careful case-study, 'An English county and education: Somerset 1889-1902' in *English Historical Review* lxxxviii (1973), pp. 286-311, so far stands on its own. There is at last, however, a detailed and fully documented study of the genesis of the 1902 Education Act in J.R. Fairhurst's unpublished Oxford D. Phil. thesis (1974), *Some Aspects of the Relationship between Education, Politics and Religion from 1895 to 1906*. It would be most helpful to have the substance of Dr Fairhurst's work more generally available in print; in the meantime, Olive Banks has dealt with some of the broader aspects of the Act's administrative and ideological context in the early chapters of her *Parity and Prestige in English Secondary Education* (London, 1955).

The very complex question of the relationships of secondary schools of all kinds to career and class structures in the society at large is only just beginning to be explored in very tentative fashion by T.J.H. Bishop and Rupert Wilkinson, *Winchester and the Public School Elite* (London, 1967), David Ward, 'The Public Schools and Industry after 1870' *Journal of Contemporary History* ii (1967), pp. 37-52, F. Musgrove, 'Middle-Class Education and Employment in the Nineteenth Century' *Economic History Review* second series xii (1959), pp. 99-111, Harold Perkin, 'Middle-Class Education A Critical Note' *ibid.* second series xiv (1961-2), pp. 122-30, F. Musgrove, 'Middle-Class Education ...A Rejoinder' *ibid.* second series xiv (1961-2), pp. 320-9, and D.C. Coleman, 'Gentlemen and Players' *ibid.* second series xxvi (1973), pp. 92-116.

Finally, the whole subject of girls' secondary schools in the nineteenth century remains virtually untouched. There are only the two rather superficial studies by Josephine Kamm, *Hope Deferred: Girls' Education in English History* (London, 1965) and *Indicative Past: A Hundred Years of the Girls' Public Day School Trust* (London, 1971).

Footnotes

1   *Report and Minutes of Evidence from the Royal Commission appointed to inquire into the Revenues and Management of certain Schools and Colleges, and the Studies pursued and Instruction given therein*, HC 1864 [3288] XX, XXI; IUP series Educa-

tion: General 9-12 (Clarendon). *Report and Minutes of Evidence from the Royal Commission appointed to inquire into the Education given in Schools not comprised within Her Majesty's two former Commissions* HC 1867-8 [3966 Pts I-XX] XXVII Pts I-XVII, 1867 [3898] XXVI; IUP series Education: General 17-33 (Taunton). *Report and Minutes of Evidence from the Royal Commission appointed to inquire into Secondary Education,* HC 1895 [C. 7862 Pts I-VIII] XLIII-XLIX, 1896 [C. 8077] XLVI; IUP series Education: General 40-46 (Bryce). They are most conveniently referred to by the names of their chairmen.

2 E.C. Mack, *Public Schools and British Opinion 1780-1860* (London, 1938); A.S. Bishop, *The Rise of a Central Authority for English Education* (Cambridge, 1971), ch. 10.

3 F.E. Balls, *The Origins of the Endowed Schools Act 1869 and its operation in England 1869-1895* (unpublished Cambridge Ph.D. thesis 1964), p. 126. I am most grateful to Dr Balls for permission to refer to his thesis.

4 E.C. Mack, *Public Schools and British Opinion since 1860* (New York, 1941), pp. 8-9 *et. seq.*

5 M.E. Grant Duff, *Notes from a Dairy 1852-1873* (London, 1897, 2 vols), I pp. 157-58.

6 *Ibid.* passim. Richard Johnson, 'Administrators in education before 1870: patronage, social position and role' in *Studies in the growth of nineteenth century government,* ed. Gillian Sutherland (London, 1972), pp. 126-29.

7 For Oxford reform see E.G.W. Bill, *University Reform in Nineteenth-Century Oxford: a Study of Henry Halford Vaughan 1811-1885* (Oxford, 1973), chs. 7-11, 13.

8 *Hansard,* third series, clxi, col. 146; clxii cols. 695-96, 983-85, 1545-46; clxiii cols. 546-47.

9 *Matthew Arnold on Education* ed. Gillian Sutherland (Harmondsworth, 1973), pp. 114, 129-30.

10 PRO *Granville Papers* 30/29/24 Pt I Memorandum Lingen to Lord President 6 August 1860. I am grateful to Dr Richard Johnson for drawing my attention to material in these papers relating to secondary education.

11 R.L. Archer, *Secondary Education in the Nineteenth Century* (London, 1921), chs. x,xii and xiii; Brian Simon, *Education and the Labour Movement 1870-1920* (London, 1965), Pt II; G.R. Searle, *The Quest for National Efficiency* (Oxford, 1971). See also the essay by R.M. McLeod below.

12 Patrick Keane, 'An English county and education: Somerset 1889-1902', *English Historical Review* lxxxviii (1973) pp. 286-311.

13 Leslie Wynne Evans, 'The evolution of Welsh educational structure and administration 1881-1921' in *Studies in the Government and Control of Education since 1860* (London, History of Education Society 1970), pp. 43-67.

14 A brief account of the general situation can be found in my pamphlet *Elementary Education in the Nineteenth Century* (London, Historical Association 1971). More detailed accounts, on which this and the two following paragraphs are based, can be found in my *Policy-Making in Elementary Education 1870-1895* (Oxford, 1973) and J.R. Fairhurst, *Some Aspects of the Relationship between Education, Politics and Religion from 1895-1906* (unpublished Oxford D.Phil. thesis 1974) esp. chs III and IV. I am grateful to Dr Fairhurst for permission to refer to his thesis.

15 E.J. Eaglesham, *From School Board to Local Authority* (London, 1956).

16 Sutherland, *Policy-Making in Elementary Education,* ch. 11.

17 Bodleian Library, *Sadler Papers,* Acland to Sadler 1 September 1892; cf. also same to same 8 October 1892.

18 Lynda Grier, *Achievement in Education: the Work of Michael Ernest Sadler 1885-1935* (London, 1952), pp. 29-32; Fairhurst, *Education, Politics and Religion 1895-1906*, pp. 10-11.

19 Bodleian Library, *Bryce Papers* UB 74, Bryce to Acland 1 February 1894; anon. (signature illegible, address King's College, Cambridge) to Bryce 5 March 1894. I am grateful to Dr Roger Davidson for drawing my attention to material on secondary education in these papers.

Biographical data in the paragraphs that follow, for which sources are not indicated, are drawn from the *Dictionary of National Biography, Burke's Peerage, Baronetage and Knightage*, J.A. and J. Venn, *Alumni Cantabrigenses* and J. Foster, *Alumni Oxonienses*.

20 Fairhurst, *Education, Politics and Religion 1895-1906*, p.10.

21 H.A.L. Fisher, *James Bryce* (London, 1927, 2 vols).

22 A. Tropp, *The School Teachers* (London, 1957).

23 Ethel Sidgwick, *Mrs Henry Sidgwick: A Memoir* (London, 1938).

24 John Bailey ed., *The Diary of Lady Frederick Cavendish* (London, 1927, 2 vols).

25 Caroline Jebb, *Life and Letters of Sir Richard Claverhouse Jebb* (Cambridge, 1907), esp. pp. 288-309, 313-34, chs. xvi-xvii.

26 Bill, *University Reform in Nineteenth-Century Oxford*.

27 *Letters to the Hon. Mrs. Edward Twistleton 1852-1862* (London, 1928), pp. 237, 302-3 and x-xi; PRO *Granville Papers* 30/29/18/12 no. 9 Lyttleton to Granville 25 August 1864.

28 *Ibid.*

29 *Gladstone Papers*, B.M. Add. MSS 44238-44240; Peter Stansky, 'Lyttelton and Thring', *Victorian Studies* v (March 1962), pp. 205-23.

30 Andrew Lang, *Life, Letters and Diaries of Stafford Northcote, First Earl of Iddesleigh* (London, 1890, 2 vols); Robert Blake, *The Conservative Party from Peel to Churchill* (London, 1970), pp. 134-5.

31 Sir Herbert Maxwell, *The Life and Letters of George William Frederick, Fourth Earl of Clarendon* (London, 1913, 2 vols).

32 *Ibid.* II pp. 294-5, Clarendon to Granville 12 August 1864.

33 PRO *Granville Papers* 30/29/18/12 no. 9 Lyttleton to Granville 25 August 1864. Parts of this letter are quoted in Lord Edmond Fitzmaurice, *The Life of Granville George Leveson Gower, Second Earl Granville K.G. 1815-1891* (London, 1905, 2 vols) I, pp. 433-5.

34 W.R.W. Stephens, *Life and Letters of W.F. Hook* (London, 1878, 2 vols); G. Kitson Clark, *Churchmen and the Condition of England 1832-1885* (London, 1973).

35 A.H.D. Acland, *Sir Thomas Dyke Acland: A Memoir with Letters* (London, privately printed, 1902); John Roach, *Public Examinations in England 1850-1900* (Cambridge, 1971), chs. 2-4.

36 T. Wemyss Reid, *Life of the Rt. Hon. W.E. Forster* (London, 1888, 2 vols). Forster had in fact been automatically, although entirely amicably, expelled from the Society of Friends on his marriage to the daughter of an Anglican clergyman – Dr Arnold of Rugby; and by the mid-1860s he and his wife were regular attenders at F.D. Maurice's Vere St. Chapel (*ibid.* i, pp. 265-66 and 347). But as Bruce put it to Granville in September 1864:

having originally been a Quaker & being a manufacturer, he would be an acceptable representative of Dissenting & middle class interests – He had no classical education – & greatly laments it – & I think he understands the wants & wishes of the more intelligent & aspiring portions of the Mid. Classes.

(PRO *Granville Papers* 30/29/19/4 no.48 Bruce to Granville 17 September 1864.

37 E.G. Sandford ed., *Memoirs of Archbishop Temple by Seven Friends* (London, 1906, 2 vols.).

38 Above, p. 100.

39 The voluminous correspondence about the creation of the Commission, including comments about the representative status of various members is to be found in the *Granville Papers,* 30/29/18/12, nos. 10*, 13, 35, 36, 37, 38, 39, 40, 42, 45, 47, 48, 49, 51, 52, 54, 56, 57, 58, 62, 63, 67; 30/29/19/4 nos. 41* and 42; 30/29/19/25 pp. 135, 139, 143, 147, 151, 155, 159, 163, 167. Items marked * were missing in September 1973. I am grateful to Dr Richard Johnson for summaries of their contents.

40 *Ibid.* 30/29/19/4 no. 35 Bruce to Granville 6 August 1864.

41 *Ibid.* 30/29/19/4 no. 42 Temple to Granville 15 August 1864; 30/29/19/4 no. 4 Lingen to Granville 11 August 1864.

42 *Ibid.* 30/29/19/4 no. 44 Bruce to Granville 15 August 1864. Granville's attitude can be inferred from the responses to his letters of invitation to serve on the Commission – many refer to 'middle-class education', apparently repeating him – e.g. 30/29/19/25 p. 143 Hook to Granville 19 November 1864.

43 *Ibid.* 30/29/19/4 no. 68 Temple to Granville – it is simply dated '1864' but content and location suggest the end of November.

44 *Ibid.* 30/29/18/12 no. 11 Emily Davies to Lyttelton 8 October 1864.

45 Melvin Richter, *The Politics of Conscience: T.H. Green and his Age* (London, 1964).

46 Sutherland, *Policy-Making in Elementary Education,* pp. 60, 78.

47 A brilliant demonstration of what can be done even for the period before the local press becomes a substantial source and without much in the way if individual school archives is provided by Margaret Bryant, 'Topographical resources: private and secondary education in Middlesex from the sixteenth to the twentieth century' in *Local Studies in the History of Education* ed. T. G. Cook (London, History of Education Society, 1972), pp. 99-135.

48 D.C. Coleman, 'Gentlemen and Players', *Economic History Review* second series xxvi (1973), pp. 92-116.

49 *Report and Minutes of Evidence of the Select Committee on the Public Schools Bill,* pp. 113-15, qq. 584-612, HL 1865 (481) X, 387-89.

50 T.W. Bamford, 'Public School Town in the Nineteenth Century', *British Journal of Educational Studies* vi (1957-8), pp. 25-36; cf. also Joyce Godber, *The Harpur Trust 1552-1973* (Bedford, 1973), pp. 65-67.

51 T.W. Bamford, *The Rise of the Public Schools* (London, 1967), chs. 1 and 2; J.R. de S. Honey, *The Victorian Public School 1828-1902: the School as a Community* (unpublished Oxford D. Phil. thesis 1969) ch. 1. I am grateful to Professor Honey for permission to consult his thesis. Cf. also W.E. Gladstone, *Autobiographica,* ed. John Brooke and Mary Sorensen (London, 1971), p. 26.

52 Bamford, *The Rise of the Public Schools,* chs. 1 and 2; Richard S. Tompson, *Classics or Charity? The Dilemma of the Eighteenth-Century Grammar School* (Manchester, 1971), pp. 90-91.

53 Godber, *The Harpur Trust,* pp. 58-61.

54 Harold Perkin, 'Middle-Class Education and Employment in the Nineteenth Century: A Critical Note', *Economic History Review* second series xiv (1961-2), pp. 122-30, p. 130. But see also F. Musgrove, 'Middle-Class Education and Employment in the Nineteenth Century', *ibid.* second series xii (1959), pp. 99-111 and 'Middle-Class Education ...A Rejoinder', *ibid.* second series xiv (1961-2), pp. 320-29.

55   Tompson, *Classics or Charity*, pp. 52-56, 59-60, 92, 96-97.

56   Michael Sanderson, 'Literacy and Social Mobility in the Industrial Revolution in England', *Past and Present* 56 (1972), pp. 75-104.

57   Tompson, *Classics or Charity*, p. 119.

58   Balls, *The Origins of the Endowed Schools Act*, pp. 36-43. For *cy près* in the context of the law of charity in general, see G.H. Jones, *History of the Law of Charity 1532-1827* (Cambridge, 1969).

59   Balls, *The Origins of the Endowed Schools Act*, pp. 7-22.

60   *Ibid.* pp. 68-100; Godber, *The Harpur Trust*, pp. 40-47.

61   Peter Searby, *Weavers and Freemen in Coventry 1820-1861: social and political traditionalism in an early Victorian town* (unpublished Warwick Ph.D. thesis 1972), pp. 401-12. I am grateful to Dr Searby for permission to consult and quote from his thesis.

62   Brian Heeney, *Mission to the Middle Classes: The Woodard Schools 1848-1891* (London, 1969); Roach, *Public Examinations in England*, ch. 2; Kitson Clark, *Churchmen and the Condition of England*, ch. 4; Honey, *The Victorian Public School*, ch. 2.

63   *Clarendon Report*, p. 56, HC 1864 [3288] XX, 68; IUP series Education: General 9, p. 56.

64   Maxwell, *Clarendon*, II pp. 269-70.

65   PRO *Granville Papers* 30/29/18/12 no. 9 Lyttelton to Granville 25 August 1864.

66   *Clarendon Minutes of Evidence*, p. 381, q. 75, HC 1864 [3288] XXI, 917; IUP series Education: General 12, p. 381.

67   *Clarendon Report*, pp. 331-37, HC 1864 [3288] XX, 341-47; IUP series Education: Genneral 9, pp. 331-37.

68   *Ibid.* pp. 32-3, HC 1864 [3288] XX, 42-3; IUP series Education: General 9, pp. 32-33. On the frustration of these hopes, see A.J. Meadows and W.H. Brock, 'Topics Fit for Gentlemen: The Problem of Science in the Public School Curriculum' in *The Victorian Public School* ed. Brian Simon and Ian Bradley (Dublin, 1975), esp. pp. 110-14.

69   *Bill to make further Provision for the Good Government and Extension of Public Schools*, (no. 32) HL 1865 V, 181-93.

70   *Report of the Select Committee on the Public Schools Bill*, p. 155, q. 990, pp. 140-44, qq. 861-64, HL 1865 (481) X, 429, 414-18. For the bill as amended by the Select Committee, see HL 1865 V, 194-205 (no. 202).

71   Sandford, ed., *Memoirs of Archbishop Temple*, I pp. 135-37.

72   *Taunton Report*, pp. 92-96, HC 1867-68 [3966] XXVII, 106-10; IUP series Education: General 17, pp. 92-96.

73   31 and 32 Vict. c. 118.

74   Endowed Schools Act 1869, 32 and 33 Vict. c. 56; *Report and Minutes of Evidence of the Select Committee on the Endowed Schools Act (1869)*, HC 1873 (254) VIII; Endowed Schools Act 1874, 37 and 38 Vict. c. 87; *Report and Minutes of Evidence of the Select Committee on the Endowed Schools Acts*, HC 1886 (191) IX, HC 1887 (120) IX; Bishop, *The Rise of a Central Authority*, chs. 11 and 12; Balls, *The Origins of the Endowed Schools Act*, chs. 4-7. In his discussion of the major and most controversial cases, as seen from the centre, Dr Balls has provided indispensable guidelines for anyone wishing to explore remodelling at the local level.

75   *Bryce Report*, pp. 138, 140, 143, HC 1895 [C. 7862] XLIII; IUP series Education: General 40, pp. 138, 140, 143.

76   *Ibid.* pp. 52-5, 61-3, 66-70, HC 1895 [C. 7862] XLIII; IUP series Education: General 40, pp. 52-5, 61-3, 66-70.

77 *Ibid*. p. 138, HC 1895 [C. 7862] XLIII; IUP series Education: General 40, p. 138.
78 Fairhurst, *Education, Politics and Religion 1895-1906,* p. 10.
79 *Ibid. passim.*
80 Olive Banks, *Parity and Prestige in English Secondary Education* (London, 1955), esp. chs. 1-8.

THE DOCUMENTS

SECONDARY EDUCATION

Education: General Volume 9

REPORT FROM THE ROYAL COMMISSION APPOINTED TO INQUIRE INTO
THE REVENUES AND MANAGEMENT OF CERTAIN SCHOOLS AND
COLLEGES, AND THE STUDIES PURSUED AND INSTRUCTION GIVEN
THEREIN. 1864

360 pp

As early as 1810–30 there was widespread criticism of Britain's
system of upper-class schools, mainly from the newly-rich middle
classes. The increasing desire of the middle classes for education
after the 1832 Reform Act made the shortcomings of the public
schools more frustrating. Apart from the work of Thomas Arnold
at Rugby, there were few efforts at reform until the Royal Commission inquiry of 1864. The commission included the Earl of
Clarendon as chairman, Lords Devon and Lyttelton, Sir Stafford
Northcote and H. H. Vaughan. Initial proposals to conduct an
examination to ascertain the attainments of public school pupils
were turned down by most of the school authorities and the commissioners had to rely for their information on questionnaires and
oral evidence. The report examined the finances and the administration of the schools, their methods of teaching and the subject matter taught. It recommended reform of the administrative
structures, especially of the ancient statutes which were attached
to the foundation endowments. Friction between staff and governing bodies was condemned and Arnold's system of staff meetings
was suggested as a model. Curricular changes suggested reflected
the still aristocratic views of the time—the classical framework
should be retained and within it the course of study should be
broadened and deepened. The report is valuable for an understanding of the effects of British conservatism on her educational
policies.

Original reference
1864   [3288] XX   Revenues and management of certain schools and
colleges, R. Com. Vol. I, Rep.

Education: General Volume 10

APPENDIX TO THE REPORT OF THE ROYAL COMMISSION ON THE PUBLIC SCHOOLS, 1864

616 pp

The appendix contains the replies to a circular questionnaire sent to the public schools tö elicit information on the property and revenue of the schools, administerial and managerial structures and procedures, the system and course of study, student numbers and other statistical data. In addition, the replies have much information on the history of the schools and on the old deeds and ordinances which governed them.

Included in the appendix are letters from members of the universities of Oxford and Cambridge on the proficiency of the public schools, the general structure of education, the merits and demerits of classical and modern subjects and on proposals for reform. A breakdown of students going from the public schools to the universities is given together with a record of their achievements. Further evidence on the efficiency of the schools is provided from the results of examinations for army commissions.

Of special interest is a letter from W. E. Gladstone, the famous statesman, requesting the commission to speak out critically on the public schools but on the other hand to recognize that European civilization was based on the union of christianity with Greek and Roman humanism. This and other letters emphasize the value of 'liberal education'.

Original reference

1864   [3288] XX   Revenues and management of certain schools and colleges, appendix, R. Com. Vol. II, Rep.

Education: General Volume 11

MINUTES OF EVIDENCE PART I TAKEN BY THE ROYAL COMMISSION ON THE PUBLIC SCHOOLS, 1864

544 pp

Part I of the oral evidence was taken from members of the boards of governors, headmasters, teachers and pupils of Eton, Winchester and Westminster schools. It gave further information on the finances and administration of the schools and clarified a number of points about the endowments and statutes. In addition, the evidence presents an excellent picture of daily life in the schools, describing the students life hour by hour and giving information on such matters as food, heating, punishments and drinking among the students (the latter was by this time under control). The commissioners were especially interested in relations between paying pupils and foundation pupils and in the system of 'fagging' (i.e. younger students acting as servants for older ones). The evidence also treats in detail the school curricula and the teaching methods. Most of the witnesses were defensive and conservative. Aristocratic tendencies and traditional values pervaded their evidence and there was little eagerness for modernization despite the obvious needs.

Original reference

1864   [3288] XXI   Revenues and management of certain schools and colleges, mins. of ev. Part I, Eton, Winchester, Westminster schools, R. Com. Vol. III, Rep.

Education: General Volume 12

MINUTES OF EVIDENCE PART II TAKEN BY THE ROYAL COMMISSION ON THE PUBLIC SCHOOLS, 1864

448 pp

Part II of the evidence covers the remainder of the public schools (see original references below) and also has an analysis of the evidence for each school and an index to all the evidence. Members of the school authorities and their legal representatives were cross-examined with respect to the written information submitted on school property and income. Evidence from provosts, fellows, headmasters, teachers and students gave a vivid account of all aspects of the schools; management, discipline, study, student pastimes, social consciousness, etc. The emphasis on modern subjects varied from school to school and within the same school often changed with change of headmaster. The character of the instruction was also influenced by the social background of the pupils.

A good deal of the evidence is concerned with the distribution of endowment monies. The founders of the schools had intended them to be used for the education of needy scholars but in many cases other practices had been adopted. The commissioners felt that in most of the schools both the financial and managerial structures were outmoded. They recognized that its history and traditions were important to a school but questioned the validity

of allowing adherance to 'sacred' systems and practices to interfere with efficiency. Of the schools examined, Rugby alone met
with their general approval and this because of the powerful
influence exercised on it by Thomas Arnold. Not all of the witnesses were happy with the state of affairs in the public schools.
Those connected with the universities and in particular Henry
Acland, *ex regis* Professor of Medicine at Oxford, were conscious
of the need for higher standards and for more emphasis on science
and other modern subjects.

Original reference
1864   [3288] XXI   Revenues and management of certain schools and
                        colleges, mins. of ev. Part II, Charterhouse, St.
                        Paul's, Merchant Taylors, Harrow, Rugby and
                        Shrewsbury schools, R. Com. Vol. IV, Rep.,
                        index.

Education: General Volume 13

FIRST REPORT FROM THE ROYAL COMMISSION APPOINTED TO INQUIRE
INTO SCHOOLS IN SCOTLAND WITH MINUTES OF EVIDENCE,
APPENDICES, 1865–1867

568 pp

Education in Scotland did not suffer from the same degree of
class distinction as in England nor did it have the same clear-cut
divisions between elementary and secondary levels. Furthermore,
it had adapted itself with greater facility to the demands of an
industrialized society. However, by 1864 the system was considered to be in need of reorganization. As well, there was strong
opposition in Scotland to the 'revised code' introduced in 1862
as a result of the Newcastle Commission inquiry (IUP volumes
Education : General 3–8). Consequently, a commission was appointed, under the chairmanship of the Duke of Argyle, to examine
all levels of Scottish education and to ascertain whether 'a plan
of national character' would be more suitable than the existing
parochial system and grant scheme.

With their first report, the commissioners submitted the evidence
taken up to March 1865 and an appendix which gives extensive
information on the educational operations of the Church of
Scotland, educational facilities in the North Western Highlands,
the number of teachers trained at institutions in Glasgow and
Edinburgh, financially-aided schools in Scotland and the overall
standard and result of Scottish education. The oral evidence
describes the general school system, covering endowed and un-

endowed schools. One of its major themes was the effectiveness of the denominational school system. Witnesses in general expressed dissatisfaction with the famous 'revised code' which made payment of parliamentary grants dependent on the efficiency of the schools. The code was expected to 'reduce Scottish education to the rudiments' and to create social distinctions between those who could pay for education and those who could not. The grant system, even as it was, was considered to be militating against poorer areas. Also included in this volume is an appendix to the first report which was not submitted until 1867. The appendix is made up mainly of replies from university professors, clergymen and others to a list of questions on the main features of Scottish education. The replies indicated a preference for a national rather than parochial education system, provided the state undertook to sponsor religious instruction.

Original references

| 1865 | [3483] XVII | Schools in Scotland, R. Com. Rep., mins. of ev., appendix. |
| 1867 | [3858] XXV | Schools in Scotland, appendix to R. Com., 1st Rep. |

Education: General Volume 14

SECOND REPORT FROM THE ROYAL COMMISSION APPOINTED TO INQUIRE INTO SCHOOLS IN SCOTLAND, TOGETHER WITH REPORTS OF ASSISTANT COMMISSIONERS, 1867

984 pp   2 maps   12 illustrations

This volume has an eight-chapter report on Scottish elementary education together with a statistical survey of the lowland country districts and assistant commissioners' reports on education in Glasgow, rural Scotland and the Hebrides. The main report was a thorough study of the elementary school system, it examined the facilities and requirements of each region and of the country in a scientific and sympathetic way. There was considerable variation in the standard of education from place to place. The average ratio between the number of students and the total population was satisfactory but in some parishes it was as low as 1 in 20. In areas of the lowlands 35 per cent of the children were not provided with school places. These facts indicated that the poorer sections of the population were worst provided for and least interested in education. In the Highlands, education was hampered by the remoteness and ruggedness of the country and the grant system had done little to improve matters. The commission reviewed the defects of the parochial system and the likely effects of the 'revised code' on Scottish elementary education. In their recommendations they attempted to suggest a parliamentary policy which, while retaining the advantages of the traditional system, would remove its defects. They proposed the judicious introduction of a national scheme incorporating all existing voluntary schools and avoiding sectarian character where possible. They further suggested that a Board of Education be set up in conjunction with the Education Department to supervise the organization of the national system and to see that sufficient school buildings and teachers were provided.

The assistant commissioners' reports are valuable sources of information on every aspect of Scottish education at the time. They provided the analysis of the systems in different socio-economic regions on which the main reports were based.

Original references

1867	[3845] XXV	Schools in Scotland, elementary schools, R. Com. 2nd Rep., appendix.
	[3845–I]	Schools in Scotland, lowland country districts, Col. Maxwell, A. C. Sellar, Rep.
	[3845–II]	Schools in Scotland, Glasgow, J. Greig, T. Harvey, Rep.
	[3845–III]	Schools in Scotland, country districts, Col. Maxwell, A. C. Sellar, Rep.
	[3845–IV]	Schools in Scotland, Hebrides, A. Nicholson, Rep.

Education: General Volume 15

STATISTICS ON SCOTTISH SCHOOLS TOGETHER WITH A REPORT ON THE COMMON SCHOOL SYSTEM IN THE UNITED STATES AND CANADA, 1867

736 pp   14 plans and illustrations

The statistics were collected by the registrars of births and deaths on the instructions of the commission. The country was divided into counties and parishes and all schools in each parish were enumerated together with their type, number of teachers and pupils, denominations, physical condition, etc. There is a comment on the total school accommodation of each parish.

Rev. James Fraser's report on the common school system of the United States and Canada was submitted to both the Argyle and Taunton Commissions (see IUP volumes Education : General 17–

32). Rev. Fraser was, among other things, required to examine the legislative approach to education in the United States and Canada especially with respect to compulsory attendance, the financing of education, the relations between central and local government in controlling education, the external and internal organization of the schools, the part played by the churches in education and the teaching of religion. His report is not only a source of extensive information; it is an interesting attempt to compare Britain's culture with that of her colonial offshoots. Fraser doubted, for example, if American taste was founded on the best models; 'they would' he reported 'consider Milton better than Shakespeare, Johnson better than Addison.' He found this cultural bluntness and lack of suppleness in other areas also— Americans did not appreciate the softer virtues of womanhood as did the British. On the other hand he credited the Americans with great energy and willingness to provide education and to embibe knowledge, which he felt, if directed with more insight and perspicacity could be very valuable. He recommended that several elements of the organization of education in the United States and Canada could be copied with profit in Britain.

Original references
1867   [3845–V] XXVI Schools in Scotland, statistics.
          [3857]   Schools in Scotland, common school system in
                         U.S. and Canada, J. Fraser, Rep.

Education: General Volume 16

THIRD REPORT FROM THE ROYAL COMMISSION APPOINTED TO INQUIRE INTO SCHOOLS IN SCOTLAND WITH AN APPENDIX, TOGETHER WITH GENERAL AND SPECIAL REPORTS OF ASSISTANT COMMISSIONERS, 1867–68

736 pp

The third report of the commission and the assistant commissioners' reports deal with middle-class schools (these were for people 'between' the labouring classes and the wealthy professional and commercial classes). The schools were of three types: Burgh schools (managed by the town councils); academies and institutions (founded by subscription) and private schools. They catered for pupils up to 16 years of age. The reports described the history, organization, finances, management, curricula, etc. of each type of school and commented on the efficiency of middle-class education. They made a number of recommendations of lesser importance but were generally satisfied that Scottish middle-class education was more extensive and more modern than most. The ratio between those receiving post elementary education and those not was much higher in Scotland than in England and elsewhere. This was particularly attributable to the insistence by the Knox religious reformers that every child should have the opportunity of university education. The commissioners urged that this equality of opportunity be allowed to continue. Their most important recommendations dealt with the establishment of an efficient examination system and with the physical condition of the schools.

Original references

1867–68 [4011] XXIX	Schools in Scotland, Burgh and middle-class schools, R. Com. 3rd Rep., Vol. I, assistant commissioner's general and special reps.
[4011–I]	Schools in Scotland, R. Com., 3rd Rep., Vol. II, assistant commissioner's special reps.

Education: General Volume 17

REPORT FROM THE ROYAL COMMISSION ON EDUCATION FOR THE MIDDLE CLASSES, 1867–68

880 pp

The Taunton Commission's inquiry into British middle-class education took four years to complete and was among the most extensive ever carried out for parliament (IUP volumes Education: General 17–32). The 650-page report proper was a study in depth of British secondary education (excluding the public schools). The commissioners sought to create an educational structure adequate to the requirements of the middle classes at a time when they had won new power and influence in the country. However, the commissioners did not consider education merely as an external structure, but attempted as well to look beneath the system for the cultural principles which enlivened it and made it specifically British. The report examined and made extensive recommendations on the organization and financing of middle-class education, the system of schools, their administration, teaching methods and courses of study. The more important proposals were that central and local authorities should be established to organize and direct education, that there should be three types of secondary schools, distinguishable by the school leaving age of their pupils, that the application of endowment funds should be coordinated and that school curricula should be reformed and modernized. Historians believe that had parliament implemented these proposals, they would have revolutionized British education. Today, we must be grateful for the exhaustive tomes of information on British schools provided by the Taunton Commission.

Original reference
1867–68 [3966] XXVIII   Schools inquiry; schools not comprised within the
             Pt. I   two recent commissions on popular education,
                      and on public schools, R. Com. Vol. I Rep.

Education: General Volume 18

REPLIES TO QUESTIONNAIRES AND CIRCULAR LETTERS, TOGETHER WITH MISCELLANEOUS LETTERS ADDRESSED TO THE ROYAL COMMISSION ON EDUCATION FOR THE MIDDLE CLASSES, 1867–68

872 pp   1 map

The two papers contain letters to ˙the commissioners on many aspects of education and replies to extensive questionnaires from trustees and headmasters of endowed schools. Among the people represented in the former are John Stuart Mill, Cannop Thirlwall, John H. Newmann and Anne G. Clough. Mill's letter condemns gratuitous education and comments on the system of 'payment by results'; Miss Clough argues the case for the education of women. This volume also has a report, presented to the British Association for the Advancement of Science, which examined the educational value of natural science and proposed that the utilization, of sense experience, inductive and deductive reasoning, and of memory, required in the study of science render it a particularly suitable form of liberal education. An appendix gives a survey of the extent to which science was being taught in schools. The replies to questionnaires came from Christ's Hospital, St. Olive's and St. John's School Southwark, Dulwich College, Birmingham Free Grammar School, Manchester School, Bedford Schools and Monmouth School. They give a comprehensive account of each school but deal particularly with the history of the endowment, the income, expenditure and social character of the school and the curriculum. Documentary evidence (balance sheets, etc.) were appended to many of the replies.

Original references
1867–68 [3966–1]   Schools inquiry; schools not comprised within the
     XXVIII Pt. II   two recent commissions on popular education,
                       and on public schools; miscellaneous papers; R.
                       Com. Vol. II, Rep.

1867–68 [3966–II]   Schools inquiry; schools not comprised within the
XXVIII   two recent commissions on popular education,
                           and on public schools; answers to questions; R.
                           Com. Vol. III, Rep.

Education: General Volume 19

MINUTES OF EVIDENCE PART I TAKEN BEFORE THE ROYAL COMMISSION
ON EDUCATION FOR THE MIDDLE CLASSES, 1867–68

888 pp

Part I of the oral evidence was taken mainly from academics working in education at either university or pre-university level. The
witnesses were asked to state their opinions on the quality of
middle-class schooling and to suggest the areas in which improvement or reform was necessary. Many of them felt that the education
provided was lacking in depth and inadequate as a preparation for
university. A lack of understanding between governors and administrators and overall poor organization are apparent in much of the
evidence of the individual schools. Proposals put forward by the
witnesses are very piecemeal, as if looking from within it, they
mistook the system's flaws for the major faults in its structure. A
case for keeping education independent of the political power is
made by some witnesses; it is suggested that education should not
be financed from public funds and that if a central system of examinations was contemplated it should be controlled by the universities rather than by the state. Remarkably enough, in view of this,
it was a politician, Sir John Pakington, who submitted the most
incisive critique of the system and the only comprehensive scheme
for its reform.

Views on the education of women were expressed throughout the
evidence, most of them admitting the need for improvement but
only in so far as improvement would prepare girls to be good
wives and mothers.

Original reference
1867–68 [3966–III]   Schools inquiry; schools not comprised within the
XXVIII Pt. III   two recent commissions on popular education,
                           and on public schools; mins. of ev. Part I, R.
                           Com. Vol. IV, Rep.

Education: General Volume 20

MINUTES OF EVIDENCE PART II TAKEN BEFORE THE ROYAL COMMIS-
SION ON EDUCATION FOR THE MIDDLE CLASSES, 1867–68

1,056 pp

Part II of the oral evidence comprises the views of clergymen, headmasters, teachers, etc., and of several deputations representing organizations with a special interest in the work of the commission. Among the latter were the College of Preceptors and the Scholastic Registration Association whose members were seeking a registration scheme for the teaching profession similar to the 1858 Medical Registration Act. These organizations argued that the absence of a recognized system of professional training for teachers was a barrier to any successful reform in education. This principle was accepted by witnesses generally, but because of sectional interests within the profession the registration question was fraught with difficulties.

Witnesses described in detail the schools to which they were attached and used their experience in support of the schemes for reorganization which they put forward. The dominant ideas in these schemes were the modernization of education to include languages, mathematics and science and the creation of a system flexible enough to provide students with the best education compatible with their school leaving age. The function of examinations in education was another widely discussed point and a memorandum on the effects of the civil service examinations was submitted by the secretary of the civil service commission on examinations.

In the report of the Taunton Commission, inefficiency in both managing and financing grammar schools was to be criticized. Evidence given here in connection with a dispute over the running of Birmingham Grammar School throws light on these criticisms.

Original reference
1867–68 [3966–IV]   Schools inquiry; schools not comprised within the
XXVIII Pt. IV   two recent commissions on popular education,
and on public schools; mins of ev. Part II, R.
Com. Vol. V, Rep.

Education: General Volume 21

REPORTS FROM ASSISTANT COMMISSIONERS APPOINTED BY THE ROYAL COMMISSION ON EDUCATION FOR THE MIDDLE CLASSES TO EXAMINE THE SYSTEMS OF EDUCATION IN SCOTLAND AND ON THE CONTINENT OF EUROPE, 1867–68

536 pp

The long tradition of Scottish education and its reputation made it worthy of consideration as a model for that of England. D. R. Fearon's report described the structure of the Scottish system, its cost, the standard of instruction, the condition of the schools and the overall effectiveness of the education provided. In comparing it with English education he pointed out that the Scottish system had adapted itself to the requirements of the people and had thereby made education popular. Mr. Fearon recommended that English educationalists, like their Scottish counterparts, should consider the public taste as it was, as a first step towards making it what it should be. The appendix to this report has information on Aberdeen Grammar School, Ayr Academy and Edinburgh and Glasgow High Schools.

In his report Matthew Arnold gave a lively and broadly based account of education in France, Germany, Italy and Switzerland. Arnold saw education as a living organism of tissue and interpenetrating parts rather than as a rigid mechanical instrument for packaging knowledge. Consequently, his report dealt with culture and cultural roots as well as with the externals of educational organization. Nevertheless, his most vehement criticisms of Britain were for her easy going, lackadaisical ways and outmoded standards of civil organization. Arnold was most impressed by German education because it had succeeded in assimilating industrial pragmatism while retaining cultural integrity. This volume also has a communication on secondary education in the Netherlands written by Baron D. Mackay.

Original reference

| 1867–68 [3966–V] | Schools inquiry; schools not comprised within the |
| XXVIII Pt. V | two recent commissions on popular education, and on public schools; education, Scotland, foreign countries; M. Arnold and D. Fearon, Reps.; R. Com. Vol. VI, Rep. |

Education: General Volume 22

GENERAL REPORTS OF ASSISTANT COMMISSIONERS ON EDUCATION FOR THE MIDDLE CLASSES IN THE SOUTHERN COUNTIES OF ENGLAND, 1867–68

680 pp   1 map

In their instructions to the assistant commissioners who were to examine middle-class education in representative districts, the Royal Commission required a detailed and exhaustive study of education in each district. They defined 'the middle classes' as gentry, clergy, professional and commercial men of limited means, and farmers and tradesmen. The investigations were to be primarily concerned with providing information. The core of each report consists of this information which covers number and quality of schools, cost, sources of income, religious restrictions, nature and method of institution, etc. Public, private and proprietary schools are dealt with and sections of each report are devoted to facilities for the education of women. The reports are not, however, merely factual, they are interspersed with conclusions, comments and recommendations. The two main reports in this paper dealt with the London metropolitan area and with some rural counties and the extra Metropolitan parts of counties around London. There was a sharp contrast between the problems manifested in the two areas. In the rural communities education was not very popular; it tended to interfere with the agrarian way of life which was conservative and self-sufficient. In London on the other hand, industrialization had brought widespread social change. It had become fashionable to live out of town and the middle classes could not afford to send their children by train to the day schools. In both the metropolitan and rural districts the assistant commissioners reported that a complete overhaul of education was urgently required. Many of the necessary reforms were specified. The assistant commissioners were C. H. Stanton, H. A. Giffard, D. R. Fearon and C. I. Elton.

Original reference
1867–68 [3966–VI] XXVIII Pt. VI   Schools inquiry; schools not comprised within the two recent commissions on popular education, and on public schools; southern counties, general Rep.; R. Com. Vol. VII, Rep.

Education: General Volume 23

GENERAL REPORTS FROM ASSISTANT COMMISSIONERS ON EDUCATION FOR THE MIDDLE CLASSES IN NORTHUMBERLAND AND IN THE MIDLAND COUNTIES, 1867–68

744 pp   1 chart

These reports are similar to those in volume 22. They deal with the counties of Northumberland, Norfolk, Flint, Denbigh, Montgomery, Stafford, Warwick, Glamorgan and Hereford. The condition of education in each county was examined in terms of the social and industrial character of the area. Statistical tables delineating educational facilities and giving exhaustive details on finance, administration, curricula and teaching methods are included. The lowly condition of the grammar schools is a feature of the reports. In his report on Stafford and Warwick, T. H. Green attributed this to the poor physical condition of the schools, the outmoded classical character of the education and the general abstension of the professional

classes from using the grammar schools. The same assistant commissioner made a clear distinction between liberal and commercial
education and suggested that modern languages should be offered
as a 'sop to commercial minded parents'. H. M. Bompas in his
report suggested that the upper middle classes were capable of providing their own education and that consequently the educational
endowments should be reserved for the lower middle class. Mr.
Bompas agreed with several other assistant commissioners in
recommending professional training for teachers and a system
of examinations for secondary schools. All the reports deal extensively with the education of women and criticize the intellectual
shallowness of girls' schooling. However, though the assistant
commissioners realized that social and moral training were over-
exaggerated in girls' schools, they were not so lucid in their positive
thinking on education for women.

Original reference
1867–68 [3966–VII]   Schools inquiry; schools not comprised within the
        XXVIII Pt. VII two recent commissions on popular education,
                        and on public schools; midland counties, North-
                        umberland, General Rep.; R. Com. Vol. VIII,
                        Rep.

Education: General Volume 24

REPORTS FROM ASSISTANT COMMISSIONERS ON EDUCATION FOR THE
MIDDLE CLASSES IN THE NORTHERN COUNTIES, 1867–68

856 pp   1 map

The main reports in this volume deal with the two great industrial
areas of the north, Lancashire and the West Riding of Yorkshire.
These were the areas which had posed the greatest difficulties for
parliamentary inquiries, both from the point of view of getting a
comprehensive picture of the facts and of making satisfactory
recommendations. In the present reports the picture is filled in in
great detail. The information covers endowed private proprietary
schools including special denominational schools, mechanics institutes, etc. In both areas there was a great deal of indifference
to education; the parents were commercially minded, the schools
were clinging to the classics and, as a result, education was perish-
ing. Even in Lancashire, where education was commercial it was
bad as such. In Yorkshire the major problem was a preponderance
of small and poorly-equipped grammar schools. J. G. Fitch, the
assistant commissioner, made a series of recommendations which
were reiterated in the report of the commission. The use of endow-

ments should be rationalized; small schools should be amalgamated or demoted to a lower status; there should be three categories of schools according to the ages at which students were to leave. Mr. Fitch further recommended teacher training, and inspection and examination of schools. The assistant commissioner for Lancashire was J. Bryce. He attacked the *laissez faire* system and blamed it for the overall lack of organization. One of his recommendations was that district boards should be set up to organize education. Mr. Bryce felt that commercial education was severely deficient. Both Fitch and Bryce were to figure prominently in deliberations on education in subsequent years.

Original reference
1867–68 [3966–VIII]   Schools inquiry; schools not comprised within the
XXVIII Pt. VIII two recent commissions on popular education,
              and on public schools; northern counties; general
              rep., R. Com. Vol. IX, Rep.

Education : General Volumes 25 to 32

IUP volumes 25 to 32 comprise the eleven original volumes of special reports and digests of information on schools in England and Wales submitted by the Taunton Commission. Each original volume is prefaced by a summary of information (tabular and textual) for the area dealt with. A tabular summary is also appended to the report for each county. The reports are divided into three sections:

(a) Endowed secondary or grammar schools: a special report by an assistant commissioner together with a digest of all information received for each school.

(b) Non-classical endowed schools: these were usually elementary schools and a digest of the information available on each one was provided.

(c) Boys' and girls' proprietary schools: a digest of the information available on these was given also.

The special reports and digests of information cover all essential features of the school (e.g. size, character, government, finance, curriculum, etc.). The special reports were the result of personal examination by the assistant commissioners; the digests of information on the other hand were abstracted from the replies to questionnaires and from reports of the charity commissioners, etc. This system provided an internal check on the accuracy of information. The accuracy was further checked by sending copies of the digests of information to the schools for correction. In the special reports the assistant commissioners isolated the main faults in each school and suggested remedies for them. The most frequent faults mentioned are outmoded endowment regulations and school statistics, lack of interest on the part of trustees or governors and overlapping and lack of co-ordination between schools. The special reports and digests are a valuable source of information for local historians.

Education: General Volume 25

SPECIAL REPORTS FROM ASSISTANT COMMISSIONERS AND DIGESTS OF INFORMATION ON SCHOOLS FOR THE MIDDLE CLASSES IN THE LONDON DIVISION AND SOUTH-EASTERN COUNTIES, 1867–68

848 pp

These reports and digests cover London, Berkshire, Hampshire, Kent, Surrey and Sussex. London and parts of Surrey and Sussex are also dealt with in a general report (see IUP volume Education: General 22). A notable feature of the special reports is the number of schools which were in extremely poor physical condition. Many of the reports give results of examinations carried out in the schools. Assistant commissioner D. R. Fearon wrote the reports for London and for Berkshire.

Original references

1867–68 [3966–IX] XXVIII Pt. IX	Schools inquiry; schools not comprised within the two recent commissions on popular education, and on public schools; special rep. London Division; R. Com. Vol. X, Rep.
[3966–X]	Schools inquiry; schools not comprised within the two recent commissions on popular education, and on public schools; special rep. south-eastern counties; R. Com. Vol. XI, Rep.

Education: General Volume 26

SPECIAL REPORTS AND DIGESTS OF INFORMATION ON SCHOOLS FOR THE MIDDLE CLASSES IN SOUTH-MIDLAND COUNTIES, 1867–68

576 pp

The counties dealt with here are Bedfordshire, Buckinghamshire,

Cambridgeshire, Hertfordshire, Huntingdonshire, Northampton, Oxfordshire and the extra metropolitan part of Middlesex. Among those who wrote the special reports were D. R. Fearon and T. H. Green. The information furnished (as in the other special reports, etc.) is very detailed and comprehensive and should be of special interest to local archives and school libraries. The history of the school and of the endowment, distinctions gained by scholars, professions of parents, the course of instruction are a random selection of topics dealt with. The tabular digests at the end of the reports for each county allow the scholar to review at a glance the number, nature and proficiency of the schools in the county.

Original reference

1867–68 [3966–XI]   Schools inquiry; schools not comprised within the
      XXVIII Pt. X   two recent commissions on popular education,
              and on public schools; special rep., south mid-
              land ˙counties, R. Com. Vol. XII, Rep.

Education: General Volume 27

SPECIAL REPORTS AND DIGESTS OF INFORMATION ON SCHOOLS FOR THE MIDDLE CLASSES IN EASTERN AND SOUTH-EASTERN COUNTIES, 1867–68

1,032 pp

This volume covers Essex, Suffolk, Norfolk, Wiltshire, Dorsetshire, Somerset, Devon and Cornwall. The state of education in Norfolk, Devon and Somerset is also discussed in general reports (IUP volumes Education : General 22 and 23). The reports from the south-western counties are especially interesting in that they represent the state of education in a district relatively untroubled by the great industrial changes. A decaying status quo maintained by its own inertia is the picture emerging from the reports; an education system based on snobbery, class distinction and jealous conservatism and clad in much moss and gowns of silk.

Original references

1867–68 [3966–XII]   Schools inquiry; schools not comprised within the
      XXVIII Pt. XI   two recent commissions on popular education,
              and on public schools; special rep., eastern
              counties, R. Com. Vol. XIII, Rep.

      [3966–XIII]   Schools inquiry; schools not comprised within the
              two recent commissions on popular education,
              and on public schools; special rep. south-western
              counties, R. Com. Vol. XIV, Rep.

Education: General Volume 28

SPECIAL REPORTS AND DIGESTS OF INFORMATION ON SCHOOLS FOR
THE MIDDLE CLASSES IN THE WEST-MIDLAND COUNTIES, 1867–68

880 pp

These reports are on the schools in Gloucestershire, Herefordshire,
Shropshire, Worcestershire, Staffordshire and Warwickshire.
Among the assistant commissioners for the district were T. H.
Green and G. Bryce (the chairman of the Bryce Commission). The
usual variety in size, condition and efficiency of schools is outlined in the reports. Many examples of outmoded statutes and
regulations are instanced, e.g. regulations for Pate's Free Grammar
School, Cheltenham, during contagious disease in the town. Mis-
management, disorganization and meaningless expenditure were
features of many schools. On the other hand those schools which
made efforts to improve faced many problems, e.g. ratepayers protested, or upper middle class withdrew. The reports include lists of
trustees and other data of interest to local and family historians.

Original reference
1867–68 [3966–XIV]   Schools inquiry; schools not comprised within the
XXVIII Pt. XII two recent commissions on popular education,
and on public schools; special rep. west-midland
counties, R. Com. Vol. XV, Rep.

Education: General Volume 29

SPECIAL REPORTS AND DIGESTS OF INFORMATION ON SCHOOLS FOR
THE MIDDLE CLASSES IN THE NORTH-MIDLAND COUNTIES, 1867–68

616 pp

The north-midland counties include Leicestershire, Rutland, Lincolnshire, Nottinghamshire, Derbyshire. Further information on
Derbyshire will be found in a summary minute submitted by R. S.
Wright (IUP volume Education : General 23). These special
reports have frequent references to disagreements between trustees
and headmasters over the running of schools. The overall impression from the reports is that the commissioners felt the educational
facilities to be far from satisfactory. The need for a more commer-
cially-orientated system is especially stressed.

Original reference
1867–68 [3966–XV]   Schools inquiry; schools not comprised within the
XXVIII Pt. XIII two recent commissions on popular education,
and on public schools; special rep. north-midland
counties, R. Com. Vol. XVI, Rep.

Education: General Volume 30

SPECIAL REPORTS AND DIGESTS OF INFORMATION ON SCHOOLS FOR
THE MIDDLE CLASSES IN THE NORTH-WESTERN COUNTIES, 1867–68

648 pp

This volume has the special reports and digests for schools in
Cheshire and Lancashire. Lancashire was also the subject of a
general report by G. Bryce (see IUP volume Education : General
24) and both of these volumes (24 and 30) are excellent raw
material for sociological research on the great industrial cities of
northern England and at the same time provide inbuilt sources of
contrast and comparison with the rural hinterlands. Many of the
proprietary schools examined were run by Roman Catholic orders;
best known of these is Stoneyhurst Jesuit College.

Original reference
1867–68 [3966–XVI]   Schools inquiry; schools not comprised within the
      XXVIII Pt. XIV two recent commissions of popular education,
                      and on public schools; special rep., north-western
                      counties, R. Com. Vol. XVII, Rep.

Education: General Volume 31

SPECIAL REPORTS AND DIGESTS OF INFORMATION ON SCHOOLS FOR
THE MIDDLE CLASSES IN YORKSHIRE, 1867–68

720 pp

These Yorkshire special reports were compiled by J. G. Fitch who
had submitted the general report on the West Riding of York (IUP
volume Education : General 24). For the purposes of presentation
the county is divided into North Riding, City of York, East Riding
and West Riding. The introductory summary provides some interesting statistics on the distribution of school endowment moneys
among the county's two million odd population. The county had
four towns of over 100,000 people, and 103 grammar schools with a
gross annual income of about £25,000. Among the towns examined
were several important centres of the woollen and iron and steel
industries.

Original reference
1867–68 [3966–XVII]   Schools inquiry; schools not comprised within the
      XXVIII Pt. XV   two recent commissions on popular education,
                       and on public schools; special rep., Yorkshire,
                       R. Com. Vol. XVIII, Rep.

Education: General Volume 32

SPECIAL REPORTS AND DIGESTS OF INFORMATION ON SCHOOLS FOR
THE MIDDLE CLASSES IN THE NORTHERN COUNTIES AND IN WALES,
1867–68

824 pp

This volume deals with Wales—Monmouthshire and the counties
of Northumberland, Durham, Cumberland and Westmorland.
General reports on Northumberland, Denbighshire, Flintshire,
Montgomeryshire and Glamorganshire will be found in IUP volume
Education: General 23. G. Bryce, J. G. Fitch and C. E. Elton
were among the assistant commissioners who compiled the reports.
The volume is particularly important for students of Welsh education because it provides extensive information, in a compact form,
that is not as readily available elsewhere. In many ways Wales was
the centre of the movement for an educational system free from
Anglican dominance; radicalism monopolized her commons representation and cultural independence was still a burning issue.

Original references

1867–68 [3966–XVIII] XXVIII Pt. XVI	Schools inquiry; schools not comprised within the two recent commissions on popular education, and on public schools; special rep., northern counties, R. Com. Vol. XIX, Rep.
[3966–XIX]	Schools inquiry; schools not comprised within the two recent commissions on popular education, and on public schools; special rep., Monmouth-shire and Wales, R. Com. Vol. XX, Rep.

Education: General Volume 33

TABULAR STATEMENT OF INFORMATION ON ENDOWED GRAMMAR AND
OTHER SECONDARY SCHOOLS IN ENGLAND AND WALES, TOGETHER
WITH A REPORT ON TECHNICAL EDUCATION, 1867–68

752 pp

These abstracts provide a concise summary of information collected on schools for the middle classes throughout the two countries. The major part of the information relates to endowed schools
both classical (i.e. grammar schools) and non-classical (the Welsh
circulating schools are included in this section) and to secondary
schools for girls. The tables give the income and expenditure of each
school, the number of pupils, the state of buildings, the courses

of instruction, etc. In addition there is a digest of the replies from the colleges at Oxford and Cambridge giving details of scholarships for the various schools and districts. The volume also gives a comprehensive account of Hume's and Betton's charities, two important endowments.

Original references

1867–68 [3966–XX]   Schools inquiry; schools not comprised within the
         XXVIII Pt. XVII   two recent commissions on popular education, and on public schools; R. Com. Vol. XXI, Rep., tables.
1867   [3898] XXVI   Schools inquiry; technical education, Rep.

Education: General Volume 34

FIRST REPORT FROM THE ROYAL COMMISSION APPOINTED TO INQUIRE INTO THE WORKING OF THE ELEMENTARY EDUCATION ACTS WITH MINUTES OF EVIDENCE AND APPENDIX, 1886

560 pp

Despite controversy and opposition, William Edward Forster's Elementary Education Bill became law in 1870. Further Acts in 1876 and 1880 achieved minor improvements in Forster's scheme. During this period the number of elementary schools increased rapidly as did the cost of maintaining them. In 1886 a commission under the chairmanship of Richard Assheton Cross was set up to inquire into the general state of elementary education and especially to review the operation of the recent legislation. The commission's first report contains oral evidence taken from Patrick Cumin, secretary of the Education Department, school inspectors including Matthew Arnold, principals of training colleges and several educational associations which represented denominational interests. The interrogation of witnesses followed a pre-arranged scheme designed to elicit information and opinion on the educational state of the population, the growth of educational legislation, the efficiency of the existing system, the denominational question and so on. Mr. Cumin gave a detailed account of the finances and administration of the system and commented on the constitution of the education department (returns and other data relating to his evidence are included in the appendices). Many witnesses raised questions of grievances and discrimination inherent in the system—non-conformists still held that public money should not be used to support denominational teaching.

Original reference
1886   [C. 4863] XXV Elementary Education Acts (England and Wales),
                        R. Com. 1st Rep., mins. of ev., appendices.

Education: General Volume 35

SECOND REPORT OF THE ROYAL COMMISSION APPOINTED TO INQUIRE
INTO THE WORKING OF THE ELEMENTARY ACTS WITH MINUTES OF
EVIDENCE AND APPENDICES, 1887

1,120 pp

The commissioners submitted evidence taken from over seventy
witnesses in 1887. The witnesses represented a lower level of educational administration than those of the first report: headmasters,
clergymen, chairman of school boards, etc. A notable exception was
J. G. Fitch, chief inspector of schools. The evidence followed the
scheme adopted in the previous report but highlighted many new
questions such as the pupil-teacher system, the half-time system, the
effectiveness of the conscience clause, the value of scientific and
technical instruction in junior schools and the desirable age for
termination of schooling. Witnesses were asked for their opinions
on the total educational result of the present system and this provided an opportunity for the expression of some interesting views.
'Payment by results' was generally condemned while conflicting
criticisms of the pupil-teacher and half-time systems were advanced.
Suggestions included the selection of inspectors from elementary
teachers and the introduction of pension schemes for teachers.

Original reference
                        R. Com. 2nd Rep., mins. of ev., appendices.
1887   [C. 5056]XXIX Elementary Education Acts (England and Wales),

Education: General Volume 36

THIRD REPORT OF THE ROYAL COMMISSION APPOINTED TO INQUIRE
INTO THE WORKING OF THE ELEMENTARY EDUCATION ACTS WITH
MINUTES OF EVIDENCE AND APPENDICES, 1887

776 pp

The third report contains further oral evidence together with appendices of returns giving extensive information on the population
density and school attendance density, the illiteracy rate, and the
employment of children.
The evidence was taken from witnesses ranging from the secretary

(Patrick Cumin) and former secretary (Ralph Lingen) of the Education Department to a representative of the working class. Many of the witnesses represented non-conformist and Roman Catholic schools; others were deputed by their organizations to raise specific points, e.g. the employment of children in the theatre. University professors, headmasters and school inspectors complemented and clarified points of evidence taken earlier.

Among the issues discussed by witnesses were the quality of teacher training, social distinction between board and voluntary schools, compulsory attendance and technical instruction. The details of school expenditure (cost of upkeep, teaching materials, etc.) and also the difficulties of teaching religion in mixed schools were examined. A number of witnesses testified that Mundella's code (1880) had improved the operation of the grant scheme.

Original reference
1887   [C. 5158] XXX Elementary Education Acts (England and Wales),
                R. Com. 3rd Rep., mins. of ev., appendices.

Education: General Volume 40

GENERAL REPORT OF THE ROYAL COMMISSION ON SECONDARY EDUCATION, 1895

488 pp

Despite the failure to implement the recommendations of the Taunton Commission (IUP volumes Education: General 17–33) for establishing a co-ordinated system of secondary education, there were several important developments in the field between 1868 and 1895, notably, the reorganization of grammar school endowments and the Technical Instruction Act of 1889. By 1895 the time was more than ripe for another re-appraisal of the situation. The Bryce Commission was appointed for this task; it was required to 'consider the best method of establishing a well ordered system of secondary education' and was to take into account all the existing sources. The general report reviewed the history of secondary education, examined the existing structures, analysed the evidence and suggestions and made extensive and detailed recommendations. One of the first comments of the report was to regret that the proposals of the Taunton Commission had not been more thoroughly acted on. As a consequence, an authority to harmonize many agencies which had control of secondary education was still the major requirement. For this purpose the commission proposed

local and one central educational authorities, their first priority to
be the provision of enough schools by organizing and making
efficient use of all existing schools, public, private and otherwise.
Secondary education should be provided in the literary, scientific
and technical fields; there should be easier access to post-primary
and higher levels of education; there was a deficiency of thorough
systematic training for secondary teachers and last but by no means
least much teaching in England had little educational value because
it failed to train the mind. These were the judgements of the Bryce
Commission on a century's educational endeavour. In the text of
the report they were documented, expanded, explained and in places
blurred a little. Nevertheless, they remained substantially true and
provided an efficient spur for ensuing legislation.

Original reference
1895   [C. 7862] XLIII Secondary education, R. Com. Vol. I, General
              Rep.

Education: General Volume 41

MINUTES OF EVIDENCE TAKEN BEFORE THE ROYAL COMMISSION ON
SECONDARY EDUCATION WITH A SUPPLEMENT, 1895–1896

624 pp

The evidence was taken from charity commissioners, the secretaries
and other officials of the Education and Science and Art Departments, the chief inspector, representatives of local educational
authorities and proprietary educational companies, representatives
of the College of Perceptors (an organization to promote a registration scheme for teachers), principals of training colleges, and
headmasters and headmistresses. Many of these witnesses, because
of their experience in administering educational organization at
different levels, were able to give valuable critiques of the system,
and even more valuable proposals on the functions, constitutions and structures of the authorities which were to emerge as a
result of the inquiry. In this respect particular attention was paid
to the constitution and working of the two educational departments. Witnesses did not mince their words in condemning the
existing state of affairs; Douglas Richmond who had been an
assistant commissioner in the Taunton inquiry referred to the
'chaos of secondary education'. A section of the evidence deals
with technical instruction and with the work of the technical
education board. This was important because the powers given to

local authorities by the Technical Instruction Acts were precursors
of the local educational authorities recommended by the commission. Another notable feature of the evidence is the important
points on the 'skill of teaching' made by a lady witness who
was principal of a teachers' training college (the commission also
included some lady members). The teaching profession is more
extensively dealt with in evidence representing the views of the
College of Perceptors. This evidence gives a good account, as
well, of conditions in private schools. The appendix has tabular
and other information corroborating the evidence and the supplement deals further with the views of the College of Perceptors
on teacher registration.

Original references
1895   [C. 7862–I]   Secondary education, R. Com. Vol. II, Rep.
               XLIV mins. of ev.
1896   [C. 8077]   Secondary education, R. Com. Vol. II, Rep.,
               XLVI supplement.

Education: General Volume 42

MINUTES OF EVIDENCE TAKEN BEFORE THE ROYAL COMMISSION ON
SECONDARY EDUCATION, 1895

576 pp

The second volume of evidence was taken from representatives
of headmasters' and teachers' associations and the Association of
School Boards; J. G. Fitch formerly inspector of training colleges;
D. R. Fearon (both these men were assistant commissioners for the
Taunton inquiry); further officials of the science and art, and
education departments; a former vice-president of the committee
of the Privy Council for Education and others. The evidence
covers many of the topics mentioned for the previous volume, but
the commissioners were keen to sound reaction to the proposals
for reform. The Headmasters' Association, for example, was
strongly in favour of a central authority; a department head from
Harrow on the other hand was not aware of the same disorder in
education as were his middle-class counterparts—he gave an
account of public school views on the work of the commission
and among other things doubted the wisdom of segregating scientific
and literary subjects. On a similar theme another witness suggested that secondary and technical education should not be
rigorously divided. The National Union of Teachers emphasized
the professional aspect of teacher training and, as a corollary, the

desirability of having training colleges adaptable to training all categories of teachers. A good deal of the evidence examines the successes and failures of the school boards in administering education.

Original reference
1895   [C. 7862–II]   Secondary education, R. Com. Vol. III, Rep.,
                          XLV mins. of ev.

Education: General Volume 43

MINUTES OF EVIDENCE TAKEN BEFORE THE ROYAL COMMISSION ON SECONDARY EDUCATION, 1895

584 pp

Many of the witnesses represented here were similar in background to those in the last volume (principals of training colleges, headmasters, etc.). In addition the volume has evidence from representatives of the Municipal Corporations Association, technical instruction committees in various parts of the country, school boards, the Lancashire Trades Council and the universities. Among the topics on which there is copious evidence are teacher training and registration, the position of private schools in the proposed reorganization schemes, examination systems and co-education. The practical aspect of teacher training is again emphasized; there is a good deal of information on the finances of teacher training colleges, and the appendices have statistics on teachers' salaries. Witnesses from Scotland give a comparative account of their secondary education system, dealing particularly with the Burgh schools and the Scottish Leaving Certificate. The provision of secondary education for the working classes is discussed by a number of witnesses and in this connection an interesting point made was that scholarships should be given not on attainment but on capacity for attainment.

Original reference
1895   [C. 7862–III]   Secondary education, R. Com. Vol. IV, Rep.,
                           XLVI mins. of ev.

Education: General Volume 44

MEMORANDA AND ANSWERS TO QUESTIONS SUBMITTED TO THE ROYAL COMMISSION ON SECONDARY EDUCATION, 1895

664 pp

Some of the memoranda were the result of detailed study on subsections of the inquiry. Topics studied include teachers' remuneration, the registration question, teacher training, the age of entrance to university and the advantages of organizing elementary and secondary education on the same basis. The last mentioned was especially important because it involved the 'municipalization' of secondary education and the consequent division of control and financial responsibility between central and local authorities. One memorandum gives an account of teacher training and registration in Germany.

An important section of the volume consists of answers from Oxford, Cambridge and other universities to a questionnaire. The main questions concerned the efficiency of the scholarship system, the effects of the university examination system (e.g. the 'locals') on secondary education, the correlation of secondary and university education and the part which could be played by the universities in teacher training. Further papers in the volume were submitted by sectional interests of various kinds to voice their opinions, and another series of replies to questionnaires came from Canada, Australia, New Zealand, the United States and several European countries and provided information on many aspects of their educational systems—recent reforms, overall effects of the system, the relationships between technical and general education, and between primary and secondary education, teacher training, co-education and other matters.

Original reference
1895   [C. 7862–IV]   Secondary education, R. Com. Vol. V, Rep.,
              XLVII   memos. and answers to questions.

Education: General Volume 45

REPORTS FROM ASSISTANT COMMISSIONERS APPOINTED BY THE ROYAL COMMISSION ON SECONDARY EDUCATION WITH APPENDICES, 1895

872 pp

The assistant commissioners were required to examine educational organization at local level in selected areas at home and to compile reports on secondary education in the United States and Canada. These investigations were to augment the information already obtained in the replies to questionnaires (see volume 44). They were particularly concerned with: overlap of educational facilities (between higher elementary schools, university secondary schools, grammar schools, technical schools, etc.); the extent of facilities provided by private and proprietary schools; the effects of science and art department grants; major deficiencies in the supply of education; the causes of the decline and inefficiency of endowed schools. Lady assistant commissioners were instructed to report especially on defects in girls' schools and reforms undertaken since the Taunton Report; differences between boys' and girls' education, and between education for girls from the industrial classes and from other classes; the preparation of girls for careers and several other matters relating to women's education. The possibilities of providing co-education and a single educational system for all classes were important considerations behind some of these queries. Some of the more important points made in the reports were that women should have more opportunity for university education, improved methods and appliances should be used for teaching science and that internal school organization was defective. The reports from America and Canada describe the general principles and character of the systems there, the co-ordination of local and central authorities, the classification of schools, training of teachers etc. Appendices to all the reports contain much ancilliary information, the most interesting of which are a statistical breakdown of pupils' occupations after leaving schools and descriptions of the methods (including demonstration experiments) used in science teaching.

Original references

1895   [C. 7862–V]   Secondary education, R. Com. Vol. VI, Rep.,
                 XLVIII   assistant commissioner's reps., Bedford, Devon,
                               Lancaster (hundreds of Selford and West Derby)
                               and Norfolk.
            [C. 7862-VI]   Secondary education, R. Com. Vol. VII, Rep.,
                               assistant commissioner's reps. Surrey, Warwick,
                               York, United States, Canada.

Education: General Volume 46

APPENDIX WITH SUMMARY AND INDEX OF EVIDENCE OF THE ROYAL COMMISSION ON SECONDARY EDUCATION, 1895

664 pp

The appendices comprise (a) information on school endowments from the records of the charity commissioners, (b) information on endowed and proprietary secondary schools in selected areas covering dates of foundation, details of constitution of governing bodies, population and character of catchment areas, condition of site and buildings, facilities (laboratories, etc.) available, total accommodation, curricula timetables and examinations, qualifications of teachers, religious instruction, etc., (c) a breakdown of where university undergraduates were educated, and (d) a breakdown of pupils attending secondary schools in London. The index covers all the evidence taken by the commission and the summary gives a complete list of witnesses and their main contributions.

Original references
1895   [C. 7862–VII] Secondary education, R. Com. Vol. VIII, Rep.,
        XLIX index.
        [C. 7862–VIII] Secondary education, R. Com. Vol. IX, Rep.,
        appendix.

EDUCATION:

SCIENTIFIC AND TECHNICAL

Roy M. MacLeod

Commentary

Introduction

The history of scientific and technical education in Britain can be seen in at least three different levels, which in context coalesce. It is, first, the history of sustained social pressure, generated by the ideas of a few small groups of 'reformers' who could combine a sense of patriotism and a zealous belief in technological progress, and who were both sufficiently knowledgeable to discern a "public problem" and politically capable of pressing for parliamentary action; and, second, a study in the problematics of institutional change, in which new administrative apparatus could be conceived, first to prompt and then to satisfy the educational demands of self-defining managerial and middle-class interests. Third, it is a study in the development of educational objectives in an industrial society, the goals of which were changing in response to varying perceptions of economic needs and political necessities.

However much they may be divided on questions of emphasis, historians of social administration, of education and of economic change, will invariably confront three central premises: first, that there came into currency between the 1830s and the 1850s a widely held assumption that national strength, which had been traditionally defined in terms of military and naval strength, and which by extension depended materially on industry, commerce and trade, now depended no less on a deliberate cultivation of the nation's educational and scientific talent; that this in turn relied upon a diffusion of the means of acquiring scientific and technical education throughout society; and third, that this diffusion, made possible through the efforts of 'reformers', revealed considerable differences in objectives, and prompted repeated attempts to redefine the concepts of 'scientific' and 'technical' education to fit the changing intellectual and industrial circumstances of the country. These factors were, together, decisive in fashioning the attitudes and assumptions upon which government policies would rest. The three reports in this series, reprinted by the Irish University Press, are important benchmarks in this development; as such, they are central to the historian's understanding of the process by which externally derived social and economic concepts have been conceived and introduced into the educational assumptions of modern Britain.

The history of scientific and technical education in this country of course considerably pre-dates the developments with which the reports in this series are concerned, and the interested student may find the bibliography given below merely a convenient point of departure. But in a sense one may be excused for beginning a discussion of this series with the Great Exhibition of 1851,[1] an event of considerable intrinsic importance, which ushered in a period of intense and unprecedented activity in eduction and a vigorous review of Government policy towards science and industry.

Perhaps more than any other single event in Victoria's long reign, the success of the Great Exhibition represented the triumph of British industry and commerce, founded upon the principles of Liberalism and Free Trade, dedicated to the progress of art and industry through the encouragement of technical change. To contemporaries, the Exhibition appeared to vindicate the virtues of peaceful competition, enshrined in material accomplishment and industrial leadership. As J B Bury wrote, it provided 'a public recognition of the material progress of the age and the growing power of man over the physical world'.[2] In conceiving and directing the Exhibition, a Committee of men of supreme importance to the cause of education, including Henry Cole[3] and Lyon Playfair,[4] had, through the leadership of the Prince Consort[5] and the Society of Arts,[6] forged a new public interest in the progress wrought by technology, and a new faith in the inevitability of stability and prosperity through a cultivated combination of hard work and sound knowledge. Within the first few years following the Exhibition, reverberations of its educational lessons were felt throughout the kingdom. 'People's Colleges' opened; essays on industrial and technical education were commissioned; and proposals for converting Mechanics' Institutes into technical colleges were heard across the industrial midlands, from Nottingham to Manchester.

For some, however, the Exhibition was not a source of unalloyed optimism. No sooner had the Great Exhibition closed than the Royal Society of Arts, at Albert's request, took steps to organise a series of lectures on the results of the Exhibition.[7] In perspective, Britain's achievements would be measured, not only by its lion's share of the prizes, but by its ability to seize the commercial opportunities displayed by the Exhibition. There were twelve lectures in the series, led by William Whewell;[8] of the twelve, eight stressed the three compelling features upon which would depend Britain's future prosperity – the provision of scientific and technical education at the secondary level in all public and private schools; the introduction of systematic scientific education in the universities; and government provision for scientific research, both 'pure' and 'applied'. The second of these objectives was already within sight, owing in part to a series of Government enquiries into the ancient universities, and in part to reforms already underway. The first and third objectives were, however, less easily realised, and it is chiefly they that form the starting point of the volumes in this series.

The era inaugurated by the Great Exhibition was heralded by the Queen's Speech from the Throne in November 1852, in which Parliament was told that

The advancement of the Fine Arts and Practical Science will be recognised by you as worthy of the attention of a great and enlightened nation. I have directed that a comprehensive scheme should be laid before you, having in view the promotion of these objects . . . .[9]

Following the efforts of Lyon Playfair and Henry Cole, a scheme emerged by which a new 'Science Division' was added to the Department of Art already existing within the Board of Trade. Within two years a new Department of Science and Art emerged, to which were transferred the Government School of Mines, and later, the Royal College of Chemistry.[10] The School of Mines was meant to provide for the metropolis a school of applied science of the highest class; while, for the country at large, it would serve as a focus for the education of a new force of scientific teachers who would diffuse scientific knowledge through the 'industrial classes'. At the same time, the Department was given the task of helping to establish Science Schools and classes, to regulate payments by results and to grant teacher's certificates.[11] The first Science Minute of the Department was issued in 1859; by 1860, nine 'science schools' were in operation, and 500 students were under instruction.

Throughout the 1860's, these classes made, however, a limited impression on science education, and did not in any case affect technical education at all. This had remained the province of the Society of Arts, which conducted a set of examinations which were still influential in many cities. But by the 1860's, the Society of Arts examinations declined, and the Mechanics' Institutes attracted fewer and fewer artisans.[12] There was widespread disagreement concerning the proper place of technical education and vocational training, coupled with a general assumption that technical training, insofar as this meant practical workshop techniques, was a private, commercial issue, and not a public responsibility. Indeed, the general absence of agreement on a satisfactory definition of 'technical education' seriously retarded a unified approach to the problem.

In the meantime, however, the importance of scientific and technical education was given fresh prominence in the national self-criticism following Britain's performance at the International Exhibition of 1862 in Paris. In the Great Exhibition of 1851, Britain had been at a distinct advantage. Not only was she displaying on home ground her best manufactures, but, having escaped the ravages of 1848 which had upturned much of Europe, she was enjoying a political stability which, however fragile it might seem to contemporaries, had put British industry in a formidably competitive position. In 1862, international circumstances remained favourable. While Britain was at peace, Italy was suffering the agonies of national unification, and Austria was locked in a struggle for national survival. France was anxiously attempting to speed her rate of industrialization, while Prussia was preoccupied with her struggle against Denmark.

Despite her advantages, however, Britain's performance in 1862 was notably less impressive than in 1851. The Society of Arts, ever watchful of the national 'image', issued a special report which expressed the pious hope that at least the Paris Exhibition demonstrated the good sense of Free Trade. But this defence could not long mask the truth. By 1867, when the next Exhibition was held, again in Paris, it was impossible to ignore the considerable improvements in the competitive position of France and particularly of Germany. There was no question that Britain's industrial leadership was severely challenged. Those appointed to investigate looked round again for reasons. Given the political context of *laissez-faire* and Free Trade, Government aid to industry was never a possibility. What did present itself, as within the realm of the 'possible', was the prospect of national self-improvement through technical education.

Beginning in 1861, a series of Royal Commissions had been launched to investigate the organization and content of British education.[13] The Newcastle Commission in 1861 had considered the state of 'popular' education, and three years later, the Clarendon Commission reported on the condition of the nine leading 'public schools'. In 1864, Lord Taunton was appointed to consider the education provided in schools which had thus far escaped parliamentary scrutiny, including the endowed schools, private schools and proprietary schools. It was in 1867, while the Taunton Commission (the 'Schools Enquiry Commission')[14] was sitting, that Lyon Playfair, then serving as a juror at the Paris Exhibition, wrote to Taunton, informing him of Britain's performance and drawing from that experience the view that 'England had shown little inventiveness and had made little progress in the peaceful arts of industry since 1862'[15]. Playfair urged Taunton, and through him, Lord Granville, Vice-President of the Council for Education, to institute an immediate enquiry into the country's need for technical education. This would necessarily include a survey of foreign attempts to generate technical skills and apply them to industry.

The Taunton Commission obligingly sent copies of Playfair's letter in the form of a circular to sixteen 'experts' in industrial manufacture, most of whom had sat as jurors to the 1867 Exhibition, asking their views. While most disagreed that the nation was in jeopardy, virtually all agreed that scientific education, for the great majority of people, was better on the Continent. The implication, as John Tyndall[16] put it, was clear. England could be industrially outstripped if her rivals were technically better equipped: 'As sure as knowledge is power this must be the result'.[17]

In his second report on technical education, Taunton recommended that an enquiry should be launched 'into the state and effects of technical education abroad'.[18] Throughout 1867 the Society of Arts lent its voice in support of the Commission's Report, and in January 1868 the Society held a Conference to discuss the future place of science in education, and the necessity for an efficient system of primary schools for children of the industrial classes.[19] In September 1867, the British Association, which for several years previously had urged Parliament to improve provision for science teaching in the schools, heard a report from its Parliamentary Committee which unequivocally insisted upon the importance of scientific education for all classes.[20] Thus prompted by a growing sense of international industrial rivalry, appeals for scientific and technical education soon acquired a momentum of their own. By 1870 they contributed significantly to demands for universal primary education, the cornerstone upon which it was believed, the edifice of secondary education could alone be securely created.

I   The Samuelson Committee

Meanwhile, events moved rapidly in the direction of special parliamentary enquiry. Emerging from the turmoil of the Reform Act of 1867, Disraeli's Government, coming into power in February 1868, almost immediately appointed a Select Committee – the first of three in the present series – under the chairmanship of Bernhard (later Sir Bernhard) Samuelson, the famous German-born ironmaster who had served on the Acland Committee in 1867 and who was Secretary of the Society of Arts Committee on Technical Education.[21] The 'Select Committee on the Provision for Giving Instruction in Theoretical and Applied Science to the Industrial Classes' was instructed specifically to find answers to questions raised by Playfair's letter to the Taunton Committee.

The Samuelson Committee convened for the first time in April 1868, met twice a week throughout May and June, held a total of 22 meetings and submitted its short final report with thundering speed in July. The Committee consisted of eighteen members, notably including George Dixon, MP (Lib., Birmingham), who would soon work closely with Forster in drafting the Education Act of 1870,[22] Lord Robert Montagu, MP (Con., Huntingdonshire), then Vice-President of the Council[23] and a strong advocate of scientific education, and Thomas (later Sir Thomas) Dyke Acland, MP (Lib., North Devonshire)[24] who had already served on the Endowed Schools Commission. In the chairman, Bernhard Samuelson we find a central figure who was to be a common denominator in all three reports in the I.U.P. series.

The Samuelson Committee interviewed a total of 56 witnesses, drawn from government educational establishments (including the Science and Art Department, the Committee of Council, and the School of Naval Architects); from the Universities of Oxford and Cambridge; from the 'few secondary schools in which science has been for some time systematically taught'; from the 'managers and teachers of science classes and Mechanics' Institutes receiving aid from the state, or supported exclusively by voluntary efforts'; and from 'the population engaged in the present staple industries carried on in the principal manufacturing towns and districts'. Rather arbitrarily, the Committee divided the educational sphere into three 'classes' – foremen and workers; smaller manufacturers and managers; and the proprietors of large industries – and a further sector – the relation of industrial education to industrial progress. The evidence of witnesses demonstrated that the first 'class' was desperately ill-equipped in numbers of both schools and teachers. For manufacturers and managers, the best instruction available was no better than that given by the best elementary schools, while for the proprietors, college and university courses were few, brief, and often irrelevant.

As to the relation of industrial education to industrial progress, the Committee expressed itself puzzled. There was, perhaps surprisingly in view of the energetic work of the Society of Arts, a strong difference of opinion on this question. This was, of course, the central issue:— Was technical education (and by implication, scientific education) vital to industrial progress, or not? There were quite possibly important social and economic factors quite separate from the *general* level of scientific and technical knowledge among the workforce, which were in their net effect more significant to the economic prosperity of individual industries. But, unfortunately, the Committee's greatest weakness was its haste. Not surprisingly, it was unable to draw firm conclusions about British industry as a whole. In fact, the issue was (and is) extremely complex, and answers were neither easy nor easily come by. In an important sense, however, this was possibly immaterial; the Samuelson Report became principally an educationalists', not an industrialists' charter. A fuller analysis could have disaggregated industry, not by class of worker or manager, but by product or process sector, and could have proceeded sector by sector to gather written and oral evidence on the relevance of different kinds of educational skills – whether scientific, technical, 'technological' (to perpetrate an anachronism) or managerial – to specific industries. This was, however, an expensive and lengthy task, and one, of course, inconsistent with the terms of reference of the Committee, and incompatible with the pressures on the Committee for quick and simple answers for Parliament. Indeed, the Samuelson Committee of 1867 reflects many of the strengths and weaknesses of Select Committee enquiries.

In retrospect, the pressure of a strong lobby of 'zealots' gave the Committee's recommendations a force which its evidence scarcely warranted. Most of this evidence focused on the educational inadequacies of existing schools and government departments, rather than on industry itself, a fact which did not escape criticism. From what manufacturers' evidence was available, for example, it appeared that industry was by no means unanimous in the view that the absence of scientific instruction was in itself disastrous. As the Committee reported, economic factors were involved:

> Although the pressure of foreign competition, where it exists, is considered by some witnesses to be partly owing to the superior scientific attainments of foreign manufacturers, yet the general result of the evidence proves that it is to be attributed mainly to their artistic taste, to fashion, to lower wages, and to the absence of trade disputes abroad, and to the greater readiness with which handicraftsmen abroad in some trades, adapt themselves to new requirements.[25]

Furthermore, the Committee defended the British workman for possessing 'in a pre-eminent degree' requisite practical experience and manufacturing skill. Nonetheless, in their next paragraph, the Committee hurried on to register itself and its conclusions, in favour of greater educational provision. Given the composition of the Committee, a conclusion of this kind was perhaps predictable; but it was a measure of the gathering consensus that a basic system of scientific and technical education was a necessary, if not itself a sufficient, condition for industrial leadership.

Despite its inadequacies, the Samuelson Report had at least four important consequences. First, the Committee had agreed that existing provision for the early education of foremen and workers was too brief and too narrow to be of lasting value. If the working classes were ever to benefit from science, elementary instruction was essential for every child. This in itself led directly to pressure for universal primary education. Secondly, the Committee argued for the reorganization of educational provision at its higher levels, including the introduction of adult science classes, the reorganization of secondary instruction, the redesignation of certain endowed schools as 'science schools', the more equitable distribution of state grants among the provinces, and the encouragement of 'superior' schools of science, supported jointly by the State, local and private benefaction in centres of industry and commerce. These recommendations laid the foundation for many decisions subsequently taken by the Department of Science and Art. Moreover, the Committee recommended improved provision for science teachers, including 'some slight addition' to their pay, and greater attention to science in their training, which contributed to the system of payment by results, and to the case for extended provision of fellowships in science at Oxford and Cambridge. Finally, in urging greater liaison between government institutions for scientific instruction in London, the Committee argued for the creation of a 'central scientific school', proposed as early as the 1850s – a proposal which years later, was embodied in the Imperial College of Science and Technology at South Kensington.

In the context of the time, however, the Committee's recommendations, apart from those respecting science education, were largely shelved. Some would undoubtedly have required new legislation, which the Government were not prepared to undertake. Indeed, Disraeli's 1868 Government was a minority government – a 'caretaker administration', dependent upon the goodwill of the Opposition. The session was accordingly difficult, with the Irish and Scottish Reform Bills consuming a good deal of parliamentary time. Moreover, the Irish Church question anticipated a general election, and Parliament was prorogued on 31 July, just two weeks after the Samuelson Committee's report was tabled. The Liberals, returned in November 1868, outlined a careful strategy of reform in education, the army and the civil service, but Samuelson's other recommendations had to wait.

With Parliamentary action momentarily in abeyance, the field was left to the technical education "lobby" outside Westminster. According to Lyon Playfair, the nation had been "much moved" by the Samuelson Report, 'and public conferences were held in London, Edinburgh and in the leading provincial towns to consider a question so grave to our interest as an industrial country'.[26] At such conferences, the thorny question was this:— given that industrial training may be desirable, of what should it consist? Apprenticeship, and the imparting of manipulative skills and 'practical' knowledge, was obviously important and was generally urged by the manufacturing interests. But what was the role of the school? 'Instruction in manipulative skill', Playfair told an Edinburgh audience in 1870, 'is not education at all; and, such as it is, belongs to the workshop, not to the school'.[27] What would 'technical education' in fact, come to mean – technical skills or scientific knowledge? Playfair and some educationalists stressed that the teaching of scientific and technical principles was also important. But if so, where would the balance be struck between science and practice, school and workshop? In 1868, the Society of Arts accepted the principle that technical education should be taken to include school work as well as workshop work. Through the 1870's, moreover, at the suggestion of Col. John Donnelly,[28] of the Science and Art Department, the Society of Arts gradually moved from its limited examination of schemes for specific industries, to a system of technical examinations for artisans generally. With the aid of the Livery Companies, inspectors were sent abroad to study different trades, and a body of experience and slow progress continued, on an *ad hoc* experimental basis.

II The Devonshire Commission

The question of science education, as opposed to technical education, had rather been submerged in the questions set by the Samuelson Committee: It already deserved treatment in its own right. Throughout the 1860's, impelled by the new discoveries in geology, zoology, chemistry and physics, T H Huxley,[29] John Tyndall, John Lubbock,[30] James Wilson[31] and others sought for science a place in the school and university curriculum equal to that held by theology and classics. Through public lectures and journals dedicated to the critical spirit, they took their campaign to the country. By far the single most visible device for the diffusion of scientific attitudes in the 1860's was the British Association which had become in its thirty years of existence a respected British institution, with a political and intellectual importance that won its pronouncements a national hearing. In August, 1866, the British Association's Parliamentary Committee reported its regret that no steps had been taken by Government to promote the study of science in schools,[32] and submitted a memorandum to the Schools Inquiry Commission, supporting the Commission's recommendations.

In 1867 the Parliamentary Committee announced optimistically to the British Association meeting at Dundee that 'the attention of the public appears to have been awakened to the necessity for introducing scientific teaching into our Schools, if we are not willing to sink into a condition of inferiority as regards both intellectual culture and skill in art, when compared with foreign nations'.[33] In 1868 the Council of the British Association meeting at Norwich considered a resolution (provisioned with arguments by Huxley and Tyndall, urging the Government to remedy defects in secondary education) which in March 1868 was printed and sent to the Education Department.[34] Meanwhile, owing to the efforts of J N Lockyer,[35] and T H Huxley, occasionally abetted by Tyndall and Playfair, who consistently argued for the importance of applying the benefits of new knowledge in a systematic fashion, the question of government provision for scientific teaching and research was brought into the foreground.

In August 1868, Alexander Strange, FRS[36], delivered a paper on the 'Necessity for State Intervention to Secure the Progress of Physical Science'. The paper aroused immediate attention. Strange, with Playfair, had recently been a juror at the Paris Exhibition. When Playfair returned to begin his struggle for technical education, Strange looked instead to the support of fundamental research. In his paper, he appealed to the spirit of one of the British Association's earliest objectives: to remove any disadvantage of a public kind which impeded the progress of science.[37]

There was no doubt in Strange's mind that State participation was vital to research. He took for granted that any abstract question whether scientific investigation should be aided or even carried on by Government had already been settled by the irresistible verdict of circumstances. William Crookes, writing in the *Quarterly Journal of Science,* agreed that science instruction could not prosper at the universities until students wanted to learn science;

and students could not turn to science until there was hope of a career.[38] At Magdalen College, Oxford, a demyship in science once went begging because, as the best candidate asked, 'What am I to do for a living, after I have completed my studies?'[39]

Following the Norwich meeting, the British Association, in November, 1868, appointed a committee of twelve, which included John Tyndall, Edward Frankland, Thomas Hirst, T H Huxley – essentially the famous 'X-Club'[40], plus Playfair and J N Lockyer (soon to become the first editor of *Nature*). The committee was asked to determine whether there was sufficient provision for the vigorous prosecution of physical science in Britain. In March 1869, the committee issued a circular to several men of science, asking:

1. Whether any course could be adopted to improve their field, whether by Government or by private initiative.
2. Whether there were grounds for asking for such initiative, and
3. Whether the interests of the community were 'sufficiently involved in the more vigorous development of scientific knowledge' to warrant the employment of state aid, either
   (a) through the creation of new institutes for experimental and observational research,
   (b) the extension of old institutions, or
   (c) the enlargement of grants to individuals for apparatus and materials.

Several months later, the committee reported its conclusion that, judged by any responsible standards, there was insufficient national provision for research. Hitherto research had paid the community 'but it had not paid the man'.[41] The community advantage wrought by research implied an obligation of support on behalf of the community itself. This obligation would not be satisfied merely by the establishment of a scientific observatory, by sponsoring physical measurements, creating one or two museums and providing out-of-pocket expenses for talented amateurs, but by allocating reasonable sums of money to individuals prepared to pursue a full-time vocation in scientific research.

Many in the British Association shared the committee's view, but others feared State interference. *Nature*, for example, published a letter from Alfred Russell Wallace, protesting against what *Nature* called the 'Science Reform Movement' because 'Experience shows that public competition ensures a greater supply of the materials and a greater demand for the products of science and art, and is thus a greater stimulus to true and healthy progress than any Government patronage.'[42]

On the other hand, there seemed grounds for arguing that 'where the State has a finger there will be patronage, and the preference of inferior agents who have the support of friendly recommendations, to superior agents who are standing alone'.[43] Already, in any case, the State was spending £140,000 a year on Museums, Gardens and Surveys, while the Science and Art Department Estimate for 1869-70 was over £225,000.[44] More important, however, was the categorical belief, evident especially among university men, that research should not be divorced from instruction which sugested that research could be properly endowed only through the universities. Benjamin Jowett, for example, argued that there was no opposition between original research and a moderate amount of teaching.[45]

Even where reformers agreed that state support was needed, they differed about how this should be distributed. On balance, those most enthusiastic for state intervention and 'Science Reform' had little experience of university life and were not Oxford or Cambridge men. This was particularly evident among the 'X-Club' and its concentric networks. On the other hand, strong arguments in favour of linking teaching with research came chiefly from the universities. In his inaugural lecture at University College, London, in October, 1869, Professor A W Williamson[46] delivered 'A Plea for Pure Science' and insisted that research should not be allowed to develop outside the context of education. Henry Roscoe[47] whose spacious laboratories at Owens College, Manchester, were among the best in England, urged that scientific research, was, through the teaching of scientific method, the best training for everyday commercial life;[48] and James Clerk Maxwell, in his inaugural professorial lecture at Cambridge in October, 1871, in a laboratory made possible by private benefaction, stressed the advantages of doing research in the university with the resources available there.[49] At Oxford, Sir Benjamin Brodie wished to found new research institutions within the universities, with staff closely connected to university teaching. In London, on the other hand, Huxley and Lockyer were strongly in favour of independent support for research, however much this research might in practice contribute to university teaching.[50]

Whatever the best connection between university science research and Government research might be, the case for support was sufficiently clear to the British Association. On 18 August 1869, the British Association Council at Exeter recounted the three Government Commissions on secondary education, and its own attempts to bring science into the curriculum, and resolved that

the study of Natural Science, whether as a means of disciplining the mind, or for providing knowledge useful for the purpose of life, is of essential importance to the youth of this country; and that it ought to form a part of education in all Secondary Schools.[51]

The Council accordingly presented a petition for Lord Lyttelton to present in the House of Lords; and for Sir William Tite to present in the House of

Commons. One week later the British Association took separately a decision to exert its influence to obtain a Royal Commission to consider:

1) the character and value of existing institutions and facilities for scientific investigation, and the amount of time and money devoted to such purposes.

2) what modifications or augmentations of the means and facilities that are at present available for the maintenance and extension of science are requisite and

3) in what manner these can be best supported.[52]

In effect, the British Association's twin pronged "attack" for the support of science in secondary education and in research was met by a single response. In February 1870, Gladstone's administration agreed to appoint a Royal Commission under William Cavendish, seventh Duke of Devonshire, to study national provision for 'scientific instruction and the advancement of science'.[53] The Duke, a disant relative of Henry Cavendish, the chemist, had taken the Tripos as revised by Babbage in1829. In 1861, he had succeeded the Prince Consort as Chancellor of Cambridge where, in October, he donated the cost of building the Cavendish Laboratory.

The Secretary of the Devonshire Commission was the ubiquitous Norman Lockyer. Two of its nine members (Sharpey and Miller) had been active in building research schools at University College. Two others (Huxley and Lubbock) were members of the 'X-Club'. One other, Bernhard Samuelson, was by now a familiar figure in educational circles.

The Commission sat for six years, met 85 times, interviewed over 150 witnesses and published eight reports and four massive volumes of evidence. Although instructed to look particularly at scientific instruction in schools, museums and universities, it soon raised searching questions about the state of British science as a whole and research in particular.[54] Some reports were more conclusive than others; some virtually assumed the truth of what they set out to prove. The first report, which appeared in March 1871, examined the institutions concentrated in South Kensington, and recommended that the Government combine the Royal School of Mines and the Royal College of Chemistry into a single science school with a single staff of professors in mathematics, physics, chemistry and biology.[55] The second report, issued in March 1872, was concerned with primary education and with endorsing improvements in the policies of the Science and Art Department which had long been sponsored by the London network. The third report, dealing with Oxford and Cambridge, appeared in August 1873; the fourth, on national museums, in January 1874; the fifth, on provincial university colleges, in August 1874; and the sixth, seventh and eighth, on secondary schools, the Scottish universities and Government provision for science, respectively, appeared in June 1875.

Over these four years, editorial comment in *Nature* and the literary quarterlies kept public interest in the Commission alive. The Commision revealed much evidence of large government expenditure on what could be considered 'scientific' research, justified on grounds of prospective naval or commercial rewards; indeed, as the history of the Arctic and *Challenger* expeditions demonstrated, this definition could be interpreted widely. Moreover, the state had increased its expenditure on science-related activities dramatically since the 1850's.[56] It was, in fact, doing a good deal, but it was not *seen* to be doing so. Much science that was supported was hampered by lack of coordination and by narrow notions of departmental control. This absence of strategic thinking, and the implied waste of scientific resources, was the chief criticism of the 'Science Reformers' who repeated in public views which they had expressed officially to the Commission. In 1870, 1871[57] and again in 1872, Alexander Strange demanded that scientists should have rewards and standing comparable to the practitioners of any other learned vocation.

It has hitherto been too much of the custom, [he said] to treat men of science as exceptions to all other professions; to assume that whilst it is quite proper to enrich and ennoble soldiers who fight for pay, lawyers who evade or apply the law according to circumstances, physicians who kill or cure as seemeth best to them, and even divines, whose missions to save souls might be deemed a sufficient privilege ... [the man of science] should work for love, and die, ... in poverty.[58]

It seemed plausible that, in the interpretation of nature, no less than in the interpretation of religion, the labourer should be worthy of his hire. W B Carpenter, the physiologist, dwelt on England's peculiar need:

If England was behind Germany in original investigations, it was not, as sometimes is said, because Englishmen are inferior to Germans in ideal power, but because the German universities are so arranged as to afford a career to men who choose to devote their lives to study. In England such men, having no means of making a livelihood by the pursuit of science, are obliged to turn their attention to a 'practical profession'.[59]

Through the early 1870s, the distressed state of scientific men was recounted again and again. 'It is known to all the world', lamented *Nature*, 'that science is all but dead in England'. By this was meant not the 'Jury' science of exhibitions and practical technology, but 'that searching after knowledge which is its own reward'.[60] 'Whether we confess it or not', Lockyer wrote, 'England so far as the advancement of knowledge goes, is but a third or fourth rate power'.[61] From the start, the solution was evident. 'It is the question of "scientific careers" that is the pressing one, and the one most difficult to settle', one correspondent agreed.[62]

The fifth report showed that Owens College (Manchester) and University College (London), as well as other university colleges united by the examination system of London University, were unable to expand their science faculties in the absence of outside help. Industry, with few exceptions, had shown little interest. City and merchant guilds were often generous, but unpredictable, sponsors. Private philanthropy in support of scientific research was rarely to be seen. Government aid, both in capital and maintenance grants, was the only real alternative. In June 1873, the sixth, seventh and eighth reports of the Devonshire Commission appeared. In the sixth report, the Commissioners found that, despite repeated attempts, little progress had been made in the introduction of science in the public or endowed schools of Britain since the Clarendon Commission of 1861 and the Taunton Commission of 1864. Readers of the IUP series will see the range of arguments presented once again. Here, perhaps it will suffice to draw attention to the Commissioners' verdict, delivered in measured tones of deliberate rebuke:

> The omission from a Liberal Education of a great branch of Intellectual Culture is of itself a matter for serious regret, and, considering the increasing importance of Science to the Material Interests of the Country, we cannot but regard its almost total exclusion from the training of the upper and middle classes as little less than a national misfortune.[63]

Perhaps the most original aspect of the sixth report was the appendix especially prepared by Norman Lockyer, after reviewing the evidence of the Endowed Schools Commission. Between September 1872 and the Spring of 1875, Lockyer himself conducted a personal survey of secondary schools, and assembled a wealth of information concerning the 'mechanics' of science teaching, including the provision of appropriate textbooks and apparatus. The experience of this piece of educational 'research' for Lockyer was, as we shall see, extremely significant to his development as an educational reformer. In this study, Lockyer found that there were 205 schools in Britain with annual endowments of over £200. Of the 128 schools which replied to Lockyer's circular, only 63 had science courses (affecting perhaps 2,400 boys, or 25% of the total registered) averaging 3-4 hours of a pupils's time per week. The position among the schools which did not reply was presumably even worse. The greatest weakness of all, he found time and again, was the sheer dearth of suitable staff. This, in turn, he reported to the Commission, was due to the time-honoured difficulty — 'the utter absence of an assured career for any student of science'.[64] In 1874, the Devonshire Commission's seventh report appeared, testifying that only two universities in Britain (Edinburgh and London), actually offered degrees in science, [65] and demonstrating widespread discrepancies in faculty salaries. It was this same question of 'pay and prospects' which guided the Commission in its eighth report, and made the development of a 'profession' of scientific graduates no less important for teaching than for scientific research.

With their eighth Report, on the 'endowment of science', the Devonshire
Commission drew its work to a close. The Government, was in fact, doing a
good deal to aid science. According to the Civil Estimates of 1869-70, the
Government spent about £400,000 on scientific museums, expeditions,
learned societies and the scientific work of central departments. But the
Commission accepted that the 'progress of Scientific Research must in a great
degree depend upon the aid of Government. As a nation we ought to take our
share of the current scientific work of the world.'[66] To ensure adequate
consideration of both science and research, they followed Strange and *Nature* in recommending that the Government create a Ministry of Science and
Education, with a council of scientific advisers; that the scientific facilities of
schools and civil departments be augmented; and that a national technical
laboratory and physical laboratory be built.[67] The Commission, in fact,
embraced the recommendations of the reformers 'it would be their own fault',
J. S. Cotton observed, 'if they let the issues remain any longer in the domain
of theory.'[68]

Unfortunately, the Devonshire Commission's recommendations proved
too sweeping for the Government to implement. After repeated prodding by
Playfair,[69] Disraeli's Government did accept certain specific recommendations — notably, by increasing the Government Grant for research, and
creating a Solar Physics Committee — but the constitutional and administrative difficulties posed by the creation of a Ministry of Education and Science,
which would embrace not only scientific research but also secondary, technical and higher education could not be quickly resolved.[70] Over the next fifty
years, many of the Devonshire recommendations were realised in some form,
each highly significant for the development of central policy towards science
and education. But none was of greater significance than the proposal that
science should form an *indispensable* part of the country's educational apparatus.

III The Samuelson Commission

While the campaign for the recognition of science was still in its infancy, the
movement for technical education gathered speed. In the late 1860's, at the
time of the Samuelson Committee, 'technical education' was a generally
unfamiliar concept, associated with the 'useful knowledge' of the Mechanics'
Institutes, but distinct (in both social and pedagogical forms) from the 'scientific instruction' meant to inform the schools and universities.[71] From the
point of view of government, this distinction was not merely of academic
interest. Scientific education could arguably be presumed to have some claim
on public educational expenditure. 'Trade subjects', however, were in a
different category altogether. According to generally accepted principles, the

subsidy of such subjects would be very near the subsidy of industry itself, and this dangerously close to policies of Protection. Moreover, through the 1870's and 1880's, strong differences of opinion about the sort of technical education desired festered within the educationalists' ranks. Huxley's view, expressed clearly to a London audience in 1877, was that technical education was 'simply a good education, with more attention to physical science, to drawing and to modern languages than is common and there is nothing especially technical about it.'[72] Others, however, including Playfair, felt that it should be rather more 'technical' in content, without sacrificing scientific principles; while others held that it should be wholly technical or commercial work, or the pragmatic business of applying techniques to industry. All agreed, however, that there should be technical education at both secondary and 'higher' levels.

Over the next forty years, the redefinition of technical education to include both practical, vocational experience and applied science gradually took hold. The movement received a great push in 1877 when a group of men including Sir W. G. Armstrong, T. H. Huxley, John Donnelly, Douglas Galton and H. Trueman Wood, (Assistant Secretary of the Royal Society of Arts) were invited by a Committee of the Livery Companies of London to advise them concerning the prospect of encouraging technical instruction.[73] In 1878, several reports were published. Huxley's views, which commanded great weight, recommended the 'diffusion of such instruction' among the industrial population; adequate training for suitable numbers of teachers; systematic arrangements for apprenticeship in industry; and provision for the best to continue their studies beyond the ordinary school-leaving age and towards careers as teachers or as 'original workers in applied science'[75]. In 1880, the plans of the 'Livery Companies Committee' were given substance by the incorporation of the 'City Guilds of London Institute for the Advancement of Technical Education'. Its first organising Director and Secretary was Philip (later Sir Philip) Magnus.[76] In 1866, the Institute opened a technical college in Finsbury,[77] and between 1882 and 1884 a Central Institute for the training of teachers was built on the Gore Estate in South Kensington. This was to become the predecessor of the City and Guilds of London Institute, later part of Imperial College.

But these developments did not fully answer the demand for technical education, particularly at the secondary level. During the 1870's, new voices were heard in support of the educationalists, notably that of A. J. Mundella, who was credited with being 'one of the earliest to mention the words "technical education" in this country'.[78] Before coming into office as Vice-President of the Committe of Council, with the Liberal Government of 1880, Mundella had travelled widely to Germany and had recognised the enormous strides made by German industry since 1870.

In April 1881, George Anderson, Liberal MP for Glasgow,[79] requested Gladstone's Government to set up a Royal Commission to visit the continent to study different schemes of technical education. Mundella was not greatly in favour, believing that 'to appoint a roving commission to travel all over Europe would be a very expensive, and, I think, a needlessly tedious process'.[80] Mundella suggested instead that Bernhard Samuelson, with experience of both the Select Committee of 1868 and the Devonshire Commission of 1870-1875, might make an unofficial study himself. 'What Englishmen do for themselves', he remarked, 'is better done than what a government does for them.'[81] In July, the issue was again raised. Mundella announced that he had spoken with four, interested men two of whom, Samuelson and John Slagg,[82] had consented to conduct such an investigation at their own expense. In fact, the Commission, when finally announced in August 1881, consisted of men who were by definition already deeply committed advocates of technical education, including Samuelson, Magnus, Roscoe, Swire (later Sir Swire) Smith,[83] John Slagg and William Woodall, MP,[84] together with Gilbert Redgrave, the Secretary appointed by the Education Department. Of the six only three were then MP's, although two of the others eventually entered Parliament.[85] Four were progressive industrialists, two were educationalists and one (Roscoe) was a practising scientist. In this extraordinary fashion, a self-confessed 'lobby' acquired the status of a traditionally 'neutral' Royal Commission.[86]

Given these unusual origins, the product of the Commission was remarkable. At a public cost of £2,600 it travelled throughout Europe to the heart of industry in Germany, Belgium, Switzerland, Holland and France. Its terms of reference — 'to inquire into the Instruction of the Industrial Classes of Certain Foreign Countries in technical and other subjects for the purpose of comparison with that of the corresponding classes in this country . . .' — gave it a virtually free hand. Sitting for over three years, the Commission produced in May 1884, five huge volumes of data and memoranda on economic, industrial and social conditions. The first volume presented reports on technical education, with recommendations, while the second contained reports by H. M. Jenkins, FGS (Secretary of the Royal Agricultural Society) on agricultural education in Europe, and by William (later Sir William) Mather (a mechanical engineer from Salford) on technical education in the United States and Canada. The remaining volumes included reports by Thomas Wardle on the silk industry, and by Professor Sullivan on technical education in Ireland.

The Commission's findings were, in a word, pessimistic. Britain still led in invention, they argued, but was falling steadily behind in the application of new technical skills. Britain had perhaps a good system of evening instruction, but European elementary and secondary education surpassed their

British equivalents. The Commission viewed with apprehension progress made in Europe in the technical training of foremen and managers, and argued that this could not have been achieved without a high degree of technical instruction and a general appreciation of learning and research.[87] Given this, their recommendations were sweeping. In the 16 years since the Samuelson Committee, British secondary schools had still not begun to offer technical instruction at a sufficient level and scale. Accordingly, the Commission suggested the transfer of all secondary education to public expense; recommended that the new teacher training courses be set up at the Normal School of Science, complemented by additional training colleges to be created by School Boards, and urged that Britain develop institutions following the model of the Zurich Federal Polytechnic.[88] When the report appeared, *The Times* put on a brave face:

> It must be regarded as satisfactory that the Commissioners have been able to terminate their labours . . . with the conviction that, whatever may be the progress of other nations in technical education and in manufactures, our own industries also are full of vigour; that we already possess considerable opportunities for theoretical instruction in the technical sciences and in art applied to industry; that these opportunities are capable of increase on their present lines; that the value of such instruction and the necessity for its further development are felt by those most directly interested; and that this development is making sure, though gradual, and perhaps somewhat tardy, progress.

But *The Times* went on to admit, in a leading article, that

> With the whole world competing for the supply of the universal market, it is vital to Great Britain that its artisans should understand how to march straight to their industrial goal by the shortest and most certain routes. Beyond a doubt the ordinary public appliances of education have not hitherto aided them as a body very efficiently in the race . . . At last, however, a serious commencement has been made of a national edifice of technical education.[89]

The Samuelson Report, according to Magnus, was 'widely circulated . . . and was for many years the recognised work of reference on all questions of technical education'.[90] Its belief that good secondary schools held the key to healthy industry became a cornerstone upon which later Education Acts were based. From the Government of the day, however, the Report met with a stony silence. The events of 1884-1885, witnessing Gladstone's leadership of the Liberal Party shaken by the driving wedge of Home Rule, left little parliamentary time for educational reorganization on the scale Samuelson required. Between July 1885 and August 1886, there were no less than three successive governments, and the issue, accordingly, went back into the public domain, where Huxley and others, long veterans of such campaigns, prepared themselves for the next phase of combat.

IV The Aftermath

The sequence of events in the wake of the Samuelson Commission are important to the history of technical education and readers of this IUP series may wish to follow further developments in greater detail. The following paragraphs will give merely an outline of the chief characteristics of this development.[91]

Following the report of the Commission in 1884, its members toured the country trying to persuade manufacturers that if Britain's commercial supremacy was undermined, continental and particularly German military supremacy would certainly result. Two years after the Samuelson Commission, a new Royal Commission on elementary education was set up under R. A. Cross.[92] The Cross Commission agreed with Samuelson that despite common knowledge of glaring deficiencies in technical education, very little had been done, and 'still less in that scientific education which is the foundation of such technical instruction as can be given in the school'[93]. Despite the parliamentary work of Roscoe, Acland, and Playfair between 1884 and 1889, during which time there were seven successive attempts at legislation, these arguments failed to make any headway. Moreover, there remained a problem of the definition of 'technical education' which hampered attempts to introduce subjects into existing curricula at Board Schools. For example, Rosamund Davenport-Hill referred in the *Contemporary Review* to 'two distinct meanings — one the teaching of a specific art or trade; the other instruction in elementary science bearing on all arts or trades and the training of hand and eye'.[94] This was a familiar difficulty, dating at least from the 1860's, but the Cross Commission in 1888 attempted to resolve the question by arguing that the one would be incomplete without the other:—

> By technical instruction we understand instruction in those scientific and artistic principles which underlie the industrial occupations of the people . . . as well as instruction in the manual practice involved in the application of these principles.[95]

In the meantime, through the initiative of Henry Roscoe and A. H. D. Acland, the National Association for the Promotion of Technical Education was created in 1887.[96] For twenty years, this body provided a forum for systematic attempts to put technical education firmly in the hands of local School Boards and firmly on the rates. Their efforts had their reward. In July 1889, after several unsuccessful attempts, Salisbury's Government (through Sir William Hart-Dyke, Vice-President of the Council) introduced and carried over bitter opposition, a long awaited Technical Instruction Act. A short amending act followed in 1891. This legislation defined 'technical instruction' and 'instruction in the scientific and artistic principles applicable to industry and special trades, but not the practice of these trades'. It gave powers to county councils and urban sanitary authorities ('local authorities' under the Act) to levy a rate not exceeding one penny in the pound for the promotion of technical education. In operation, the Science and Art Department, with Donnelly as its chief, helped local authorities by providing examinations on both scientific principles and their applications. The newly created London County Council (LCC) inaugurated several 'maintained' technical schools, and many provincial cities, including Birmingham, Huddersfield, Leicester, Manchester and Salford, created new or expanded technical schools. Meanwhile, several new polytechnics were proposed. By the mid 1890's, 'technical education' had taken on an even wider meaning, embracing both scientific, technological and general education, both at the secondary level and at the more advanced level of the polytechnic.[97]

In 1889, the Association, given a new lease of life, added 'Secondary Education' to its title, and began to press for means to increase the funds available to local authorities for the support of technical education. The situation was transformed in the wake of the Local Taxation (Customs and Excise) Act, 1890.[98] The Act was intended to direct to the local authorities, newly created under the Local Government Act, 1888, certain surplus funds created for compensating publicans whose licenses were not renewed. During its passage, Acland tried to insert an amendment which would give local authorities the power to use these sums for technical instruction; the amendment failed, but three years later, G. J. Goschen, then Liberal Chancellor — a man of strong German associations, one feels, and a willing convert to technical education — moved that this 'whisky money' be made over to County Councils for either technical education or the relief of rates. As one MP quipped, local authorities were thus enabled to 'distil wisdom out of whisky, genius out of sin, and capacity for business out of beer'.[99] Many local authorities snapped at the chance of 'whisky money'. In 1892-93, £472,560 was used for technical education in this way; by 1900-01 the figure had risen to £836,847 (rather more than the total income received by all the schools from their endowments).[100] This contrasted with the sums of £12,762 and £106,209, raised in the respective years by the penny rate provided under the Technical Instruction Act, 1889. By all accounts, local authorities used their funds rigorously, and technical schools became a source of local prestige.

The battle for education won, educational reformers turned themselves to the even more formidable task of rationalizing the structure of education. By the end of the century what Lord Goschen called 'the chaos of local government' was reflected in the multiplicity of educational authorities up and down the land. It was clear that the School Boards, created under the 1870 Act to administer elementary education, had also created higher-grade schools where scientific education was often tailored to local circumstances.[101] Moreover, the Science and Art Department, beginning with science classes in elementary schools, had gradually extended their grants to secondary schools. Many of these (92 up to 1895) were recognised as 'organised science schools', and over 3,000 students received some science instruction. But the Science and Art Department, in expanding in this direction, without legislative provision, made for innumerable difficulties of confusion and overlapping. Finally, the Technical Instruction Act, which gave powers to County Councils and County Boroughs, extended the range of authorities eligible to be called 'educational' even further.

In the meantime, many of the old campaigners had left the field of battle. Huxley died in 1895, and Mundella in 1897. Only Magnus and Lockyer survived well into the present century, and lived to write the history of the movement they helped to launch.[102] Nevertheless, their campaign continued. Stimulated by international rivalry and the threat of German competition — vividly captured in Ernest Williams's *Made in Germany*[103] — the educationalists won new ground in 1895 with the appointment of the Royal Commission on Secondary Education (the Bryce Commission). The Bryce Commission summarised several of the recommendations which had emerged over the years in the wake of the Devonshire and Samuelson Commissions. It proposed a strong central Ministry of Education, and recommended placing secondary education into the hands of reconstituted local education authorities. It also recommended that

ample provision must be made in schools for scientific teaching . . . [and] the chief tongues of modern Europe . . . and that full opportunities to boys and girls to prepare themselves for the particular occupation which they intend to follow in after life, whether industrial or commercial, ought to be supplied by the teaching of the practical arts . . .[104]

The Bryce Commission's Report gained greater urgency from a second visit of Magnus, Woodall, Swire Smith and Redgrave to Germany in 1896.[105] Their report was widely read and reviewed, and in Magnus's view, hastened progress towards reorganising educational administration. This was completed by the Education Act of 1902, which swept away the School Boards and constituted 'local authorities' as 'local educational authorities' in their place. In the meantime, by the Board of Education Act, 1899, the old Department of Science and Art was dissolved, and replaced by a single Board of Education with a unified secretariat. The century opened with the beginnings of a coherent structure for primary, secondary and technical education for all of England and Wales.

In 1906, the National Association for the Promotion of Technical and Secondary Education was wound up, its duty done. An important era appeared to be ending. In 1910, Philip Magnus felt confident enough to write:

The necessity of the higher scientific and technical instruction and of its specialisation to industry and commerce is generally realised. No one doubts it. The questions now engaging attention are the kind of training that should lead up to it, the best means of providing avenues through which the children of our elementary schools may pass to the higher technical institutes, the character of the teaching most suitable for children after the elementary school age, and the relation between university and technological instruction.[106]

After years of work, the way had been cleared, administratively and politically for a 'silent social revolution' in British scientific education that was to become a central part of the history of Britain in the twentieth century. The principles stated, it remained for a new generation, made next to familiar with the threat of international industrial and technological competition, to attempt their implementation.

Footnotes

1 On the Great Exhibition itself, see C. R. Fay, *Palace of Industry*, 1851, (Cambridge, 1951); and 'The Great Exhibition (i) How it all began, (ii) Frustration and Fruition', in K. W. Luckhurst, *The Story of Exhibitions*, (London, 1951), pp. 85-116. On the aftermath of the Great Exhibition, see W. L. Burn, *The Age of Equipoise*, (London, 1964). See also D. S. L. Cardwell, *The Organization of Science in England: A Retrospect*, (rev. ed. London, 1972), pp. 76-81. Cardwell ably summarizes the chief points at issue in the wake of the Great Exhibition and should not be ignored by the student. This section of his book does, however, oversimplify many of the issues and neglects the industrial contribution to the structure of the educational debate.

2 J. B. Bury, *The Idea of Progress* (London, 1920), p.329.

3 Henry (later Sir Henry) Cole, (1808-1882); civil servant; assistant keeper of the Record Office, 1838; served on managing committee of exhibitions of 1851, 1862 and 1871-4; British commissioner at the Paris Exhibitions of 1855 and 1867; joint secretary of the Science and Art Department, 1853, and sole secretary, 1858-73; KCB, 1875. Cf. H. Cole, *Fifty Years of Public Life* (London, 1884).

4 Lyon (later Sir Lyon) Playfair, (1818-1898); educated at St Andrews, Glasgow and Giessen; assistant to Thomas Graham at University College, London; honorary professor of Chemistry at the Royal Institution, Manchester, 1842-45; professor in the School of Mines, Jermyn Street, 1845; FRS, 1848; President of the Chemical Society, 1857-9; helped organize the Great Exhibition; CB, 1851; Secretary of Science to Department of Science and Art, 1853, and Secretary for Science and Art, 1855-8; professor of chemistry at Edinburgh, 1858-69; Liberal MP for universities of Edinburgh and St Andrews, 1868-85; Postmaster General, 1873; chairman and deputy speaker of the House of Commons, 1880-83; Liberal MP for South Leeds, 1885-92; Vice-President of Council, 1886; raised to peerage, 1892: GCB, 1895. Cf. Wemyss Reid, *Memoirs and Correspondence of Lyon Playfair* (London, 1899).

5 Albert, Prince Consort of England (1819-1861), son of Duke of Saxe-Coburg-Gotha; educated privately, then at Brussels and Bonn; married Queen Victoria, 1840; placed by Peel at the head of the Royal Commission on the rebuilding of the Houses of Parliament, 1841; Chancellor of Cambridge University, 1847, where he successfully

advocated alterations in the curriculum; projected the idea of the Great Exhibition; died of typhoid fever in December, 1861.

6 Cf. D. Hudson and K. W. Luckhurst, *The Royal Society of Arts, 1754-1954*, (London, 1954). With the strong support of the Prince Consort, the Society of Arts received its Royal Charter in 1847.

7 *Second Report of the Commissioners for the Exhibition of 1851*, HC. 1852, pp.72-74.

8 Whewell, 'The General Bearing of the Great Exhibition on the Progress of Art and Science', *Lectures on the Results of the Exhibition delivered before the Society of Arts, Manufacturers and Commerce, at the suggestion of HRH Prince Albert, President of the Society* (London, 1852). William Whewell (1794-1866) was Master of Trinity College, Cambridge, 1841-66; he supported the election of the Prince Consort as Chancellor in 1847, and assisted in the introduction of the Moral Sciences Tripos and the Natural Sciences Tripos, he published distinguished works in the natural and mathematical sciences, philosophy and theology.

9 'The Queen's Address to both Houses of Parliament', *Hansard*, 3rd series, 123, c. 19. For comparative comments on the development of art education, see Celina Fox, *Critical Commentary: Fine Arts and Design, supra*, pp.68-93.

10 The Government School of Mines and Science Applied to the Arts was founded in 1851 in association with the Geological Museum in Jermyn Street. The Royal College of Chemistry was created in 1845 with the aid of the Prince Consort. It thrived briefly under the direction of A. W. Hoffman, but fell into financial loss until its 'rescue' in 1853. See G. Roberts, *The Royal College of Chemistry*, (1845-1853): A Social History of Chemistry in Early Victorian England (unpublished Ph.D. thesis, Johns Hopkins University, 1973).

11 H. Butterworth, *The Science and Art Department*, (Unpublished Ph.D. thesis, University of London, 1951).

12 Cf. Thomas Kelly, *A History of Adult Education*, (Liverpool, 1970).

13 J. W. Adamson, *English Education, 1789-1902*, (Cambridge, 1930), chaps VIII-X. For general reviews of these developments, cf Richard Johnson, *Critical Commentary: Education, supra*, pp.5-29, and Gillian Sutherland, *supra*, pp.137-159.

14 *Report of Commissioners on Education in Schools in England not comprised within Her Majesty's two recent Commissions on Popular and Public Schools*, (the "Schools Enquiry Commission"), HC 1867-68, (3966), XXVIII (parts 1-17).

15 *Report of the Schools Enquiry Commission Relative to Technical Education*, p.261. HC 1867, XXVI. Letter from Playfair to Taunton, 15 May 1867, 266-70.

16 John Tyndall, (1820-1863), natural philosopher; teacher at Queenwood College, Hampshire; studied at Marburg with Bunsen, 1848-1850; FRS, 1852; professor of natural philosophy at the Royal Institution, 1853; succeeded Faraday as Superintendent, 1867-87; made important investigations on heat, sound and light, succeeded Faraday as scientific adviser to Trinity House and the Board of Trade, 1866. Well-known for popularising science. Cf. A. S. Eve and C. H. Creasey, *Life and Work of John Tyndall*, (London, 1945).

17 *Report of the Schools Enquiry Commission relative to Technical Education*, p.10, HC 1867, XXVI, 261.

18 *Ibid.*, p.264.

19 For an account of the Society of Arts Conference in January, 1868, see the *Journal of the Royal Society of Arts, XVI*, 31 January 1868, p.183; and for the report arising from the conference, see *J. Roy. Soc Arts., XVI* (1868), 627.

20 Report of the Parliamentary Committee, *Report of the British Association for the Advancement of Science*, [Dundee], (London, 1867).

21 Bernhard (later Sir Bernhard) Samuelson (1820-1905); manager of Manchester Engineering firm, 1842-6; began famous Britannia ironworks at Middlesbrough. Liberal MP for Banbury, 1859 and 1865-85, and for North Oxfordshire, 1885-95; baronnet, 1884; FRS, 1881; presented technical institute to Banbury, 1884. Samuelson also served on the Royal Commission on Elementary Education in 1887, and was chairman of Select Committees on the patent laws, (1871-2), and the railways (1873).

22 George Dixon (1820-1898), merchant of Edgbaston. In 1868, helped found the National Education League; attempted to amend Education Act of 1870 in accordance with 'advanced' Liberal views; member of first Birmingham School Board, 1870; MP for Birmingham, 1867-76; 1885-98.

23 Lord Robert Montagu, (1825-1902), liberal Conservative MP, Huntingdonshire, 1859-74; advocated legislation on sewage disposal, cattle plague, and prevention, and vaccination; helped found School of Naval Architecture.

24 Thomas (later Sir Thomas) Dyke Acland, (1809-98); scholar and educational reformer; Liberal MP for North Devonshire, 1865-85; served actively on the Endowed Schools Commission, 1864-73 and in the debates in Committee on the Education Bill of 1870.

25 *Report from the Select Committee on Scientific Instruction*, HC. 1868 (432), I, vii.

26 *Hansard*, 3rd series, 197 c. 204.

27 Adamson, *English Education*, p.398.

28 John (later Sir John) Donnelly (1834-1902); Royal Engineers, retired with honorary rank of major-general, 1887; assisted Sir Henry Cole in reorganizing Science and Art Department, 1858; Inspector of Science, 1859; arranged for payment of teachers by results of examinations of pupils, 1859; became 'director of science', 1874; supervised science schools and institutions throughout the country; secretary and permanent head of Science and Art Department, 1884-1889; CB, 1886; KCB, 1893.

29 Thomas Henry Huxley (1825-1895); M.B. London, 1845; assistant surgeon on HMS *Rattlesnake*, 1846-50; FRS, 1850; lecturer on natural history at Royal School of Mines, 1854; naturalist to Geological Survey, 1855; served on many royal commissions, including that on the sea fisheries of the United Kingdom, 1864-5, the Royal College of Science for Ireland, 1866, on Scientific Instruction and Advancement of Science, 1870-75, on vivisection, 1876, and on Scottish Universities, 1876-8; Hunterian professor at Royal College of Surgeons, 1863-69; Fullerian Professor at the Royal Institution, 1863-7; President of the Royal Society, 1883-5; Privy Councillor, 1892. Cf. Cyril Bibby, *T. H. Huxley: Scientist, Humanist and Educator*, (London, 1959).

30 Sir John Lubbock (1834-1913), fourth baronet and first Baron Avebury; banker, scientist and author; educated at Eton; Liberal MP for Maidstone, 1870 and 1874, London University, 1880-1900; promoted the Bank Holidays Act (1871), and the Act for Preservation of Ancient Monuments (1882); Privy Councillor, 1890; baron, 1900; FRS, 1858; author of numerous scientific and ethical works.

31 James Wilson (1836-1931), schoolmaster and antiquary; educated at St John's College, Cambridge; senior wrangler, 1859; Fellow, 1860; mathematical master in Rugby, 1859-70; ordained, 1879; headmaster of Clifton, 1879-90; archdeacon of Manchester, 1890-1905; Canon of Worcester, 1905-26.

32 Report of Parliamentary Committee, (22 August, 1866), *Report of the British Association*, [Nottingham], (London, 1866).

33 Report of Parliamentary Committee, (September, 1864), *Report of the British Association*, [Dundee], (London, 1867).

34 *Report of the British Association*, [Norwich], (London 1868).

35 Norman (later Sir Norman) Lockyer (1856-1920); astronomer; clerk in the War Office, 1857; pioneered observations of sun-spot spectra, 1866 and of solar promi-

nences, 1868; secretary to Royal Commission on Scientific Instruction and Advancement of Science, 1870; transferred to Science and Art Department, 1875; director of Solar Physics Observatory and professor of astronomical physics, Royal College of Science, 1890-1913; editor of *Nature*, 1869-1920; FRS, 1869; CB, 1894; KCB, 1897. See A. J. Meadows, *Science and Controversy: A Biography of Sir Norman Lockyer*, (London, 1972).

36 Lieutenant-Colonel Alexander Strange (1818-1876), educated at Harrow; Madras Light Cavalry; trigonometrical survey of India; Inspector of scientific instruments for use in India, 1861; FRGS, and FRAS, 1861; FRS, 1864. Cf. J. G. Crowther, *Statesmen of science*, (London, 1965), pp.237-269.

37 'On the Necessity for State Intervention to Secure the Progress of Physical Science', Address to the Mathematics and Physics Section, *Report of the British Association*, [Norwich], (London, 1868).

38 [W. Crookes], 'On the Teaching of Natural Science at the Universities', *Q. J. Sci.*, VI, (October, 1869), 500.

39 *Ibid.*

40 Roy MacLeod, 'The X-Club: A Social Network of Science in Late-Victorian England', *Notes and Records of the Royal Society*, 24, (1970), 305-322.

41 [W. Crookes], 'On National Institutions for Practical Scientific Research', *Q. J. Sci.*, VI, (January, 1869), 48.

42 'Government Aid to Science' *Nature*, I, (1870), 279-88.

43 W. Crookes, *Q. J. Sci.*, VI, (1869), 48-9.

44 See *Nature, I*, (1870), 589-90.

45 Benjamin Jowett, 'Suggestions for University Reform, 1874' in Lewis Campbell, *The Nationalization of the Old English Universities*, (London, 1901), pp.183-208.

46 Alexander Williamson (1824-1904), chemist; educated at Dijon, Heidelberg, Giessen and Paris; professor of practical chemistry, University College, London, 1849-87; President of Chemical Society, 1863-5, 1869-71; President of the British Association, 1873; FRS, 1855; helped introduce science degrees in London University.

47 Henry (later Sir Henry) Roscoe, (1833-1915), educated at University College, London, and Heidelberg; researched with Bunsen on the measurement of chemical action of light; professor of chemistry, Owens College, Manchester, 1857-85; knighted, 1884; Liberal MP, South Manchester, 1885; PC, 1909.

48 H. Roscoe, 'Original Research as a Means of Education', Address at the opening of Owen's College, *Nature, VIII*, (1873), 538 ff.

49 J. Clerk Maxwell, *Introductory Lecture on Experimental Physics*, (London, 1871).

50 *Nature* pointed out that almost all continental researchers taught as well, and that even 'in this country the greater number of our most distinguished men of science are professors and teachers', 'The Royal Commission on Science', *Nature, I*, (1870) 375. See also, *The Academy*, (1 December 1872), 460.

51 *Council Minutes*, (18 August, 1869), *Report of the British Association*, [Exeter], (London, 1869).

52 *Council Minutes*, (25 August 1869), *Report of the British Association*, [Exeter], (London, 1869).

53 The Commission (hereafter the 'Devonshire Commission') included the Marquis of Lansdowne; Sir John Lubbock; James Kay-Shuttleworth, MD; Bernhard Samuelson, MP; W. A. Miller (London); H. J. S. Smith (Oxford); William Sharpey (London); George Stokes (Cambridge); T. H. Huxley (London). Historical commentaries on the Commission can be found in D. S. L. Cardwell, *The Organization of Science in*

England: A Retrospect, (London, 1972), pp.119-126, and in Crowther, *Statesmen of Science* (London, 1965), pp.222-33.

54 *Nature,* IV (1871), 302.

55 The first brief report was printed in full in *Nature,* III (1871), 421.

56 Cf. 'Government and Scientific Investigation', *Spectator,* XLIV (1871) 882-4; Cf. also Anon., *Correspondence between the Royal Geographical Society and the Government* (London, 1873).

57 C.f. *J. Roy. Soc. Arts,* XVIII (1870); reported in 'The Relation of the State to Science', *Nature,* I (1870), 589-91.

58 'On the Necessity for A Permanent Commission on State Scientific Questions', *J. Royal United Services Institution,* XV (1870), 537-66, reprinted in *Nature,* IV (1871), 133, 'On Government Action in Science', *Report to the Mathematics and Physics Section of the British Association* (1871), p.56.

59 *The Academy,* (1 December 1872), 460.

60 'A Voice from Cambridge', *Nature,* VIII (1873), 21.

61 'Our National Industries', *Nature,* VI (1872), 97.

62 *Nature,* II (1870), 25.

63 *Sixth Report of the Devonshire Commission,* HC. 1575 [C. 1279], XXVIII, p.10, para. 46.

64 *Appendix to the Sixth Report of the Devonshire Commission,* p.60.

65 *Seventh Report of the Devonshire Commission,* HC. 1875, [C. 1297], XXVIII, pp.3, 6.

66 *Eighth Report of the Devonshire Commission,* H.C. 1875 [C. 1298], XXVIII, p.2. Both reports were abstracted at length in *Nature,* XII (1875), 285-8, 305-8, 361-3, 389-92, 469-70. The seventh report, dealing with the universities of London, Scotland, Trinity College, Dublin and Queen's University, Ireland, was discussed in *Nature,* XIII (1875), 21-2.

67 *Eighth Report of the Devonshire Commission,* p.47. See Strange's letter to *The Times* (6 February 1874); 'A Minister for Science', *Nature,* IX, (1874), 277. A Science Council of thirty members were proposed anonymously by Strange in *Nature,* XII (1875), 431.

68 *The Academy* (4 September, 1875), 252.

69 Cf. *Hansard,* 3rd Series, 227 c. 551.

70 Lewis Gunn, 'Organizing Science in Britain, Some Relevant Questions', *Minerva,* 5, (1967), 167-97.

71 Cf. 'What is true technical education?', *The Economist,* (25 January 1868), 87-8.

72 T. H. Huxley, 'Technical Education', (1877), *Collected Essays,* III, (London, 1893) pp.411-12.

73 See G. T. Millis, *Technical Education: Its Development and Aims* (London, 1925), p.56. A. Albu, 'Introduction', to E. E. Williams, *Made in Germany* (London: 1896, 1973), pp. xxvii-xxviii.

74 Philip Magnus, *Educational Aims and Efforts* (Longmans, 1910), pp.86-7.

75 Livery Companies' Committee, *Report on Technical Education,* (London: privately published, 1878). A volume of essays prepared by Sir William Armstrong, G. J. C. Bartley, Col. John Donnelly, Capt. Douglas Galton, T. H. Huxley and H. Trueman Wood.

76 Philip (later Sir Philip) Magnus (1842-1933), Secretary and Organizing Director of the City and Guilds of London Institute, 1880-1913; MP for London University,

1906-1922; a consistent advocate of education — particularly technical education — he sat on several commissions and was a staunch supporter of Lockyer's British Science Guild. See Frank Foden, *Philip Magnus: Victorian Educational Pioneer* (London, 1970), esp. pp.128-129.

77 On Finsbury Technical College see E. G. Walker, 'Finsbury Technical College', *Central, 30* (1933), pp.35-48, H. E. Armstrong, 'The Beginning of Finsbury', *Central, 31* (1934), pp.1-14.

78 *Hansard*, 3rd series, 260. c. 537; cf. W. H. G. Armytage, *A. J. Mundella, 1825-1897: The Liberal Background to the Labour Movement* (London, 1951).

79 George Anderson (1881-95); retired merchant; published pamphlets on National Education; (Dod's *Parliamentary Companion, 1881*).

80 *Hansard*, 3rd series, 260. c. 542.

81 *Ibid.*, c. 543.

82 John Slagg (1841-1889); Liberal MP for Manchester (1880-85); MP for Burnley (1887-89); merchant at Manchester Chamber of Commerce.

83 Swire Smith (1842-1918), knighted, 1898; Liberal MP for Keighley Division of Yorkshire, 1915-1918: Member of the Royal Commission on Technical Instruction, 1881-1884; Vice-Chairman of the Royal Commission on Technical Instruction, 1909; LL.D., University of London, 1912.

84 William Woodall (1832-   ?), Liberal MP for Stoke on Trent; partner in china works; magistrate for Staffordshire; 'in favour of the equalisation of the borough county franchise, a simplification of its land laws'. (Dod's *Parliamentary Companion, 1881*).

85 Swire Smith in 1915 and Roscoe in 1885.

86 Given Mundella's surprising reluctance, it has been argued that the Commission was in fact engineered by Samuelson, with Magnus and Mundella acting as accomplices, to by-pass the Government's reservations towards a full-scale enquiry. Cf. Michael Argles, 'The Royal Commission on Technical Instruction, 1881-1884: Its Inception and Composition', *Vocational Aspects*, II, (1959), 98.

87 *Second Report of the Royal Commission on Technical Instruction*, 1884, [C. 3981] I, pp.508-510. In England, on the contrary, opportunities for applied research were rare and advanced technical instruction virtually non-existent.

88 The development of polytechnics could be fostered in London under the provision of the City of London Parochial Charities Act, 1883.

89 *The Times*, 16 May, 1884, quoted in M. Argles, 'The Royal Commission on Technical Instruction', *Vocational Aspects*, II, (1959), 103.

90 Magnus, *Educational Aims and Efforts*, p.94. One version was published by Francis Montague, *Technical Education: A Summary of the Report of the Royal Commission Appointed to Inquire into the State of Technical Instruction*, (London, 1887).

91 For further reading, see the well chosen excerpts from reports and legislation of the period in J. Stuart MacLure, *Educational Documents – England and Wales, 1816-1963* (London, 1969). For legislative details of the 'Technical Instruction Movement', Cf. Philip Magnus, 'Technical Education', *Encyclopedia Britannica*, 11th ed (1910-11).

92 *Royal Commission on Elementary Education*, first Report, HC 1886 (4565), XXV; second Report, HC. 1887 (5056), XXIX; third Report, HC 187 (5158), XXX; Final Report, HC 1888 (5485), XXV.

93 Adamson, *English Education*, p.407.

94 R. Davenport-Hill, 'Technical Education in Board Schools', *Contemporary Review, 53,* (1888), 672-685.

95 *Final Report of the Royal Commission on Elementary Education*, 1888, HC. (5485),

XXV, p.217. The celebrated debate between Armstrong and Playfair on the nature of technical education, in terms of its 'civilizing' and conceptual satisfactions and its vocational objectives, is extremely instructive. See W. G. Armstrong (Lord Armstrong), 'The Vague Cry for Technical Education', *Nineteenth Century*, 24 (July 1888), 45-52; 'Lord Armstrong on Technical Education', *Nature*, XXXII (1888), 313-14; Lyon Playfair, 'Lord Armstrong and Technical Education', *Nineteenth Century*, 24 (September 1888), 325-333; W. G. Armstrong 'The Cry for Useless Knowledge', *Nineteenth Century*, 24 (November 1888), 653-668.

96 See the Annual Reports of the National Association for the Promotion of Technical (and Secondary) Education, 1888-1906; and the *Record of Technical and Secondary Education*, published bi-monthly by the Association from November 1891 to December 1906.

97 For changing definitions and their significance, see P. W. Musgrave, 'The Definition of Technical Education', *Vocational Aspects, 16*, (1904), 105-111.

98 Cf. Adamson, *English Education*, p.409.

99 G. A. N. Lowndes, *The Silent Social Revolution* (Oxford, 1937), p.40. In fact, the disposition of the 'whisky money' was influenced strongly by the temperance party during a sessional crisis which endangered the safety of several Liberal Unionist seats. Cf. the allusive evidence of Arthur Elliot, *The Life of George Joachim Goschen, first Viscount Goschen, 1831-1907* (London, 1911), p.167. P. R. Sharp, 'Whisky Money and the Development of Technical and Secondary Education in the 1890's', J. of Educational History and Administration, 4 (1971), 31-36.

100 *Ibid.*, p.40. For contemporary criticism of the school, see Lowndes, *ibid.*, chap. IV, pp.47-63.

101 *Ibid.*, p.40.

102 Philip Magnus, *Industrial Education* (London, 1888); *Educational Aims and Efforts* (London, 1910); R. D. Roberts, *Education in the 19th Century* (Cambridge, 1901). For an account of Lockyer's advocacy of technical education see Norman Lockyer, *Education and National Progress: Essays and Addresses, 1870-1905*, (London, 1906).

103 Ernest Edwin Williams, *Made in Germany* (London, 1896; reprinted, Harvester Press, 1973). Cf. also, G. R. Searle, *The Quest for National Efficiency* (Oxford, 1971).

104 *The Royal Commission on Secondary Education* HC. 1895 [C. 7862], p.284.

105 Cf. *Report on a Visit to Germany with a View to Ascertaining the Recent Progress of Technical Education* (HMSO, 1896): Magnus, *Educational Aims and Efforts*, p.121.

106 Philip Magnus, *Educational Aims and Efforts* (London, 1910), pp.126-7.

Bibliography

The reader interested in pursuing the subject of technical education will find many suggestive references in the text and footnotes to primary and secondary sources of particular importance. The following list is therefore intended as only a brief supplementary guide to further reading, and as such includes many items of a contextual and general nature. In many cases, bibliographies to specific themes form part of these treatments.

John William Adamson, *English Education, 1789-1902* (Cambridge: Cambridge University Press, 1930).

Michael Argles, "The Royal Commission on Technical Instruction, 1881-1884: Its Inception and Composition", *The Vocational Aspect of Secondary and Further Education*, II (1959), 97-104.

Michael Argles, *South Kensington to Robbins* (London: Longmans, 1964).

W. H. G. Armytage, *The Rise of the Technocrats* (London: Routledge and Kegan Paul, 1965).

Eric Ashby, *Technology and the Academics* (London: Macmillan, 1959).

Cyril Bibby, *T. H. Huxley: Scientist, Humanist and Educator* (London: Watts, 1959).

E. J. T. Brennan, (ed), *Education for National Efficiency: the Contribution of Sidney and Beatrice Webb* (London, 1975).

W. H. Brock, (ed), *H. E. Armstrong and the Teaching of Science, 1880-1930* (Cambridge, 1973).

W. L. Burn, *The Age of Equipoise* (London: Allen Unwin, 1964.

H. Butterworth, "The Development of Technical Education in Middlesbrough, 1844-1903", *Durham Research Review*, III (September 1960), 27-34.

D. S. L. Cardwell, *The Organisation of Science in England: A Retrospect,* (London: Heinemann, 1957, 1972).

J. G. Crowther, *Statesmen of Science* (London: Cresset Press, 1965).

Frank Foden, "Technical Education in England", *Pedagogica Historica,* VI (1966) 68-97.

Frank Foden, *Philip Magnus: Victorian Educational Pioneer* (London: Vallentine, Mitchell, 1970).

D. Hudson and K. W. Luckhurst, *The Royal Society of Arts, 1754-1954* (London: John Murray, 1954).

T. Kelly, *A History of Adult Education* (Liverpool: Liverpool University Press, 1970).

David S. Landes, *The Unbound Prometheus: Technological Change and Industrial Development in Western Europe from 1750 to the Present* (Cambridge: Cambridge University Press, 1970).

David Layton, *Science for the People: The Origins of the School Science Curriculum in England* (London: George Allen and Unwin, 1973).

G. A. N. Lowndes, *The Silent Social Revolution* (Oxford: Oxford University Press, 1937).

A. J. Meadows, *Science and Controversy: A Biography of Sir Norman Lockyer* (London: Macmillan, 1972).

Stuart MacLure, *Educational Documents: England and Wales, 1816-1963* (London: Chapmune Hall, 1965).

G. T. Millis, *Technical Education: Its Development and Aims* (London: Edward Arnold, 1925).

J. Monagham, "Some Views on Education and Industrial Progress a Hundred Years Ago", *The Vocational Aspect of Education,* XX (1968), 187-194.

P. W. Musgrave, "The Definition of Technical Education, 1860-1910", *The Vocational Aspect of Education,* XVI (1964), 105-111; "Constant Factors in the Demand for Technical Secondary and Further Education, 1860-1900", *British Journal of Educational Studies,* XIV, 1966; reprinted in Musgrave, P. W. (ed.), *Sociology, History and Education: A Reader* (London: Macmillan, 1970), pp.65-74; 143-157.

K. O. Roberts, "The Separation of Secondary from Technical Education", *The Vocational Aspect of Secondary and Further Education,* XXI (1969), 101-105.

G. W. Roderick and M. D. Stephens, "Scientific Studies in the Public Schools and the Endowed Grammar Schools in the 19th Century: The Evidence of the Royal Commissions", *The Vocational Aspect of Secondary and Further Education,* XXIII (1971), 97-105.

G. W. Roderick and M. D. Stephens, *Scientific and Technical Education in Nineteenth Century England* (Newton Abbot: David and Charles, 1972).

Michael Sanderson (ed), *The Universities in the Nineteenth Century* (London: Routledge and Kegan Paul, 1975).

Michael Sanderson, *The Universities and British Industry, 1850-1970* (London, 1972).

Geoffrey R. Searle, *The Quest for National Efficiency* (Oxford: Blackwell, 1971).

Mabel Tylecote, *The Mechanics Institutes of Lancashire and Yorkshire* (Manchester: Manchester University Press, 1957).

P. F. R. Venables, *Technical Education: Its Aims, Organization and Future Development* (London: G. Bell and Sons, 1956).

Ernest Edwin Williams, *Made in Germany* (London: Heinemann, 1896; repr. Harvester Press, 1973, with introduction by Austen Albu).

THE DOCUMENTS

SCIENTIFIC AND TECHNICAL

Scientific and Technical Volume 1

REPORT FROM THE SELECT COMMITTEE ON THE PROVISIONS FOR GIVING INSTRUCTION IN THEORETICAL AND APPLIED SCIENCE TO THE INDUSTRIAL CLASSES, WITH MINUTES OF EVIDENCE, APPENDICES AND INDEX, 1867–68

608 pp   4 tables

The 1835 Select Committee inquiry into the means for extending knowledge of the arts and of design (IUP volume Industrial Revolution: Design 1) manifested an early concern among manufacturers for the maintenance of British industrial primacy. After the Great Exhibition of 1851 which revealed weaknesses in England's industry, the Department of Science and Art was established to encourage scientific and technical education with a view to placing industry on a better technical footing. As the foreign challenge strengthened and Victorian optimism waned, especially after the Paris Exhibition of 1867, concern for the future of British industry sharpened—this was especially illustrated in Dr. Lyon Playfair's letter to the Taunton Commission on the technical advances of foreign manufacturers (IUP volume Education: General 33) and by Sir Bernhard Samuelson's speeches and reports on technical education in Europe. Accordingly, in 1867, a Select Committee was established with Samuelson as chairman to investigate the question. The committee reviewed the field under two headings (a) the state of scientific instruction and (b) the relationship between scientific education and industrial progress. Witnesses interviewed represented the Education and Science and Art Departments, universities (both old and new) in Britain and Ireland, colleges and institutes of science and technology, secondary schools, mechanics institutes, the Science and Art Department science classes and the principal industries of the large cities. The report and evidence provided a concise appraisal of British thinking and practice in the field of technology and technological education on the eve of the big Royal Commission inquiries, they examined the educational requirements and facilities of management, foremen and workmen in British industry and suggested a basis for the gradual orientation of education towards the second phase of the Industrial Revolution.

Original references

1867–68 (432) XV	Provisions for giving instruction in theoretical and applied science to the industrial classes, Sel. Cttee. Rep., mins. of ev., appendix.
(432–I)	Provisions for giving instruction in theoretical and applied science to the industrial classes, Sel. Cttee. Rep., index.

Scientific and Technical Volume 2

FIRST, SUPPLEMENTARY AND SECOND REPORTS OF THE ROYAL COMMISSION ON SCIENTIFIC INSTRUCTION AND THE ADVANCEMENT OF SCIENCE WITH MINUTES OF EVIDENCE, APPENDICES, ANALYSIS OF EVIDENCE AND CORRESPONDENCE RELATING TO THE FIRST REPORT, 1871–1872

816 pp

The appointment of the Royal Commission was a further expression of Britain's fears that she was falling behind rapidly in technological and scientific development. The commission was required to examine both the teaching of science and the facilities for scientific research. It was chaired by William Cavendish, seventh Duke of Devonshire, a relative of Henry Cavendish the famous scientist and a vigorous proponent of scientific and technological progress in his own right. Other famous names on the commission were T. H. Huxley, James Kay-Shuttleworth and Bernhard Samuelson. The second report, the main one in this volume, dealt with scientific instruction in teacher training colleges, elementary day schools and in the special science classes organized by the Department of Science and Art. In each of these areas the history of scientific instruction was reviewed and its current condition thoroughly examined. At the same time the reasoning behind the provision of scientific instruction for working-class children was examined. Among the many issues which this involved were the likely effects on industry of scientifically and technically educated workmen, the correctness of attempting to teach science to elementary school children, etc. The commissioners made suggestions and recommendations on these and many similar questions e.g. younger children should be prepared mentally for scientific instruction. They were extremely critical of the revised code introduced in 1861—it had made the teaching of science virtually impossible and had rendered elementary education narrow and rigid. Evidence from more than a hundred witnesses including T. H.

Huxley, Edward Frankland and Robert Applegarth is included in this volume. The witnesses represented all levels of scientific education from the universities and royal colleges to the science and art department classes and included besides those already mentioned many of the great men of the time both in education and in science. The evidence with a large appendix of corroborating documents and statistics covered science in the universities and schools and in industry, and together with the remaining evidence in later volumes provides a very extensive account of Britain's attitudes to technological progress and of her facilities for coping with it.

Original references

| 1872 | [C.536] XXV | Scientific instruction and the advancement of science, R. Com. 1st Rep. (reprint), supplementary Rep., 2nd Rep., mins. of ev., analysis of ev. |
| 1871 | [C.422] LVI | Scientific instruction and the advancement of Science, correspondence relating to 1st Rep. |

Scientific and Technical Volume 3

THIRD, FOURTH AND FIFTH REPORTS OF THE ROYAL COMMISSION ON SCIENTIFIC INSTRUCTION AND THE ADVANCEMENT OF SCIENCE WITH MINUTES OF EVIDENCE, APPENDICES AND ANALYSIS OF EVIDENCE, 1873–1874

768 pp

The third, fourth and fifth reports dealt respectively with Oxford and Cambridge Universities, scientific museums and collections, and recently-founded voluntary institutions giving advanced scientific instruction (University and King's Colleges, London, Owens College, Manchester, the College of Physical Science, Newcastle-on-Tyne and the Catholic University of Ireland). Each report was a critical survey of the structure, facilities and efficiency of the institutions dealt with and of the reorganization and improvements which were considered necessary. The report on Oxford and Cambridge, for example, discussed the universities themselves, the various colleges, the special scientific institutes, the distribution of finance, the teaching staffs, the course of study and examinations and scholarships for the study of science. The discussion was geared towards elucidating the actual and proper place of scientific instruction and research in the universities. The report on scientific collections especially emphasized their usefulness for research and suggested that the different collections be expanded and co-ordinated from this point of view. This and the fifth report summarized the history of the institutions examined and assessed their rate of development. The fifth report recommended that state aid should be given to many of the new colleges. A notable exception to this was the Catholic University of Ireland which both on religious and academic grounds was considered unsuitable for state assistance. The evidence in this volume is a continuation of that in the last and deals mainly with the Scottish and Irish universities and with the Standards Department of the Board of Trade. The list of witnesses includes many eminent names e.g. Sir Stafford Northcote, Rev. Thomas Fowler, C. William Siemens, and George B. Airy. The appendices have an account of German scientific education, science syllabuses, statistics, etc. It should be noted that the analysis of evidence in this volume refers to many of the subjects dealt with in the last volume.

Original references

1873	[C.868] XXVIII	Scientific instruction and the advancement of science, R. Com. 3rd Rep., appendices.
1874	[C.884] XXII	Scientific instruction and the advancement of science, R. Com. 4th Rep., appendices.
	[C.1087]	Scientific instruction and the advancement of science, R. Com. 5th Rep., appendices.
	[C.958]	Scientific instruction and the advancement of science, R. Com. mins. of ev., appendices, analysis of ev.

Scientific and Technical Volume 4

SIXTH, SEVENTH AND EIGHT REPORTS OF THE ROYAL COMMISSION ON SCIENTIFIC INSTRUCTION AND THE ADVANCEMENT OF SCIENCE WITH MINUTES OF EVIDENCE, APPENDICES, ANALYSIS OF EVIDENCE AND INDEX, 1875

552 pp   8 illustrations

The sixth, seventh and eighth reports deal respectively with scientific education in endowed secondary schools, with the Irish and Scottish universities and the University of London and with scientific progress and research generally. The sixth report which is illustrated with plans and sketches of laboratories and scientific equipment was based on personal examination and replies to questionnaires in a special inquiry conducted by Mr. Lockyer, the secretary of the commission. (The findings of this inquiry are contained in a lengthy appendix to the report). Some information was obtained from 128 of the 202 schools shown by the Taunton Commission to have endowments greater than £200 per year; however, the report is more solidly based on a thorough examination of science teaching in about 20 of the better-known schools including many of the public schools. Scientific education in the secondary schools left much to be desired; only 63 of 128 schools taught science, only 13 had laboratories. The report described the existing facilities in detail and discussed their extension. The seventh report examined the universities in London, Edinburgh, Glasgow, St. Andrews, Aberdeen, Dublin, Belfast, Cork and Galway and completed, with the third report, a survey of science in the universities. Having reviewed the whole field of scientific education the commission endeavoured in their final report to summarize the state of science in Britain and to suggest an overall policy to parliament. Many elements of the latter are remarkably modern, e.g. a central state authority to co-ordinate research, and direct state involvement in large-scale scientific investigations (meteorology, solar physics, etc). The report describes many projects already under the control of state departments, topographical, hydrographical, geological, meteorological and others, and also examined the financial assistance being given by the state to promote research.

Original references

1875	[C.1279] XXVIII	Scientific instruction and the advancement of science, R. Com. 6th Rep., appendices.
	[C.1297]	Scientific instruction and the advancement of science, R. Com. 7th Rep., appendices.
	[C.1298]	Scientific instruction and the advancement of science, R. Com. 8th Rep., appendices.
	[C.1363]	Scientific instruction and the advancement of science, mins. of ev., analysis of ev., index.

Scientific and Technical Volume 5

FIRST REPORT AND SECOND REPORT VOLUME I OF THE ROYAL COMMISSION ON TECHNICAL INSTRUCTION, 1882–1884

632 pp   1 plan

This commission was chaired by Bernhard Samuelson and was instructed to examine the technical and other education of the industrial classes abroad in order to compare it with that of the corresponding classes in Britain, and to examine the influence of technical education on industry at home and abroad. The first report dealt with recent improvements in French education, success n reducing the illiteracy rate in France, legislation enacted and the controversies which had arisen. The report described many aspects of the French system and gave many interesting statistics on it.

The second report, volume I, is the general report of the commission. It has four sections dealing with (a) technical education on the continent, (b) the influence of technical education on large manufacturing concerns abroad, (c) establishment of technical education at home (universities, polytechnics, laboratories, schools, handicraft classes, etc.) and (d) conclusions and recommendations. The latter section covers progress abroad relative to Britain, technical education and industry, training of technical teachers, agricultural education and organization of a system of the technical schools. The first section deals with technical education in France, Germany, Switzerland, Austria, Belgium, Holland and Italy. The system in each country is thoroughly described and critically evaluated. Apprenticeship schools, schools for artisans and foremen, technical universities, industrial art schools, galleries and museums are discussed. The manufacturing concerns studied in the report include a number of famous German engineering works e.g. Siemens and Halske of Berlin. The commission recommended the creation of much more extensive facilities for technical education in Britain and spelled out how this could be achieved.

Original references

| 1882 | [C.3171] XXVII | Technical instruction, R. Com. 1st Rep. |
| 1884 | [C.3981] XXIX | Technical instruction, R. Com. 2nd Rep., Vol I. |

Scientific and Technical Volume 6

THE SECOND REPORT VOLUME II OF THE ROYAL COMMISSION ON TECHNICAL INSTRUCTION, 1884

544 pp   2 plans   4 tables

The volume comprises a report by H. M. Jenkins, secretary of the Royal Agricultural Society, on agricultural education in France, Denmark, Belgium, Holland and the United Kingdom, together with a report by William Mather on technical education in the United States and Canada. The former examined institutions at all levels connected with agricultural education in each country: agricultural institutes in Germany, the Royal Veterinary and Agricultural Colleges of Denmark, university departments of agriculture, agricultural research stations, etc. A large number of appendices provide a wealth of information on many aspects of agriculture and agricultural education both at home and abroad e.g. school syllabuses, research and finance. The report made recommendations for the expansion of British agricultural education at higher (gentlemen farmers and farm managers), intermediate (tenant farmers and farm bailiffs) and lower (peasant farmers and workmen) levels. For the lower level Jenkins suggested a system of special farms where youths could serve an apprenticeship. The report on technical education in the United States and Canada was based on inspection of over a hundred educational and manufacturing establishments. It set out to show the influence of America's system of free and graded public schools on her industrial progress. The report gave a general review of the public schools system and a description of scientific and technological training in colleges and universities. It paid special attention to technical, industrial and manual training schools and assessed their integration into the industrial system and their effects on it. In addition it examined influences other than education which tended to improve the American industrial population. Though obviously impressed by the tremendous technological potential of North America, Mather had quite a few critical comments. He found for example that free education produced too many people willing to take white-collar jobs only. Mather's report complements the report compiled by Rev. G. Fraser for the Argyll and Taunton Commissions and they can be usefully studied ir. conjunction.

Original reference
1884   [C.3981–I] XXX   Technical instruction, R. Com. 2nd Rep., Vol II.

Scientific and Technical Volume 7

THE SECOND REPORT VOLUME III OF THE ROYAL COMMISSION ON TECHNICAL INSTRUCTION, 1884

912 pp

This volume includes: a report on technical education in Russia by William Mather; a report on the British silk industry; a scheme of technical education for Ireland submitted by William K. Sullivan; the evidence relating to England taken by the commission. Mather's report on Russian education paints a picture in sharp contrast to his American report. Serfdom, he says, was still effectively in existence in Russia; only military and civil officials were admitted to what educational institutions existed; others had to depend on private tutors or on the facilities provided in Russian possessions which had retained their own social framework (Finland, Poland, etc.). Mather described the conditions and the social background of rural and urban life. His report, though short, is an absorbing document, bearing, on a small scale, the same relationship to the nineteenth-century Russian novelist as many other parliamentary reports bear to Dickens. The report on the British silk industry described the development and current condition of the industry, paying particular attention to the larger centres (Derby, Coventry, Manchester, Nottingham), discussing foreign competition, strikes and level of technical knowledge, and contrasting the industry with its continental counterparts. The report is fortified with statistics and tabular information on imports and exports, etc. Dr. Sullivan's scheme for Irish technical education is also provided with an extensive appendix including replies to a long questionnaire on the suitability of technical education for Ireland sent to clergymen and local officials throughout the country.

Original reference

1884   [C.3981–II] XXXI   Technical instruction, R. Com. 2nd Rep., Vol III.

Scientific and Technical Volume 8
THE SECOND REPORT VOLUME IV OF THE ROYAL COMMISSION ON TECHNICAL INSTRUCTION, 1884

824 pp   13 plans, 1 table

The final volume of the report has two sections of evidence, one general and one relating to Ireland. The former covers many aspects of the inquiry including the relative merits of British and continental systems of technical instruction, British engineering and machinery manufacture, instruction in agriculture, art and technical subjects, apprenticeships and glass processing and other industries. A number of questions relate to technical education in Japan. The evidence on Ireland was taken in the main cities and represents the views of academics, manufacturers, architects, property owners, the officials of various committees and societies, clergymen, workmen, etc. Notable witnesses were Dr. William K. Sullivan and Michael Davitt. The topics and institutions discussed included the universities and institutes of learning, the facilities for technical education, the special requirements of Ireland in this field, the state of several branches of science in Ireland, agriculture and industry, with specific reference to the state of several industries. Numerous suggestions and proposals were put forward by witnesses.

Original reference

1884   [C.3981–III] XXXI (I) Technical instruction, R. Com. 2nd Rep., Vol IV.
      [C.3981–IV]   Technical instruction, R. Com. 2nd Rep., Vol V.

Index